D0829194

Meditations for Christians Who Try to Be Perfect

❧

Meditations for Christians Who Try to Be Perfect

JOAN C. WEBB

MEDITATIONS FOR CHRISTIANS WHO TRY TO BE PERFECT. Copyright © 1993 by Joan C. Webb. All rights reserved. Printed in the United States of America. No part of this book may be used or reproduced in any manner whatsoever without written permission except in the case of brief quotations embodied in critical articles and reviews. For information address HarperCollins Publishers, 10 East 53rd Street, New York, NY 10022.

FIRST EDITION

Library of Congress
Cataloging-in-Publication Data
Webb, Joan C., 1948–
       Meditations for Christians who try to be perfect /
Joan C. Webb — 1st ed.
          p. cm.
       ISBN 0–06–069272–3 (pbk.)
       1. Perfectionism (Personality trait)—Religious aspects—Christianity—Meditations. 2. Burn out (Psychology)—Religious aspects—Christianity—Meditations. 3. Peace of mind—Religious aspects—Christianity—Meditations. I. Title.
BV4908.5.W43 1993
248.4—dc20   92–54530
                                                         CIP

93 94 95 96 97 98 BANWI 9 8 7 6 5 4 3 2 1

WORD TO THE READER

One day in April 1987 I sat in my office surrounded by the ever-present piles of papers and stacks of files. I was the president of a growing new company, and we had just reached a potential one million dollars in sales, up from a hundred thousand dollars the previous year. This was great news, but to me it did not symbolize success. In my mind I was in a dreary and depressing POW camp. "Get me out of here!" I wanted to scream.

Every simple detail of a normal day had become overwhelming to me. I had learned to cope by functioning like a machine. But this particular April afternoon I could not seem to move the crank. An important client waited impatiently on the other end of the telephone for information and the name and address of our showroom. I could not answer his questions. I could not remember where to find the information. "What shall I do?" I wondered. "What *can* I do?" How I concluded the conversation I do not remember.

A few days after this experience, which had become all too common, I realized I could no longer "gut it out." Reluctantly I admitted, "This is enough! I can't keep going. Something has to give!" I knew I was severely burned out.

Suddenly I was forced to start making some tough decisions. (Most of my life I had lived with the misconception that I had no choices.) First I decided to admit my need and see a counselor. This decision involved risking rejection by my husband and loss of respect from my colleagues. I did it anyway.

This move initiated a difficult journey; had I known how difficult it would be, I might never have embarked on it. I slowly began to understand that my burnout was a result of workaholic behavior. Sixty-, seventy-, or eighty-hour work weeks were not uncommon. I could not permit myself to say no to a new job or client. Sometimes I was shocked to realize that I had skipped the last five meals. I felt compelled to keep working and doing. In an effort to relieve the many physical symptoms of the burnout and give myself some time to think, I decided to take a month off. Incredibly, I ended up working forty hours a week during that month. However, it helped to open my eyes to the reality of my need.

It was the malignant anger inside that troubled me the most. I genuinely believed that I had never been angry before. What was I supposed to do with this ugly, raw emotion I was feeling? When I dug past the burnout and the workaholism, I discovered a defective pattern of misbeliefs. I believed the lie that I must make all things right for my family, my clients, my business associates, and anyone else who came across my whirlwind path. I believed that I must appear perfect so that others would be attracted to my God. I believed that it was my responsibility to see that my husband was always happy, healthy, and satisfied with life. "Peace at any cost" and "Don't rock the boat" were my unspoken mottoes. I was angry at not being permitted to be the person I thought God wanted me to be. All my time and energy was involved in fixing life so it would work for other people. The "me" God created was lost in the shuffle.

For the first year I did not have a label for any of this. I was simply trying to climb out of a deep, dark hole. I admitted my dire need of God, made the difficult decision to leave the business (which had become the mirror image of my self-destructive family patterns), and practiced saying no when it was beneficial to do so. But the most stressful part of my recovery came when I attempted to speak the truth about my feelings, desires, and thoughts to my husband. The fear of rejection and emotional abandonment was so great that I would become nauseated and begin to shake.

Many days I felt as if I wanted to run away and hide. But one night a light bulb blinked on in my mind. "It's the system," I said. "I don't want to live in this system anymore—it's faulty." I read the books *Codependent No More* by Melody Beattie and *Women Who Love Too Much* by Robin Norwood. Gradually I realized that it was not escape from my life or relationships that I wanted but a changed pattern of thinking and behaving within my life and relationships. "If I could just learn a new, healthy way of living and loving," I thought.

Weeks turned into months, and more than anything I wanted to know if this desire to change was God's idea for me. Did God really want me to stay in the shoulds and oughts and have tos of the seemingly unselfish patterns I had learned and practiced for so long? Or did God want me to continue on this journey to health, freedom, and recovery? I studied Jesus' healthy life-style and relationships. I read what the Bible said about God's attitude toward feelings, truth, and objectivity. I asked many questions and searched for insight to help combat the destructive thinking and behavior. One of the helpful books I read was *Forgive and Forget (Healing the Hurts We Don't Deserve)* by Lewis B. Smedes.

What I learned from this searching process affirmed my desire to continue getting out of the faulty system. I kept a journal of my thoughts, feelings, and discoveries. It took huge quantities of courage to combat my feelings of fear and discomfort as I broke from the familiar system. Often I felt sucked back up into the old vacuum. During this time I read *When Helping You Is Hurting Me (Escaping the Messiah Trap)* by Carmen Renee Berry. I found evidence of myself on almost every page.

After a while I began to talk with others who were hurting in a similar way. We met one-on-one. Increasingly we discovered that we needed encouragement to keep going. It was a big step even to admit we had a need. With the old system the denial of human needs was great—a machine has no needs. But a human being does. We were finally accepting that we were imperfect human beings. We repeatedly asked each other questions such as these: Does God really love me, or is his love as punitive and conditional as the other "loves" I have known? What does God's Word have to say about the destructive patterns of behavior that result in burnout? Is this the way God wants us to live? Does God call this "love"? Is the longing to be free of fear and unhealthy shame acceptable to God? What did Jesus say about all this? Can we be certain that it is God who is encouraging us to change? If so, how can God help us in attempting to leave this faulty system?

The meditations that follow grew out of our search for answers to these questions. They are also the result of admitting powerlessness over obsessive thoughts and compulsive behaviors. They are the product of recognizing a need for God and submitting to his plan of salvation and leadership. They are the result of acknowledging that we have choices, and these include the choice to grow, to change, and to recover.

It is indeed a process . . . and not always easy. If we wish to be healthy in mind and spirit, we cannot ignore the pain of past defective relationships and systems. Pretending that hurt, disappointment, abuse, anger, addictions, injustice, disease, and death do not exist is not the answer.

Once we acknowledge the truth of these realities, however, we are free to admit our need of God. You and I can then pray, "God, I have been trying to do and be what I cannot without you. To erase the pain I have used my own detrimental ways of coping. I admit that this has not worked. Please help me."

Perhaps you find reflections of your own life in this story. You may be struggling with similar issues. Maybe you want to do everything: have a happy family, a prosperous career, meaningful friendships, worthwhile community and church involvement, a successful ministry, as well as a healthy body, soul, and mind. And you want to do everything "right"; you may even strive to have "right" or perfect thoughts and emotions about all this. The potential for burnout with this life-style is enormous. To avoid burnout you and I need daily reminders to reorient destructive thinking and behavior.

I invite you to join me on an adventure, a journey. It takes commitment, because this new way of thinking and behaving is not familiar. The truth is, only God is absolutely perfect; we humans are not. But God promises to help, to guide, to teach, and to give us courage. We can change. We can grow. We can heal. As you read these meditations I hope you will be encouraged in your own process of changing, growing, and healing. This is the promise for those of us who wish to avoid burnout:

> *"The Lord will guide you always;*
> *he will satisfy your needs in a sun-scorched land*
> *and will strengthen your frame.*
> *You will be like a well-watered garden,*
> *like a spring whose waters never fail."*
>
> ISAIAH 58:11 (NIV)

We can be confident that God will guide "those who want to do everything right" to a more balanced and realistic life-style.

Meditations for Christians Who Try to Be Perfect

Read Isaiah 40:28–31: "He gives strength to the weary. . . . Those who hope in the Lord will renew their strength" (vv. 29, 31).

High achieving, goal-oriented, capable, overly conscientious people are candidates for burnout. Myron Rush, former president of Management Training Systems and author of the book *Burnout,* defines burnout as "the type of stress and emotional fatigue, frustration, and exhaustion that occurs when a series of (or combination of) events in a relationship, mission, way of life, or job fail to produce an expected result."

Some of us who are certain that our commitment to hard work will bring us what we desire are flabbergasted when we run out of energy, enthusiasm, and faith. Defeated, we ask, "Is there any hope for renewal and recovery?" "Yes!" says our Creator. "Though you stumble and fall, you will one day soar on wings like eagles, run and not grow weary, walk and not faint. Trust me. I will renew your lost strength."

Lord, I'm too exhausted to feel. An unbalanced lifestyle has eroded my inner being and threatened my relationships. You can help restore what has been destroyed. I'm now asking for your help.

Read Psalm 42:9–11: "I say to God . . . , 'Why have you forgotten me?' . . . My bones suffer . . ." (vv. 9–10).

"I'm working harder than ever, yet accomplishing far less," a busy executive said. "Just the thought of getting out of bed in the morning, dressing, and going to face people makes me gag. I used to enjoy being with others, but lately people irritate me. Everyone blames me for everything. I want to run away and never come back. I hate the person I've become. Everything just keeps getting worse. Why won't God help me?"

These words reveal classic burnout symptoms. Unless steps are taken to reverse the debilitating process, this person will become another charred statistic.

Although there are no simple remedies for burnout, the first step to becoming mentally strong again is to accept responsibility for one's own life and health. Accepting responsibility means making decisions to reverse self-destructive thoughts and behaviors.

A person facing severe burnout cringes at the mere thought of doing something. Doing is what propelled him to this devastation. This time, however, the doing is not in the name of accomplishment, success, or service. This doing is to regain life. I know. I remember. This burnout victim was me.

Lord, my mind hurts, my heart hurts, and my body hurts. Don't abandon me now. I need help.

Read Ecclesiastes 2:17–25: "A man can do nothing better than . . . to find satisfaction in his work. This too, I see, is from the hand of God, for without him, who can eat or find enjoyment?" (vv. 24–25).

When I began sharing my story, I noticed that a few people retreated when I mentioned the word *workaholism.* "I can't identify," they said, laughing. Yet I have a hunch that more than care to admit experience workaholism's self-destructive patterns. In her book *Working Ourselves to Death,* Diane Fassel contends that although workaholics may work a great deal, they are not always working. Some avoid work, some work in obsessive spurts, others procrastinate. Pressured by church and family, housewives may become work addicts "all in the interest of being perfect wives and mothers." In the zealous pursuit of excellence, schools produce youth obsessed with perfect performance in athletics *and* academics.

Work addiction often surfaces when we confuse who we are as God's unique and valuable creation with what we can or cannot do. God will help us uncover the distorted ideas we have about ourselves and our work. After facing the issues honestly, we can learn to labor at our daily tasks without being controlled by them. God wants us to find peace and satisfaction in this area of our lives.

Lord, help me assess the role work has in my life.

Read Luke 9:25: "'What good is it for a man to gain the whole world, and yet . . . forfeit his very self?'"

The Japanese have a name for it. It's called *karoshi,* or death by overwork. In their efforts to make Japan the most productive nation in the world, some Japanese have forfeited much. Many have sacrificed family life as well as their own lives. According to some reports, the death toll from overwork has been as high as ten thousand per year. These people are driven by the corporate leadership to routinely work overtime, take little or no vacation, work weekends, ignore physical signs of stress, and never complain. The heartbroken families have recently begun to say that the price for gaining the world's admiration is too high.

We would do well to learn from this human disaster. Are you and I forgoing healthy relationships with our spouse, children, and family for the sake of our work addiction and perfectionism? Some of us overwork to obtain economic superiority. Most of us overwork to prove our value, desperate to gain approval and respect. What is your rationale for obsessive work habits? Is it worth the price?

Lord, my family and life mean more to me than "gaining the whole world." But I've become so entrenched in this way of life, I don't know how to stop. I don't want to commit karoshi. Please give me courage and direction.

Read Ecclesiastes 2:10–11: "I denied myself nothing my eyes desired. . . . My heart took delight in all my work. . . . Yet when I surveyed all that my hands had done and what I had toiled to achieve, everything was meaningless, a chasing after the wind."

"I want to be a rich workaholic. I just want to be rich and work all the time and enjoy my job." I recently read this quotation from an eighteen-year-old girl in my local newspaper. This girl's statement rang warning bells in my mind. "If she only knew what she is really wishing for herself," I thought. Experts agree that true workaholics suffer from neurotic obsessions to work. Symptoms may include compulsive rushing and busyness, constant thinking about work or performance, continual list making, the refusal or reluctance to take time off, and severely diminished family or social life. Workaholism is a progressive disease. If left unattended it will kill us.

But we can decide to reverse the direction we are going in. It won't be easy, but with God's loving and understanding help, we can learn to change first our thinking and then our behavior. Life can and will have new meaning.

Lord, release me from bondage to performance and work. I want to live in freedom now, so that at the end of my life I can look back and smile. I need your strength to help me change.

Read Psalm 139:17 and 23–24: "How precious it is,
Lord, to realize that you are thinking about me constantly! Search me, O God, and know my heart; test
my thoughts. Point out anything you find in me that
makes you sad, and lead me along the path of ever-
lasting life" (TLB).

I became so wrapped up in the daily routine of cranking
out work that I lost me. I didn't know me anymore. The
person I thought I knew was buried under layers of smoldering ashes. The "together" image I saw in the mirror
encased an emotionally dying woman.

It sounds overdramatic, but it's true. The question
that haunted me was, "Can I be found?" I didn't know
when or if I'd ever come back. Yet step by step, little by
little, God picked up the burned-out fragments, repaired
them, and pieced them back together.

God knew where I was all the time. He never stopped
thinking about me. When the time was right, he reintro-
duced me to myself. Then, when I could handle it, he
showed me how to change my self-destructive life-style
so I wouldn't get lost again. How great is his love!

*Father, you know me inside and out. Please share
your thoughts with me. Help me to be the person I'm
capable of becoming.*

Read Romans 8:18–20: "Yet what we suffer now is nothing compared to the glory he will give us later. For all creation is waiting ... hopefully for that future day ... sin, death, and decay ... will all disappear" (TLB).

"Perfectionism is the belief that it's possible for everything to be exactly as we think it should, and that this would make us totally, blissfully happy," writes author Veronica Ray in her pamphlet entitled *I'm Good Enough.*

If you and I had everything just the way we wanted, it would not be perfect. Our dreams, thoughts, desires, and goals are laced with flaws. Perfection on this earth is not possible.

One day everything and everyone who trusts in God will be flawless. Although it may not be how we envision a perfect eternity, it will be the way God wants it. And we will delight in it.

We will worship the triune God with perfect pitch, complete adoration, and unimpaired service. It will happen. Letting go of our need to do and make everything perfect now releases us to hope in the glorious future God has planned for us later.

Lord, you are not only good, you are perfect. I give up my obsession with earthly perfection in anticipation of the coming best.

Read Genesis 1:1–2: "In the beginning God created . . . " (v. 1).

I remember the day it dawned on me that I had been attempting to mold my world and its inhabitants into perfection—to re-create according to my own image. Driving down the highway, I cried, "O God, forgive me for trying to craft myself a perfect life—perfect parents, perfect spouse, perfect children. I have trampled on your territory. Who do I think I am?"

In the beginning of time as we know it, God created, and he has been creating ever since. The Hebrew word for *create* used in the first verse of the Bible is *bara.* This is a God word. Human beings are incapable of producing this way. Creating out of nothing is God's job alone.

Trying to craft myself a perfect world in which to live made me tired. Eventually I burned out. How relieved I was to learn that it is not my responsibility.

God Almighty, the Creator of all, I acknowledge that I have sometimes tried to interfere in your creation process. I want to learn to leave the crafting process to you. You are the strong and capable one, not I. There is peace in being satisfied to be one of your "created" and not the one responsible for re-creation.

Read Ecclesiastes 7:18: "Try to avoid going too far in doing anything. Those who honor God will avoid doing too much of anything" (NCV).

"Everything, everything, EVERYTHING!" the young working mother's voice grew louder with each word. "This has been my unspoken motto: I must do all things and do each right. But I want to change."

Many of us, like this woman, live in an inner whirlwind. We want it all and at the same time are anxious that we will have nothing. Anne Wilson Schaef says: "Our biggest fear is not knowing enough or not being enough. . . . We have become addicted to busyness, and if we are not busy we feel worthless, at a loss, and even frightened."

When my friend shared her "Everything" motto with me, I understood. Here is a recent excerpt from my journey: "Yesterday was not a wasted day! I wrote in my journal; I was quiet enough for God to give me new insight. I called my husband at work to thank him for his support, and he suggested we meet for lunch. But my stomach was knotted. I still often feel compelled to measure myself and my day by busyness and accomplishments. I am learning, though, to enjoy others, life, and God. That is enough. I do not have to DO IT ALL!"

Lord, I want to let go of my need to do everything. Thank you for my progress thus far. I will trust you for the continuing process.

Read Isaiah 26:3: "You, Lord, give true peace . . . to those who trust you" (NCV).

"Usually I feel a quiet inner panic that if I fail to stay in high gear, everyone and everything will turn on me," said an overworked teacher.

Some of us, like this teacher, feel as though we have a judge and jury peering over our shoulder. Maybe we have a person or group of persons who tries to push us beyond our human limits. Or perhaps the slave driver is in our own head. In either case, we have a choice.

We can choose not to be railroaded by ourselves or others. When we learn not to be controlled by unrealistic expectations and refuse to react with panic to unplanned circumstances, we can relax and live!

Our best at any given moment in any specific situation is all we have. Though our best may vary according to the unique conditions of each situation, that's OK. Our best is good enough. We can admit the fear that our personal contributions to life will not be good enough. Then, with God's help, we can move past the panic to live in peace.

Lord, I'll relax and trust you. Please remove the destructive results the internal and external slave drivers have on my life. My OK-ness comes from you.

Read 1 Kings 17:1–6: "Then the word of the Lord came to Elijah: 'Leave here, turn eastward and hide in the Kerith Ravine. . . . I have ordered the ravens to feed you there'" (vv. 2–4).

When we first meet the sensitive and depression-prone prophet Elijah, he has just given King Ahab distressing news about the coming drought. Most likely he found delivering this negative news stressful. God acknowledged this probability and came to comfort and provide for Elijah. God did not chide Elijah for "unproductive" time at the ravine. God will not be angry with us if we choose to retreat and rest for a while. We do not need to do or perform endlessly with no break for recuperation. When we are so exhausted that we have little energy left to pray, God does not reject us. Perhaps we could say no to a weeknight meeting and stay home to sit by the fireplace or read a fun book or go on a date with our spouse or take a nap.

God is in control, and we do not mess up his universal plans when we step back and relax.

Lord, sometimes I need to take a break. Thank you for providing for me whether I am busy or inactive.

Read Philippians 4:19: "And my God will meet all your needs according to his glorious riches in Christ Jesus."

> Some of us need to stop thinking and do,
>   while others need to stop doing and think.
> Some need to stop asking and give, though
>   others need to cease giving and ask.
> Some of us need to stop crying and smile,
>   yet others need to stop smiling and cry.
> Some need to stop confronting and give in,
>   while others need to quit compromising
>   and confront.
> Some of us need to stop waiting and run,
>   though others need to stop running and
>   wait.
> Some need to practice discipline and orga-
>   nize, yet others need to cease structuring
>   themselves into a box and relax.

What do you need?

God is big enough to help us all. His power and resources are unlimited. He will meet us at the precise point of our individual needs.

Lord, cause me to be aware of my unique shortcomings. Then help me boldly address my needy areas with your strength. I promise to cooperate with the maturing process. I'll trust you to meet my needs.

Read Psalm 55:4–8: "'Oh, that I had the wings of a dove! I would fly away and be at rest . . . far from the . . . storm'" (vv. 6, 8).

"All people in burnout develop the feeling that they want to run away and hide from the world. Part of the reason for this is that they *do* need to get away from the source of the problem," says Myron D. Rush, former president of Management Training Systems. Specialists in the field of burnout recovery insist the first step toward healing is to remove the victim from the fire. This is a difficult step for most to take. It was for me.

Struggling with the question of whether to leave the business I helped start, I repeated, "I can't leave my baby!" My husband listened and finally responded, "Please stop calling this your baby. Your children are in the other room." His words shocked me into reality.

I left the business hoping that I might begin to heal. I continued to work free-lance, and six months later I still wanted to run away and hide. My family and I agreed I must go away to recuperate. So while struggling to gain equilibrium, I left. At intervals during my time away, I felt as if I might not return, but I did.

Each burnout victim's circumstance is unique, and so is the "get away" solution. Yet this truth remains: wherever we go, God never leaves us alone.

Lord, please see me safely through this recovery.

Read Jeremiah 17:7–8: "Blessed is the man who trusts in the Lord, whose confidence is in him. He will be like a tree planted by the water that sends out its roots by the stream."

We lived for a while in the desert. Dust and rolling sagebrush swept across the barren landscape. However, a built-in sprinkler system kept our yard lush and green. When the sun beat down and the temperature topped 100 degrees day after day, we did not worry about our flowers or fruit trees as long as we had this consistent flow of water.

During my recovery from burnout I felt as if I were trying to install a sprinkler system in a cracked and parched wasteland. But Jeremiah's words gave me hope.

God desired that I be blessed and joyous, not overworked and dried up inside. His plan to refresh me included the transfer of my worries and burdens to him. As I began to trust him I noticed that my parched spirit slowly regained new life. I clung to the hope that I might once again be healthy, producing fruit, not by determined performance and overdoing but by God's power within.

God will irrigate our parched souls if we let him.

Thanks for the hope, Lord. I know I'm powerless to water my spirit alone. I accept your help.

Read Psalm 20:6–7: "Some trust in chariots and some in horses, but we trust in . . . God" (v. 7).

"How have you been since you left the showroom?" my client asked, referring to my recent resignation as president of a growing young company.

"I'm in the process of adjusting my life-style to include some balance," I explained. "I'm trying to learn to say no to working harder and longer. It's difficult, though."

"It *is* hard to say no sometimes, isn't it?" he responded. "I was recently picked up by the police on a drunk-driving charge." He paused and stared out the window. "I think we all have to find a way to cope. Drinking is mine, maybe working is yours."

We need something bigger than ourselves to help us deal with the harsh realities of life. The psalmist knew people who trusted in chariots and horses. Overworking, overdrinking, trying to control food or other people give us a similar sense of power. We may harness and ride this power to help handle the frustration, disappointment, and pain of living. But many of us have discovered that this is not enough. Our power sources turned on us—to destroy us.

An unlimited power source is available. We can find strength in trusting God. He is ultimate power.

Lord, the power sources I trusted have failed me. You are stronger. I want to trust you instead.

Read Joel 2:25–26: "'I will repay you for the years the locusts have eaten. . . . You will have plenty to eat, until you are full, you will praise . . . your God, who has worked wonders for you.'"

"I've worked and struggled away so many years," said a friend of mine. "My relationships are damaged. I haven't been true to myself or become the person God created me to be. My mind and body feel fried. And I'm angry. I wonder if I will ever be whole and happy again."

Some of us have experienced severe pain as a result of our perfectionistic and workaholic life-style. Perhaps we thought if we just tried harder, everything would get better. But we're disappointed. Our hopes are tarnished, and our dreams eaten up by destructive "locusts." Sometimes it is difficult to believe that life will ever be different. The ache is so deep, the scars so disfiguring. Can our desolate personal fields destroyed by the locusts of our past ever be lush again?

God promises those of us who choose to believe him that he will repay us for the destructive years. We cannot begin to guess how he will accomplish this. All we can do is let go, trust, and let him work his wonders. It's an adventure worth our faith.

Lord, sometimes I'm so afraid. But I want to trust you. Work your wonders in my tangled-up life.

Read 1 Thessalonians 2:4: "We are not trying to please men but God, who tests our hearts."

Pleasing God is possible because he has no unrealistic expectations. He just expects us to be the person he created us to be. This is reachable because it is natural. When we try to please people, we are attempting to accomplish the impossible. How do we decide which human being to satisfy or placate—a parent, a child, the boss, our spouse, a friend, the pastor, a neighbor, a sibling? Each of these people has a different image of us, and often their expectations are not consistent with our personality, gifts, or talents. Trying to be everything others want is a crazy-maker.

Cooperating with our Creator to become the person he planned us to be will release us to freedom. God knows what is in our hearts. When he "tests" our hearts, he brings forth what is best in us. When we allow God to guide in the quest to become our true selves, we please him. He understands us and expects us only to fulfill our God-given talents and gifts. This is a natural process of spiritual, mental, social, and emotional growth. Just for today are you willing to cooperate with God?

Lord, I want to please you by becoming the genuine "me" you had in mind when I was born. Instruct me.

> *Read Ecclesiastes 4:7–8:* "I saw something . . . that was senseless. I saw a person. . . . He always worked hard. But he was never satisfied with what he had. He never asked himself, 'For whom am I working so hard? Why don't I let myself enjoy life?'" (NCV).

"I just have to work harder. If I don't get it all done, everyone will be mad at me," moaned an exhausted student.

"What was your goal for today?" I asked.

"I needed to read five chapters in sociology, finish the rough draft for an English term paper, learn my lines for drama class, and write letters to my grandma and boyfriend."

"How much do you still have to do?" I asked.

"Well, I've completed all those things. But I should be ahead of schedule. I canceled my baby-sitting job last night so I could get ahead. I just have to try harder."

Some of us feel like we are always on the brink of disaster even though we are experiencing obvious daily success. Rather than congratulate ourselves when we reach our goals, we change the rules. More! More! Harder! Harder! Faster! Faster!

With patience and practice we can learn to stop changing the rules on ourselves, accept our current accomplishments, and enjoy life. Let's begin today.

Lord, temper my striving to work harder, faster, longer, and more! I want to enjoy my life.

Read Colossians 3:12: "Clothe yourselves with . . . gentleness."

Tony, the perfectionist, is his own worst enemy. He convinces himself that his needs, ideas, plans, and desires are inferior. He believes he must prove his significance by always helping others, consequently he never says no. Daily he berates himself for failing to live up to his impossible standards. He finds it very difficult to live with himself. Tony needs to develop a gentle friendship with the person who lives within him. Perhaps you do, too. The definition of gentleness includes choosing to be kind instead of nitpicking and condemning. How can you be kind to yourself today? What action can you take?

You might write yourself an encouraging note or invite a friend to meet you for a cup of coffee. Tony decided to take a break from his studies, walk to the ballpark, and watch a ball game. Decide for yourself what you need, and then do it. Being gentle with yourself is acceptable to God.

Lord, please help me today to be as kind and gentle with myself as you are with me.

Read Titus 1:7–8: "Since an overseer is entrusted with God's work, he must be . . . self-controlled."

Some of us have the mistaken idea that to be effective leaders we must whip ourselves into excellent performance. We may say to ourselves, "You didn't accomplish enough today. Get with it! Are you lazy or something? You'd better forget about eating any dinner. You can't afford to take any time off. Hurry up. You've got to finish this project before you go to bed." We would not think of making oppressive demands like these on others, yet in the guise of being self-controlled, we treat ourselves poorly.

Perhaps we can readjust our definition of self-control to be more balanced. Although we are responsible for our behavior, thoughts, and growth, we do not need to whip ourselves into action. Positive reinforcement may be much more helpful. Today ask, "What do I need to support and help myself?" The answer may surprise you. Maybe you need a hug, a break, a word of encouragement, a visit with a friend, or forgiveness. We cultivate self-control by being firm but gentle; honest yet kind; and fair but understanding.

Lord, I take responsibility for my own emotional, mental, physical, and spiritual progress. Please help me learn to practice positive self-control.

Read Romans 11:6: "And if by grace, then it is no longer by works; if it were, grace would no longer be grace."

Often we begin with a genuine desire to help others and to make a significant contribution before we die. But as years roll by, our goals unfulfilled, we feel compelled to step up the pace. We want to make more money, perhaps to give it away to family or charities, so we work harder and longer. When others do not change in the way we feel they should, we increase our efforts to serve and fix. When dreams to develop our God-given talents fail, we try to make up for lost time.

Carol Travilla, author of *Caring Without Wearing*, lists five unrealistic expectations that contribute to burnout mentality:

> There should not be any limits to what I can do.
>
> I have the capacity to help everyone.
>
> I am the only person available to help.
>
> I must never make a mistake.
>
> I have the ability to change another person.

God never expects more than we are able to give. We do not have to do it all. Because of God's grace we have choices.

Lord, help me today to make wise and balanced choices about my work, service, and contributions.

Read Ecclesiastes 4:6: "Better one handful with tranquillity than two handfuls with toil and chasing after the wind."

In the years before I hit my final burnout slide, I experienced sobering mental glimpses of the downhill course I was taking. Although I tried to fight it, I had the overwhelming feeling that I must keep both hands completely full with projects, sales, and clients. If a sale threatened to fall between my fingers, I panicked.

One day an associate and I were so busy trying to finish projects and meet deadlines that it was almost comical. But I wasn't laughing. "Do you ever worry you won't get it all done and clients will go elsewhere and everyone will be angry?" I asked. She looked at me strangely and answered, "No."

"Is something wrong with me?" I wondered momentarily and then continued racing through my day. I needed both hands full to feed my obsession.

But more than that, I felt compelled to prove that I was worthy to be alive. I wanted desperately to please my husband and make him proud of me. I was chasing after the wind. Today I realize I do not need both hands full with projects and work. Life feels more balanced with one hand toiling and the other touching tranquillity.

Lord, please help me to remember that it's possible to balance work with sane daily living.

Read Psalm 127:1–5: "Unless the Lord builds the house, its builders labor in vain. . . . In vain you rise early and stay up late, toiling for food to eat" (vv. 1–2).

During a recent business dinner, an associate asked me about the book I was writing. When I mentioned the topic of perfectionistic thinking, workaholic behavior, and burnout, he nodded and said, "Well, those things are not worth dying for!"

Soon after this I read an article about a new trend in our society called downshifting. Author Amy Saltzman first coined the term and defines downshifters as men and women who choose to leave all-consuming jobs for a slower pace so they can experience more enjoyment in their lives.

Some of us may be beginning to realize that striving and working all the time is not what God had in mind when he made us. There is more to life. Life includes enjoying nature, pursuing hobbies, developing talents, deepening relationships, serving others, and knowing and enjoying God. *Life* is worth living for.

God, teach me the meaning of life. Slow me down to listen.

Read Mark 11:25: "'If you hold anything against any-one, forgive him.'"

For years I put myself in an impossible position trying to be perfect all the time. While trying to please others and do everything right, I silently shamed myself; expected too much; crushed creativity; robbed myself of nourishment, fun, sleep, and relaxation. I let anger turn to resentment, stuffed it down and became depressed. I wronged myself, others, and God in the process.

One morning during my recovery from burnout I realized that one person I most needed to forgive was myself. I wrote in my journal: "I've harmed you, Joan. I'm sorry. It's OK for you to nurture yourself and become the person God wants you to be. I'll try to be kinder and more forgiving now." Being gentle and toler-ant with ourselves is not self-indulgent. God wants us to have compassionate hearts toward all people, ourselves included. Forgiveness is freeing.

Lord, do I need to forgive myself?

Read Psalm 55:4–8: "My heart is in anguish within me" (v. 4).

Many of us have the idea that in order to be mature, respected adults we must renounce all our feelings. We may think that if we are to be real men or women of God we must never admit a need. We must always have an answer and always appear in total control. Perhaps as children we were taught that it was weak or cowardly to admit to disappointment, hurt, sadness, discouragement, anger, or even happiness. But what we learned is a misconception.

King David led his people to victory many times. Nations looked up to him. But he made mistakes. He experienced the rejection of trusted co-workers. He felt angry, jealous, and hurt. David was a truthful man who allowed himself to think and feel and be. In the psalms he often expressed sadness, discouragement, and confusion. His acceptance of reality and the resulting feelings of disappointment and pain led him again and again to God. And God called him "a man after my own heart." Like David we can think, feel, and share, as responsible, mature men and women of God.

Lord, sometimes I feel happy, sometimes I feel sad, hurt, and disappointed. Thank you for not rejecting me because I feel.

Read Isaiah 43:1–4: "But now, this is what the Lord says—he who created you. . . . 'Fear not, for I have redeemed you; I have summoned you by name; you are mine. When you pass through the waters, I will be with you. . . . When you walk through the fire, you will not be burned; the flames will not set you ablaze. For I am the Lord, your God, the Holy One . . . , your Savior; . . . you are precious and honored in my sight, and . . . I love you.'"

Are you tired? So tired that you no longer feel loved or even likable?

Are you angry? Do you wonder what you can possibly do with the built-up resentment and hostility?

Are you confused and nearly hopeless? Do you believe that you have no choices?

Are you exhausted, frightened, sad, and alone?

I was, too. And I wanted so much to be renewed, to feel, to think straight again, and to be released from the overwhelming resentment and isolation. I didn't know how this could happen. Then, with the feeble strength I had left, I said, "I can't, Lord. Help me." And he did.

It was not easy. It took time. But I am thankful that after walking through the fire, I was not irreparably burned. I've been redeemed; given my life back. I am loved by the Holy One, my Savior, the Creator. And so are you.

I don't know what's next, Lord. Please help me.

Read Isaiah 58:11: "'And the Lord will . . . satisfy your desire in scorched places, . . . and you will be like a watered garden, and like a spring of water whose waters do not fail'" (NASB).

Each morning I climbed out of bed, put on makeup, dressed, and went to work. Yet the person who once lived inside me was gone, charred. An invisible inner machine smiled, talked, and worked. "I'm burned out," I admitted to a friend. "I've fried my brain. I doubt I'll ever be the same."

In his book *Burnout,* Myron Rush writes, "When you burn both ends of a candle, it may produce twice as much light, but the candle burns out twice as fast. People experiencing burnout suddenly discover that all of their mental, emotional and physical energies have been consumed."

Have you ever seen the effects of a forest fire? Once-luscious green trees become scorched and barren. Ground that was formerly lush with wildflowers and lacy ferns appears parched and desolate. But God's handiwork and time can replenish what the devastating flames have stolen. And God will patiently replenish the burnout victim, too. He promises to satisfy your desire in scorched places and water your heart's garden with a spring that will never fail.

O Lord, please renew my scorched mind and soul. I want to be like a well-watered garden.

Read Luke 5:15: "Crowds of people came to hear him and to be healed. . . . But Jesus often withdrew to lonely places and prayed."

Jesus' days were filled with counseling the confused, encouraging the disappointed, hugging children, protecting the abused, feeding the hungry, questioning false teaching, challenging the weather, crusading for justice and fair play, withstanding ridicule, teaching his staff of apostles, and loving his opponents. Increasing crowds clamored around Jesus daily.

Jesus was extremely busy. Yet he knew the limitations of his human body and soul. He realized he needed to separate himself from the day-to-day demands. Although Jesus acknowledged the people's tremendous need, he did not call himself selfish when he *often* withdrew to replenish his mind and spirit.

Learning to take care of ourselves is worthwhile and nurturing. Jesus did it; so can we.

Lord, help me challenge my faulty impressions of giving and loving. If Jesus acknowledged his need to retreat and pray, then I will permit myself to do the same.

Read Matthew 6:28: "'And why do you worry . . . ?
See how the lilies of the field grow. They do not labor
or spin.'"

My client raced around the corner toward me, overcoat
flying in the breeze, briefcase banging against the wall.
He announced breathlessly, "I don't feel like I'm getting
anything done or that I've achieved my goals for the day
unless I'm at least a half hour late for each meeting." He
was an hour and a half late for our appointment. He
must have felt real accomplishment that day!

Anne Wilson Schaef proposes the following questions: "What kind of creed have we accepted that tells us
that we are of no value unless we are working ourselves to
death? . . . What belief have we accepted that suggests
that, if we are not rushing and hurrying, we have no
meaning?"

Jesus asked similar questions. "Why are you so worried? Look at the lilies. Aren't they lovely? But you don't
see them racing and rushing around trying to prove their
right to exist, do you?" We do not need to race constantly to prove our worth. We are valuable to our Creator and Savior just because we are.

*Lord, remind me daily that I need not rush about to
prove my value.*

Read Genesis 2:2–3: "God had finished the work he had been doing. . . . He rested from all the work of creating that he had done."

"My doctor says I must take a day off each week to rest. He says that if I don't, I will almost certainly experience total physical and emotional exhaustion," commented the youth pastor of a large metropolitan church. "But I don't see how I can manage that. I just don't have time to take off."

Many of us identify with this overworked pastor. We believe that we do not have time to rest and relax. One of the burnout warning signs is the attitude that "I've got to keep going. I can't stop now. I'm on a roll. I can do it. I don't need to rest." But if we do not pace ourselves; if we do not stop to rest, eventually we will burn out. The risk is great.

God rested after he completed the seventh day of creation. He rested not because he was tired but to set an example for us. Stopping to rest is acceptable to God. It does not make us any less valuable or worthwhile to admit that we need to cease working and creating to rest. God loves us when we work, when we rest, and when we play.

Lord God, change my misconceptions about accomplishments, relaxation, and recreation. Please teach me how to live a balanced life.

Read Psalm 23:2–3: "He makes me lie down in green
pastures, he leads me beside quiet waters, he restores
my soul."

Our family has lived in our present house for fourteen
years. Yet this morning I walked up the hill that over-
looks our housing development for the *first* time. A
pleasant view stretched out before me. Above the tree-
tops I noticed the new steeple on the oldest church in our
community. To the south I saw the high school our children attended. I recalled the days long ago when my son
and daughter slid down the snowy hill on their sleds.
Although I knew where they were, I never went along.

In one sense, I did not have time to do this exploring
today. Yet I'm glad I did, because after twenty minutes I
returned to my work with a renewed attitude. I am not a
machine, cranking out productivity. I am a living,
breathing part of God's creation. He has given me this
day as his current masterpiece to enjoy.

Are you overwhelmed and pressured by a heavy work-
load? Do obligations and deadlines threaten your joy? I
suggest you take a minivacation. Walk by a quiet stream,
sit in the grass, climb a hill. Do something you have
never done before. This respite is a gift from a loving
Creator.

*Lord, I have so much to do. But I'm going to take a
break. Breathe fresh air into my mind and soul.*

Read Matthew 14:13–14 and 23: "When Jesus heard what had happened, he withdrew ... to a solitary place.... The crowds followed him.... He ... healed their sick.... After ..., he went up on a mountainside by himself to pray."

"Jesus, we have bad news," said the messengers. "Your cousin, John, has been beheaded while in prison. We just came from the burial."

When Jesus heard these distressing words, he decided to go away by himself. But the crowds interrupted him, begging for attention. Jesus remained flexible with his schedule, attending to the people's immediate needs, healing the sick, and feeding the hungry. When he was finished, he resumed his original plans—to be alone and pray.

Some of us make detailed daily agendas and become frustrated when something or someone interrupts those plans. Daily interruptions, however, are inevitable. The issue is how we react to them. Some surprises are easy to deal with. We can adjust and still meet our scheduled obligations. Others are major upsets and totally out of our control. Learning to alter or modify our plans will help reduce frustration levels. Jesus' calm example of flexibility shows us the less stressful way to handle daily interruptions.

Lord, things don't always go as I plan. Please help me relax as I deal with life's daily surprises.

Read Ephesians 5:16: ". . . redeeming the time . . . " (KJV).

When I was a child, I memorized the verse ". . . redeeming the time, because the days are evil." I wanted to heed the message, making the best possible use of my God-given time. I thought "redeeming time" meant making each moment productive. Over the years it came to mean filling each minute of every day with activity and accomplishment. Rushing and busyness characterized my life.

Occasionally I paused long enough to realize I was not in control of my time. Time was controlling me. I then resolved to step back and adjust, only to be sucked up into the excessive doing once again. If I made perfect use of my time, I thought, I could accomplish much and God would be pleased with me. This was not only a lie but an impossibility. Speeding through life is not a productive way to redeem the time. A better way to redeem life's opportunities is to slow down, relax, and enjoy myself, others, and God.

Some days I practice this philosophy, some days I do not. I will never do it perfectly. But God knows my desire to redeem my time effectively.

Lord, how would you have me spend my time today?

Read Psalm 127:1–2: "In vain you rise early and stay up late, toiling" (v. 2).

The deadline for an important project is approaching. Similar jobs have taken longer than the time we have. How then can we finish on time? "Just work harder and longer," we say. But is that wise advice? Can we ignore the reality of our time limitations? "Contrary to Conventional Wisdom . . . the next time you are faced with a difficult task, remember a passionate 90 percent is better than a panicked 110 percent," writes Robert J. Kriegel in his book *If It Ain't Broke . . . Break It!* If a deadline extension is impossible, perhaps we can alleviate some of the time panic by:

> limiting the number of hours spent on each specific phase of the job;
>
> curtailing ineffective rehashing and worry;
>
> asking for assistance;
>
> being satisfied with the best we can do at the moment and not expecting perfection.

You and I are not indispensable. We cannot stuff additional accomplishments into a limited time span merely by willing to do so. Going faster and trying harder may crush creativity and decrease productivity. When we work in cooperation with our limitations, we experience less stress.

Lord, help me to be reasonable about my expectations and to realize that less is sometimes more.

Read John 3:16–17: "For God did not send his Son into the world to condemn the world, but to save the world through him" (v. 17).

Why do we work so hard, serve so arduously? Why do we drive ourselves to perfect God's will? Are we afraid we'll be rejected if we take a break or say no? Perhaps we wish to assure ourselves that we will not be ridiculed or condemned.

Many of us long to be accepted unconditionally, to be free of shoulds, oughts, and have tos. We hunger for good news to feed our souls. We are tired of striving yet always falling short. When we stop trying so hard and let ourselves feel, we may realize that our fear of rejection is overwhelming.

Jesus did not come to give us more to-dos. He does not stand over us ready to chide when we fail. He gives no dirty looks when we are tired and cannot go on. God sent Jesus not to condemn us but to save, deliver, protect, and make us whole.

Some of us have felt shameful criticism from family or fellow church members. We work strenuously to avoid further rejection. We may believe that if we surrender to Jesus we will experience additional religious condemnation. However, it is not God's plan to heap condemnation on us. He sent Jesus to release us to freedom. This is good news.

Lord, in you I find freedom and acceptance. Thank you.

Read John 4:6: "And Jesus, tired as he was from the journey, sat down by the well."

"I feel I should never give in to being tired," confided a friend of mine. "Everyone will be disappointed in me if I don't get it all done. I must not let them down."

Some of us believe that we prove our spirituality by having all the answers, doing everything, and helping everyone. When this is our creed, we cannot afford the luxury of fatigue.

"Jesus, tired as he was from the journey, sat down by the well." This simple phrase from Scripture gives us a glimpse into the everyday life of our Savior, Jesus. Although Jesus never sinned, he did tire. Fatigue is a normal human reaction to performing ordinary daily activities. While Jesus was on earth he experienced the limitations of a human body.

We don't need to expect ourselves or those we love to keep going indefinitely, without stopping to rest. Allow yourself and others time for recuperation. Slow down. Relax. Jesus did. It's all right.

Lord, help me to remember that I'm not committing a crime by succumbing to fatigue. I want to learn to stop and rest without experiencing shame. Please help me.

Read 2 Corinthians 13:4: "[Jesus] was crucified in weakness, yet he lives by God's power. Likewise, we are weak in him, yet by God's power we will live."

"I hate weakness," I said to a colleague. Other people's lack of commitment irritated me. The inability of management to carry through on the dismissal of an employee exasperated me. My own decreasing stamina unsettled and concerned me. If I admitted my weakness, it would prove I was fallible just like everyone else. That was unthinkable. "Of course I can cut it," I told myself. "I'll just try harder."

While on earth, Jesus lived with the same restrictions that we face. He was limited by time, space, hunger, exhaustion, and a human body. We may dislike our human frailties and limitations, but we cannot alter the fact that they exist. Trying to make our surroundings, ourselves, and others perfect is a stress builder.

It may take some time for us to learn to accept our human imperfections and weakness. Because Christ lived on this imperfect earth, he understands our frustrations. By the power of his death and resurrection, we can experience God's working in our human frailties.

Lord, I'm a limited human being living in an imperfect world. Help me to accept my weaknesses and the power you offer me.

Read Romans 3:23: "For all have sinned, and come short of the glory of God" (KJV).

Do you want to do everything right? Do you wish you could hide when you make a mistake? Are you secretly certain your ideas and opinions are best? Do you get impatient inside when a loved one's behavior does not meet your expectations? Do you try hard to be perfect in thought and deed?

The dictionary defines the word *perfection* as the state of being complete in every way; without defect; flawless; completely accurate; pure, most excellent, or faultless. This defines the nature and character of God, not human beings.

Perfectionism, the dictionary indicates, is the theory that moral, religious, or social perfection can be attained by mortals. Some of us live as if we believe this theory. And we are worn out.

We find relief when we begin to change our beliefs. Paul's words may be interpreted: "All human beings fail to measure up to God's perfect expectations. They misunderstand and misinterpret his flawless ways, so they lack what it takes to possess the dignity, honor, and perfect character of God." Not one of us is perfect or without fault. We all need God. In this truth we are released to cease our striving, ask for forgiveness, and find rest.

God, I'm so relieved that I don't have to keep up this facade. Only you are perfect. I need you.

Read Philippians 4:13: "I can do everything God asks me to with the help of Christ who gives me strength and power" (TLB).

"The sky is the limit. You can do anything you want to do. Dream, work hard, and everything will be yours," concluded the commencement speaker. But can we do *anything?* Will all dreams come true? Newlyweds plan a large family but discover they cannot conceive. A young man's dream of being a pilot is crushed when he loses his eyesight. We can plan, pray, and work, but some dreams will not come true. They are beyond our control.

Other things may be in our personal control, but only within human limitations. After working ten hours at the office, a mother plans to cook dinner, attend a son's concert, sew a costume for her daughter's play, and still get a good night's sleep. Is it reasonable?

Have we used Philippians 4:13 to back up our belief that we can do everything? "I can do *all* things," we contend, "through Christ who helps me." But God does not require us to do all things.

Here's a more reasonable rendering of Paul's statement: "All that God wants me to do I can do through Jesus' power." It's a relief to know I can rely on God's strength and be myself.

Lord, I wish to be only who you want me to be. Help me to adjust my unrealistic expectations.

Read 1 Timothy 4:4: "For everything God created is good, and nothing is to be rejected if it is received with thanksgiving."

I wanted to be a perfect wife. I longed to be everything my husband desired and make him happy that he married me. But my original objective turned into an obsession. I felt compelled to change my personality, values, beliefs, talents, and hopes to match his. It looked good, but it felt awful.

Eventually my unrealistic "wifely" expectations led to burnout. The outward me could no longer live in such intense disharmony with the inner me. I knew I had to do something or crumble. Yet the thought of changing the way we related to each other was extremely frightening.

"You won't like me when you get to know the real me," I said trembling.

"Yes, I will," my husband assured me.

At first I didn't believe him. Over time I grew more comfortable with letting him see the real me. I am learning to combine who I am on the inside with who I have the capabilities to be on the outside. The two are merging—slowly. And I am grateful.

Lord, please help me to be the person you created me to be. The me you made is good enough. I do not have to be perfect. What a relief.

Read Hebrews 13:5: "Be satisfied with what you have" (TLB).

How often have you said (aloud or silently), "When I finish school . . . " or "After I get married . . . " or "As soon as I get that promotion . . . " or "When I pay off the bills . . . " or "If my spouse would just shape up . . . *then* I'd relax and enjoy my life"?

Some of us are never really satisfied. We live in the future, longing for what might be. Our now is not quite good enough—yet.

Stop for a just a moment. What is the reality of your present? Why do you think it isn't enough? Is it in your control to change it? Do you need to do something that will help you be more content with your life?

Today is life's stepping stone to tomorrow. Today is a gift from God, worth enjoying or grieving. Several years ago I realized this truth and wrote the following words in my journal: "JCW, don't live in the future, always waiting, longing for what is not. Be satisfied and thankful for what is. Accept reality as a basis for continued growth. Stop fearing the present, wishing for different circumstances, dreaming of a future that may never be. Live now."

Lord, some things I can change. Others are not in my power to control. Help me know the difference and enjoy life now.

Read 1 Corinthians 13:9–12: "For our knowledge is fragmentary. . . . When the complete and perfect comes, the incomplete and imperfect will vanish away" (vv. 9–10 Amplified).

As a child I did not always get what I wanted, so I dreamed of being a teenager. "I'll be free to do what I want and go where I please when I can drive," I thought. But my bubble burst. "It's not quite how I figured it'd be," I thought. "But just wait till I'm on my own with a family, job, money, and perfect freedom." Then after marrying my ideal mate, pursuing a career, and parenting children, I asked, "Why isn't everything better? What happened to my dream, my God-given calling? Where did I go wrong?"

In his book *Inside Out,* Larry Crabb writes, "The simple fact we must face is this: *Something is wrong with everything.* No matter how closely we walk with the Lord, we cannot escape the impact of a disappointing . . . world."

Imperfect lives, marriages, children, friends, churches, relationships, houses, jobs, careers, ideas, and solutions. Accepting reality releases us from the tyranny of perfectionism. We are then free to relax, trusting in God's perfect eternal plan.

Lord, my life, marriage, children, and dreams will never be perfect. As paradoxical as this seems, I know admitting this is the way to a more peaceful and fulfilling life. Thanks.

Read Romans 11:29: "For God's gifts and his call are irrevocable."

"Perfectionists minimize their moral and ethical plus-side and magnify their failings," write Miriam Elliott and Susan Meltsner in the book *The Perfectionist Predicament.*

We sometimes hang our heads in shame when circumstances prevent us from attending a church meeting or a sick child keeps us from our private prayer time or we make a mistake and don't meet up to our unrealistic expectations. God will be mad at us, we may conclude.

But God will never withdraw his love or break his promises even if we fail to believe or obey him. Once we accept the invitation to be his child, he will never change his mind. God's gift of grace, as well as his promises to comfort, love, and protect, is an undeserved benefit. He gives us gifts and then employs us for service according to those talents. This call, his gifts, and the promises are irrevocable.

Lord, I know you've called me to love and serve you. Everything that you've given me is forever. I'm filled with gratitude.

Read Ephesians 5:19–20: "Sing . . . in your heart to the Lord, always giving thanks to God the Father for everything."

I drove up to the motel entrance, turned off the engine, and walked into the lobby. Glancing around, I determined that the motel was not adequate for my needs. I decided to find another one. So I climbed back into the van to scout out the city's motels. The next one had no vacancy, but I didn't like the atmosphere anyway.

At the next motel I walked down the hallways, examined the café and pool area, and was almost ready to retreat to the van to continue my hunt when I stopped. "When will anything be adequate?" I whispered. "Don't worry that something better is just around the corner. This motel is good enough." I unloaded the van and stayed the night.

Some of us are constantly on edge, anxious to appear perfect in our personal attitudes and actions, concerned that our house, children, relationships, jobs, vacations, exercise, volunteer time, and church involvements be fault-free. When we accept our imperfect reality as "good enough," we are free to enjoy the moment, have fun with others, practice thankfulness, and relax inside.

Lord, I am a human being living in an imperfect world. I am "good enough" because of your grace. I will let go of trying to make everything "right."

Read Ephesians 6:14: "Stand firm then, with the belt of truth buckled around your waist."

"Of course the truth hurts. You would, too, if you got kicked around so much," said Franklin P. Jones. Some of us are experts at kicking and stepping on the facts. Perhaps we believe we are better people by ignoring what is painful or negative. However, we may need to reach down and retrieve what is left of our honesty from the floor of our lives and examine it. The facts may include

> We harm our health when we overwork or fail to rest or eat a balanced diet.
> We hurt our families and friends when our projects or causes take priority over time with them.
> Our do-everything-right attitude often leads to burnout.

There is profound wisdom in the biblical command to stand firm and buckle on the belt of truth. When we stop running long enough to stand still and acknowledge the truth about our unbalanced behavior, we actually take the first step toward enjoying life more fully. We become better family members, friends, and associates when we greet each day with honesty and openness. At first, facing the truth may hurt, but accepting reality will result in positive change and enhanced productivity.

Lord, I will face the truth of my past and present life, surrounding myself with it so that I can grow and become the person you created me to be.

Read Ephesians 4:22–24: "With regard to your former way of life, . . . put off your old self, . . . be made
new in the attitude of your minds; and . . . put on the
new self."

I went to a motel with the sole purpose of writing for
four uninterrupted days. After working for several hours
I decided it was time to take a meal break. (That step
alone was an accomplishment.) Preparing to go down-
stairs to the café, I had the urge to take a book so I could
do more research while eating, thereby making the "best"
use of my time. Instead I went to dinner empty-handed,
sat quietly, ate, and then returned refreshed to the room
to write.

Because I ate fried fish for dinner (my normal diet does
not include fried foods), I had an upset stomach. Previously I would have berated myself for making a poor
menu choice. But I heard myself saying, "It's OK, Joan.
This won't last forever." Later that evening I remembered
that I needed to find a guest speaker for a writers' meeting.
But I didn't panic. Instead I called a fellow board member
and asked for assistance. We can change.

*Lord, thank you for simple reminders that with your
help, I am changing.*

Read John 17:4: "'I have brought you glory on earth by completing the work you gave me to do.'"

None of us can house every homeless person or save each starving child. When we try to do more than God asks of us, we wander away and get lost in the desert. While trying to remedy all the world's problems from the desert, we deplete our energy supply. Eventually we burn up all our reserves.

Jesus protected children, comforted the grief-stricken, fed hungry people, restored sight, and taught many about God, but he did not do everything. There were those he did not talk with, heal, or feed. Yet when he prayed to his Father, he said, "I've finished the work you gave me to do."

Because it is impossible for any one of us to do it all, we need only determine what part God expects of us. When we exercise our specific talents and gifts to accomplish our God-given tasks, we do not have to feel guilty because we can't do more.

Lord, empower me with your indwelling Spirit so that I can complete the work you've given me to do. I will try not to steal someone else's job. And when I don't understand because so much is left undone, I will hand it all to you.

Read Isaiah 40:29–30: "He gives strength to the weary and increases the power of the weak. Even youths grow tired and weary and young men stumble and fall."

"This year I've decided to be natural and not try to hide my needs or problems," a college student said to me. "Last year I tried to do more than a human being could reasonably do. It was unnatural. So I guess I'll lower my unrealistic expectations for perfect grades and say no to a few extracurricular activities. I really want to learn to laugh, enjoy others, and have fun."

Learning to be natural is difficult for some of us. We have pushed ourselves beyond human limits. Perhaps hidden within our drivenness is an attempt to think and act like God—superhuman. It is not possible. At the end of this unreasonable journey is confusion and pain.

There is relief in being the "you" and "me" God created us to be. Popular recording artist Amy Grant sings, "All I ever have to be is who you made me." We find inner power cooperating with God, who works in our natural and ordinary being.

Lord, thank you that I don't have to be any more or less than who you created me to be.

Read 2 Corinthians 2:15–17: "For we are to God the aroma of Christ" (v. 15).

While taking my afternoon walk, I noticed several white, bell-shaped flowers clinging tenaciously to the straggly weeds along a hidden trail. "What a shame that the beauty and fragrance of these flowers is wasted on this secluded spot," I thought. "They'd show better in my yard with the geraniums, marigolds, and ferns. I wonder if anyone else has noticed them here." "God has," said a small voice inside my mind. I chuckled. "There I go again. Trying to maneuver even nature to be better and more effective."

We do not have to be extraordinary to be worthwhile or of use to God. It is a challenge for some of us to be content with the natural beauty inherent in living an ordinary day or doing an ordinary task. Our silent obsession is proving to others (and ourselves) that we are worthy of existence. Learning to appreciate the calm satisfaction of being the fragrance of Christ to God is possible. We need to remind ourselves daily that, like the obscure white flowers, we please God when we bloom contentedly where we are.

Master Creator, when I feel driven, I miss the beauty and fragrance of the ordinary. I want to fill my day-to-day world with the aroma of Christ. Please help me.

Read Matthew 6:27: "'Who of you by worrying can add a single hour to his life?'"

"Sometimes I get this strange sensation in my gut, like someone just slugged me," said a friend of mine. "For years I didn't realize that my fear was causing it. Now I recognize that the pain surfaces when I'm afraid my wife will be angry or disappointed in me."

My friend has been conditioned to feel anxious. When he makes an incorrect turn off the highway, his wife berates him. If he goes shopping but buys the wrong brands, she will respond, "How stupid!" When he sings a solo and hits a flat note, she jokes about it. Even when they aren't together, he worries he'll make a mistake and she'll find out. His need to be perfect and please her is an obsession.

Worrying about another's response to us robs our lives of freedom and joy. Although we may wish that the person would behave differently toward us, becoming excessively anxious will not change what that person thinks and does. We begin to relax when we believe it is not our responsibility to control how another person thinks or reacts. God loves and values us regardless of what someone else says. We are worthwhile. We can smile and live.

Lord, I'm tired of feeling like I've been slugged in the stomach. Please help me release my fear.

Read Psalm 73:22–24: "I saw myself so stupid. . . .
But even so, you love me!" (vv. 22–23 TLB).

I made out the grocery list carefully so I would not forget anything. I checked off the items as I put them in the grocery basket. When I came to the soft-drink aisle, I consulted my list for the brand my family wanted. I reached for the appropriate twenty-four pack and loaded it in the cart. After reviewing the list, I smiled with a sense of completion. Then I checked out and drove home to put it all away.

As we were emptying the bags, I heard a groan.

"What's wrong?" I asked.

"You got caffeine-free diet soda instead of caffeine-free regular soda. How could you do that? Couldn't you tell the difference?"

I immediately felt the shame of not doing it right. I had tried hard to please everyone by getting all the correct items. How could I have failed?

Then, to my amazement, I heard the following words come from my mouth: "I made a mistake." "No big deal!" I thought. "I goofed, but it doesn't make me less valuable."

Slowly I am learning to live with my humanness and imperfection. It's OK. God loves me anyway.

Lord, may I release myself and others from the rigid rules of perfectionism, even in the little daily areas of our lives.

Read Luke 7:18–28: "'Are you the one?'" (v. 19).

Dare we admit we have questions? If our faith wavers, will God abandon us?

John the Baptist's depressing circumstances seemed insurmountable. Would he ever be released from prison? Did anyone care? Why hadn't Jesus tried to get him out? Had his hard work, sacrifice, and faith been in vain?

Finally one gloomy day John called two of his friends and said, "Go ask Jesus if he's the one God promised or if we should keep looking." John's inner uncertainty did not shame him into silence. He asked a direct question, and Jesus responded. John's doubt did not lower him in Jesus' estimation. "Among those born of women there is no one greater than John," said Jesus.

Some of us who try to do all things right all the time expect to have "perfect" faith. But that is not possible twenty-four hours a day, seven days a week, fifty-two weeks a year, an entire lifetime. Even the "greatest man born of a woman" (the same man who years before baptized Jesus) needed reassurance to "keep on keeping on" in the confusing times. Jesus is patient with our imperfect doubting days. We can be too.

Lord, I'm tired of trying so hard to prove my faith. Like John, I bring you my honest questions. Thank you for listening.

Read Genesis 1:3–4: "And God said, 'Let there be light,' and there was light. God saw that the light was good."

"It dawned on me." "A light blinked on in my mind." "The fog lifted and I finally understood." "Let's shed some light on the subject." These are phrases we use to describe what happens when we gain insight or discern a previously hidden truth. Many of us feel as if we are "in the dark" about how to live more effective lives. We need the light bulb to be turned on in our minds and spirits. As children we may have been discouraged from talking, thinking, or asking questions. In adulthood our thoughts become confused, our perception foggy, and our reality-base hazy. We want to think and behave responsibly in life's inevitable ups and downs but aren't certain how.

God is the one who created light. First he created physical light, and then he created inner light to help us understand who he is, who we are, and what he wants. In his own timing he sent his Son, who was called the Light of the World. He offers meaning to our lives. We can ask God for insight. He wants to shed light on our confusion and help us understand what we need to do to live more balanced lives.

Lord, all light bulbs of understanding originate with you. Give me the insight to live responsibly.

Read Luke 18:27: "Jesus replied, 'What is impossible with men is possible with God.'"

Several years ago I invited an older woman to have lunch with me. On the scheduled day she left a note on my porch apologizing for breaking our date. I knew she was having trouble with her two married daughters, but I didn't anticipate the contents of her note. "I don't think we can be friends," it read. "You've never been through anything like this. God certainly is not helping. It's best we not see each other again."

My immediate response was to reach for the phone and tell her she misunderstood. I had only wanted to enjoy lunch together. I wanted to assure her that, since I had experienced hurtful times, too, I would pray for her and her family. I wanted her to think well of me and God. If I could just set her straight—lovingly, of course.

But I didn't call. I didn't write. In fact I didn't even panic. I decided to let God work in this woman's life unhindered by me. No longer did I need a crisis to feel valuable. The new behavior was not totally comfortable, but I walked through the unfamiliar feelings and survived. Positive change is possible.

Lord, changing is difficult. But with you as my helper, I can change destructive thoughts and habits.

Read Genesis 15:1–6: "'Do not be afraid, Abram. I am your shield, your very great reward'" (v. 1).

Sometimes it is difficult to understand the things that happen to us after we decide to trust God to help us change. We want to believe that God is working for the best in our lives, but we may see little clear-cut evidence.

For ten years Abram and Sarai saw no evidence of the fulfillment of God's plan for them. God had promised them that their lives would change. God said Abram would be the father of a great group of people, yet he and Sarai remained childless. As Abram contemplated adopting a servant as his heir, God reaffirmed his intentions. "Don't worry, Abram. I'm your protection and your reward. You will have a son."

Like Abram, we can be assured that God will keep his promises to us. When we sincerely ask him to save us from our destructive thoughts and habits, and remain committed to the process, we need not be afraid. He is helping us, even when we do not understand or see the evidence. The change may not take place as rapidly as we wish it would, but it will happen. God is our shield; our assurance that change is possible. The God of Abraham is our reward. We can trust him.

Lord God, you've promised to help me, and I believe you. I trust you even when it's hard.

Read Jeremiah 31:3: "'I have loved you with an ever-lasting love.'"

While enjoying a few days away on retreat, I listened to a new folk music tape while I ate breakfast. To the background of a peaceful guitar, a soloist sang the following words: "God is in love with his people. God is in love with me."

Tears filled my eyes. "What a liberating idea!" I thought. Immediately my longing heart was bathed with hope. Then a disturbing question threatened my contentment: "But is this true?" When I returned to my room, I searched my Bible and concordance for an affirmation. "The Lord appeared . . . saying, 'I have loved you with an everlasting love,'" I read.

"It is true," I whispered. God is in love with me. And God is in love with you, too. You might write this verse on a small card and put it on your desk or your car visor to remind you daily of God's constant love. For time immemorial he has loved you and me.

Lord, I'm amazed that I need not perform to draw you near. Neither is it necessary to strive to win your approval. You smile at me as a lover who is completely enamored with his mate. My heart catches a moment of pure joy as I contemplate this truth. Help me continue to believe this when my mind and emotions insist otherwise.

Read Galatians 5:22–23: "The fruit of the Spirit is . . . gentleness."

It was the first week of the new year. The speaker closed her remarks with the following question: "What special characteristic would you like for God to develop in you this year?"

As I drove home I contemplated my response. "I want to be less obsessive, less intense. I want to balance giving with taking and then be comfortable with it. I want to learn to accept the person God made me to be. I want to be less judgmental of myself and others." Then a light bulb flashed in my mind. "Gentleness!" I concluded. "I want to be more gentle."

At home I looked up the word *gentle* and read this definition: "kind, and moderate, a mild breeze, one with the velocity of no more than 12 miles per hour." I smiled as I imagined going through each day at a moderate pace. Those of us who run through life at top speed are like a high-velocity wind, sometimes a hurricane, sometimes a whirlwind. Practicing gentleness with ourselves and others is learning to live like a refreshing gentle breeze.

Lord, manifest the fruit of gentleness in me. Will it hurt? I'm scared and tired of hurting. Help me.

Read 1 Thessalonians 5:11: "Therefore encourage one another and build each other up, just as in fact you are doing."

"I'm ashamed to say this," admitted a friend of mine. "But I've gone back to square one. I feel like such a failure. I thought I was doing well, but I guess I need help in continuing to change." She hesitated and then asked, "Will you call me later to follow up on my decision? I need accountability."

Those of us who try to do everything right often function in isolation. While our public worlds appear increasingly successful, our private lives crumble. We long for someone to understand our confusion and pain. It takes courage to reach out of our hurt and ask for help.

One of the most valuable steps we can take when we start our journey out of excessive doing, working, or serving is to be involved in a buddy system. We need encouragement and support to stay emotionally and spiritually healthy. God did not plan for his children to grow or heal in isolation. As frightening as this seems to us who have always been strong and able, we really do need each other. Perhaps today is a good day to reach out to a caring and safe buddy.

Lord, I've always worked and plodded through alone. Please lead me to a safe place where I can share my heart.

Read Hebrews 10:25: "Let us not give up meeting together, . . . let us encourage one another."

When I first moved to Minnesota, I was amazed at the many geese that inhabit the beautiful lakes. Over the years I have appreciated their unique habits. In flight each bird creates an uplift for the bird following behind. When flying in the familiar V formation the entire flock experiences 71 percent more flying range than a lone goose does.

When the lead bird gets tired, it flies back into the flock, and another bird takes over at the point position. Those in the rear ranks of the formation honk to encourage the front lines to keep up the speed needed to complete the journey.

We can learn from the behavior patterns of the geese. It is to our advantage to accept the help and community of those who share common goals and values. None of us can be the energizing leader all the time. Like geese we need to share the difficult tasks. We are interdependent.

Lord, sometimes I get so busy I neglect my need for community. Help me remember to look for the encouragement and support I need.

Read Matthew 11:1: "After Jesus had finished instructing his twelve disciples, he went on from there to teach and preach."

Some of us are overworked and exhausted because we neglect to train others to help us with our jobs or ministries. Perhaps we think we can manage on our own. Yet many times we become so busy and stressed out that we no longer have time or patience to teach others. Instead of enlisting the help and support of competent people, we beg God for strength to carry on alone.

While God does impart power, strength, and stamina when we need it, he also expects us to follow his plan and work together to alleviate stress. This is a new idea for those of us who have tried to do everything just right without imposing on others. We may be conditioned to believe it is selfish and lazy to enlist the assistance of others.

During his earthly ministry, Jesus engaged the help and support of twelve men. He could not be at each synagogue meeting, visit every sick person, comfort all the bereaved, or even convince every person to follow him. He sent out his disciples to increase his ministry and prevent complete burnout. We, too, need that kind of wisdom.

Lord, I am not omnipresent or omniscient. Help me to learn to ask for assistance when I need it. Train me to train others.

Read John 4:34–38: "'Thus the saying "One sows and another reaps" is true. I sent you to reap what you have not worked for. Others have done the hard work, and you have reaped the benefits of their labor'" (vv. 37–38).

Those of us working in service and ministry-related jobs need one another. We cannot do all the planting, cultivating, and harvesting alone. Nor can one alone bring in the results. The seed must be planted first, and we may not know when that has been done. We cannot force a bumper crop if the preparation work has not been completed.

Some have a gift for alerting people to an existing problem or need. They often work in uncharted territories. They may not see the results of their work. Others feel called to implement new programs or give information after the initial need has been recognized. Still others come in after all the preparatory work has been done. They reap the harvest. They witness the positive changes.

Each step of the process is valuable. We can learn to relax and do our job, expecting God to have someone else do the part we cannot do.

Lord, what job do you want me to do? Is it what is right in front of me? Help me not to be jealous of someone else's crop or job. I realize we need one another in this gardening process.

Read Psalm 119:96: "To all perfection I see a limit."

For months I meticulously planned a statewide writing seminar. I wrote confirmation letters, signed contracts, made phones calls, and took notes. Schedules and menus were verified, deposits made, and attendance counts submitted. I arrived at the hall on the designated morning to discover the speaker and board members standing on the sidewalk in the cold. All the doors were locked. A security guard drove by, felt sorry for us, and opened a door. Once inside, we noticed there was no podium, microphone, or breakfast setup. Half an hour later we learned that the mix-up was due to someone's faulty alarm clock.

We had no control over these circumstances, but we had a choice. We could try to force through our perfectly planned agenda and experience increased stress, or we could smile, be flexible, and bypass the frustration.

We chose to laugh and start the seminar late. The situation confirmed again that trying to be a perfect person in an imperfect world is impossible.

Lord, there are obvious limits to all our perfect planning. Help me learn to be more flexible and to adjust to changing circumstances.

Read Isaiah 6:1–13: "Then I heard the voice of the Lord saying, 'Whom shall I send?' . . . And I said, 'Here am I. Send me!'" (v. 8).

"I can't do it!" said the middle-aged husband and father. "I've hurt too many people. There's so much to change. I can't bear the pain." With that he packed his bags and left town.

Some of us, like this man, are overwhelmed by the problems our past life-style has caused. Change seems impossible. The huge task of reordering our attitudes and behavior is formidable.

When God called Isaiah to be a prophet, he gave him an enormous job to do. Although Isaiah was willing, he felt inadequate for the task ahead. It must have required a great deal of courage and faith for him to change his life-style and do what God wanted. Once we decide that God wants us to change, we, too, need courage and faith to move ahead. Even though we have no guarantee that others will agree with our decisions, like Isaiah our initial move is to say, "Lord, here I am." Then we can trust him to help us take the next step. God will not leave us alone.

Lord, the task of changing my beliefs and behavior looms before me like an insurmountable wall. I can't do it without you. So here I am, please help me.

Read Matthew 10:39: "'Whoever loses his life for my sake will find it.'"

"Lord, my husband is not mine," I prayed. "I release my hold on him. He is yours." I contemplated the ramifications of my decision and continued, "I cannot predict the future; he may choose to leave. I give up control of his life and mine. The result is yours."

It seems like the ultimate paradox. We give up what we long for; we let it go in order to find what is missing. Letting go involves faith, trusting that the decision to surrender is OK, that the process will be worthwhile, and that God is in complete control of the result.

In his book *Inside Out,* Larry Crabb describes the surrendering process: "As we walk a path that seems to lead toward death, a sense of life quietly grows within us."

We let go, not into the unknown space, but up to God. The difference is significant. Resignation means giving up; hope releases to a powerful and loving God.

Lord, I release the grip I have on my world. In exchange I regain life.

Read Deuteronomy 31:6: "'He will never leave you nor forsake you.'"

Some of us are afraid that those who profess to love and care about us will one day decide to leave. We may expect this to happen because of a previous disappointing experience. Perhaps a father left when he was needed most. Maybe that special trusted friend betrayed our confidence. A spouse who promised to love for better or worse may have reneged on that promise when the going got rough. Now we fear that it will happen again.

Sometimes that fear transfers over to our relationship with God. Will God really stay with us even when we're not perfect, even when we fail or make a mistake?

There is good news for us. God has promised never to leave us. It is not in God's nature to abandon his children. Never. *Never.*

Dear God, you say that you will never forsake me. Help me to believe you will always be with me and for me.

Read Psalm 118:24: "This is the day the Lord has made, let us rejoice and be glad in it."

Yesterday, after doing preliminary research, I met with a client, earning enough money to pay off several bills. I called my editor and followed up on several business leads. After ordering my son's graduation announcements, I picked up my daughter's prescription at the pharmacy and dropped by the grocery store. While working on this book, I washed four loads of laundry and stopped to make dinner. I called my parents long-distance and ironed some clothes.

Today, after writing for a few hours early this morning, I took a walk and noticed the crocus flowers pushing through the semifrozen ground. I entered a magnificent old cathedral, sat down in a back pew, and sang quietly. I wrote in my journal, finished a letter to my lonely aunt, and hugged a new friend. After dinner I sat alone and enjoyed the view out my window, browsed through an old book, and played a few favorite hymns on the piano.

"Which day is more valuable?" I wondered. Although I enjoyed today more, I realize my life does not consist solely of one kind of day. No matter what a day brings, it is a gift from God and a reason to celebrate.

Lord, you made this day and gave it to me to enjoy. Thanks.

Read Isaiah 42:5–6: "He who created the heavens, ... who spread out the earth and all that comes out of it, who gives breath to its people and life to those who walk on it ... will take hold of your hand."

"My life is on automatic pilot," said the burned-out mother, wife, and business executive. "I'm tired of rushing around, working all the time, and fixing other people's problems. I want to live again."

When we are deep into the addictive life-style of overworking and people pleasing, we do not really live; we merely exist. Perhaps we thought we possessed the strength, intelligence, and stamina to keep it all going. Eventually, however, we discovered the truth: We cannot do it all. And we're tired!

God is the one who is able to keep our world in motion. Life originates from him. At our birth he gave us physical breath; now he can and will restore our spiritual and physical vitality. God is our guide while we travel the unfamiliar road toward balanced living. He walks with us, helps us over the inevitable rough spots, and renews us to health.

Lord, I've lost the strength to carry on. I cannot go on the way I have been. Please give me back my life. And hold my hand in the process.

Read 2 Corinthians 5:7: "For we walk by faith, not by sight." (KJV).

When I made the decision to face my burnout-prone life-style and get well, I was filled with fear. Initially I was afraid to admit my need to see a counselor. Then I was afraid to tell my husband. Next I was uneasy about leaving the business I helped start, fearful that I would not make enough money. I was nervous about turning down clients, afraid I would no longer be of value to my family, society, or God. I was anxious about discovering why I had become enslaved by work. I was alarmed that I might never recover from burnout, that I would not retrieve the "me" I lost. I was afraid I would be labeled selfish if I stopped helping or fixing others' problems. And when my life started to change for the better, I was apprehensive it might all blow up. Through it all, I feared I might never "feel" again.

Then little by little my fear gave way to faith. I just kept walking. Step-by-step I walked not around, over, or under the fear, but through it. I began to experience what the apostle Paul meant by the words "Walk by faith, not by sight."

Lord, sometimes I'm still afraid. Please walk with me through the uncertainty and dread.

Read Isaiah 33:2: "O Lord, be gracious to us; we long for you. Be our strength every morning."

Can I learn to live with my ambivalent feelings, thoughts, and behaviors? So imperfect, jerked back and forth between benevolence and self-preoccupation, wandering aimlessly between restlessness and peace. I am rarely satisfied. I want more growth, more joy, more contentment, more insight, more knowledge, more wisdom, more love. Will I ever have enough? Probably not.

Can I come to terms with this reality? I want to. We who want to do everything right have a difficult time accepting the imperfect process of change. David Stoop, author of *Living with a Perfectionist,* suggests we face the lifelong challenge of accepting our humanness "one day at a time. This means that each day is the only part of the process [we] can see and affect, so [we] are satisfied with growth that comes in small steps."

One day at a time I will let go of what cannot be. One day at a time I will relax and appreciate the joys I have. One day at a time I will trust the truly perfect one, claiming his unconditional love—just for today.

Lord, one morning at a time I wait for you. You are my strength for renewal and change.

Read Jeremiah 33:3: "'Call to me and I will answer you and tell you great and unsearchable things.'"

Have you dreamed of slowing down but can see no way to do so? Perhaps you are one of many in service-related careers or ministries who are on the fast track to burnout.

Awareness is an important step in changing this destructive life-style of overworking or overdoing. The following questions may help you identify your need:

> Do you have a difficult time relaxing?
>
> Are you crankier than you used to be?
>
> Do you always rush from one project to another?
>
> Are you exhausted on an ongoing basis?
>
> Do you feel depressed or hopeless?
>
> Are you increasingly angry and don't know why?
>
> Do you spend less time with friends and family?
>
> Do you work hard and long but accomplish little?
>
> Is life becoming a drag?

If you answered yes to several of these, you may be headed in the opposite direction of real life. The prospect of changing is frightening and overwhelming, yet there is a way. You can admit your need, ask God for help, and take active steps to reshape your thoughts and behavior. God is patiently waiting. Call on him.

Lord, help me take an honest look at myself, and give me courage to make the necessary changes.

Read Matthew 11:28–30: "'For my yoke is easy and my burden is light'" (v. 30).

"Although I want to follow Christ," a friend said, "I'm tired of trying so hard to do it right. How could Jesus say that his way is easy?"

For many years we may have had shoulds and oughts and have tos impressed into our thinking. You should do this. You have to do that. You ought to do this. No, you cannot do that. Most of all, do not feel that. When human rules are added to God's laws, our burdens become heavy, our way cumbersome. This is not the life Jesus wants for us.

Jesus said, "The yoke—the work, job, life, or ministry—that I have for each of you is unique. I made it for you, and I promise that it will fit. So take what I have to teach you. Live for me, not for the approval of those who make the burdensome rules. If you are tired, if you are burned out, come to me and I will give you rest. I promise."

Lord, I am tired. I take off the burden of human rules, and I accept what you have for me. Teach me. I rest in you.

Read Ecclesiastes 6:10: "God is more powerful than man is" (NCV).

My husband and I sat in the concert hall with our guests. I was engrossed in the beautiful music when it dawned on me. "I'm enjoying this concert for the sheer pleasure of it, without being preoccupied with my guests' thoughts, feelings, or reactions." I smiled. What uncomplicated delight! For years my personal pleasure and satisfaction was shadowed by an overzealous sense of responsibility. When I invited another person to attend a church service, meeting, or concert, I felt duty-bound to see that he or she gained insight and enjoyment.

I have now realized I am not responsible for the perceptions, outlook, or gained insight of someone else. My attitude robbed myself and others of experiencing our individual joys and insights. Those of us who want to do and make everything right often live by the false rule that we should be in total charge of all that goes on. A warped sense of responsibility causes us to believe we are more powerful than we are.

God wants to release us from this unnecessary responsibility. He is the one in charge of the world, not us. When we give him our shoulds and oughts, we begin to live in genuine freedom.

Lord, I'm responsible only for my own fulfillment, not anyone else's.

Read 1 Corinthians 6:20: "Honor God with your body."

"Our bodies have limits, no matter how determined we are. We can go only so long without sleep, absorb so much information, make so many decisions, and do well at so many things," writes singer and author Annie Chapman.

This fact distresses those of us who want to do everything and do it "right." We push ourselves beyond reason, and then when approached with another task or "opportunity," we cannot refuse. "If I could just accomplish more," we reason, "what pleasure and glory it would bring to the Creator."

For the sake of a deadline, crisis, or uncontrollable circumstance, we may need to work extra hours or go with less sleep. But when the deadline or crisis is past, we need to recognize our limitations and rest for however long it takes and in whatever way fits our situation. We honor God when we admit our physical limitations and work within them.

Lord, I want to honor you. Please help me to treat my body with respect and wisdom.

Read Psalm 107:9: "He has satisfied the thirsty soul, and the hungry soul He has filled" (NASB).

I glanced at the gas gauge. "I'll make it," I reasoned. "Don't have time to stop now." An hour later the red warning light blinked on. "Uh-oh, really getting low," I thought. "Probably should stop and get gas, but just don't have time. I think I can make it to the next exit."

But I did not make it to the next exit. The car sputtered and rolled to a stop. The tank was empty. No gas, no power, no go. "I wish I had heeded the warning light," I muttered as I started the hike to the gas station I passed several miles before.

"In the busyness of our day and life, it may seem like a waste of time to slow down, to stop what we're doing, and take [a] break. It is no more a waste of time than stopping to put gas in our car when the tank is almost empty." These are the insightful words of Melody Beattie from her book *The Language of Letting Go.*

God does not expect us to run our lives on empty. He promises to fill up our longing souls. We need time alone—and with him.

Lord, I know my red warning light is flashing. Help me slow down and fill up before I run out of inner strength.

Read Ephesians 2:4–9: "For it is by grace you have
been saved, through faith—and this not from yourselves, it is the gift of God—not by works, so that no
one can boast" (vv. 8-9).

I have frequently had the impression that everyone wants
something from me. No wonder I've often wanted to run
away. Then maybe the demands would stop and I would
no longer have to perform. Perform! Perform! Always
trying desperately to prove that I'm worthy to be loved.

Well, Lord, what do *you* want from me?

What's that you say? You want no special favors. No
extraordinary works. No outstanding performances. No
unreasonable expectations to make you look good. Just
faith?

Lord, that sounds too good to be true. But to be honest, I'm so exhausted I don't even have much of that.

OK, Lord. I want to get this straight now. You say
you'll *give* me the faith I need? I don't have to work it up?

Whew! Thanks, Lord. That's amazing! No wonder
it's called amazing grace.

*Lord, thank you for accepting me even when I'm
tired and have little energy left to trust. I gladly
receive your free gift of grace.*

Read Luke 6:43–45: "'For out of the overflow of his heart his mouth speaks'" (v. 45).

Jesus taught that a human being's words and actions are the result of what he thinks and believes. Several faulty thought patterns thwart our growth as mature individuals:

Absolutes such as, "I must never be afraid of the future."

Personalizations such as, "When the boss criticizes a co-worker, he is referring to my performance, as well."

Overgeneralizations such as, "This is how I am, I'll never change."

These self-defeating thoughts keep us from maintaining healthy relationships with others and ourselves. Growth will take place as we learn how to challenge our existing thought processes and believe the truth. For example, we can exchange the first absolute listed with, "Sometimes the unknown future scares me, but with God's help I'll gain courage to move through the fear."

Changing from the inside out helps us to become the people God created us to be. Lasting change is possible. When we alter the way we think and believe, new, balanced behavior will follow.

Lord, help me to be aware of my faulty thought patterns. I know this might be a painfully long process, but I'm willing to start.

Read Isaiah 42:3: "A bruised reed he will not break."

"What a day! Everything has gone wrong!" moaned a friend. "Our car broke down, and it cost eight hundred dollars to have it repaired this morning. When I finally got back home, the washer overflowed and flooded the kitchen floor. Then the school nurse called to tell me that my son has chicken pox!

"I wonder if God is punishing me." Her voice broke as she continued. "Maybe he doesn't think we give enough time or money to our church."

I knew she had had a difficult childhood. "Maybe you're associating God with the father who slapped you for accidentally spilling your milk or ridiculed you when you mispronounced a word or made you go to bed without dinner because you accidentally soiled your pants," I suggested. "A seven-year-old car that breaks down, a child who contracts chicken pox, a washer that malfunctions and overflows are all inevitable consequences of living in an imperfect world. These things just happen."

God's love and acceptance are unconditional. He doesn't slap us for trying to grow or learn. With our heavenly Father we are free to acknowledge our imperfections and admit our need of help.

Father, how comforting to know that you will lift me up and hold me when I am weak and needy.

Read Revelation 21:4: "'[God] will wipe every tear from their eyes. There will be no more death or mourning or crying or pain.'"

"Life is difficult. This . . . is a great truth because once we truly see this truth, we transcend it. . . . Once it is accepted, the fact that life is difficult no longer matters," writes M. Scott Peck in *The Road Less Traveled.* Several years ago while attending a personal growth workshop, I completed a questionnaire concerning the developmental tasks of adulthood. After acknowledging my roles as wife, mother, friend, executive, writer, and child of God, I contemplated my childhood, marriage and babies, career shifts, and dreams lost. When I realized the inherent changes in coping with aging, relationships, and inevitable disappointments, I suddenly exclaimed, "It's a lie! Life is not simple! I've been fed a lie!"

As long as I believed that life was easy, I ignored reality, asked few questions, rarely complained, and remained confused. Once I admitted that life is difficult, however, I began to relax and to cease the silent demand that imperfection go away.

Lord, someday all the crying, sorrow, and pain will stop. Until that time I'll admit the truth that life is difficult and stop trying to be so perfect.

Read Job 28:12–24: "'Where does understanding dwell? . . . God understands the way to it and he alone knows where it dwells'" (vv. 20, 23).

One day last year my teenage son lost his billfold. He became aware of the loss late one evening after driving home from a date. He looked in his pockets, in the car, in his room, and throughout the house. He searched the driveway and the yard, but in the dark it was difficult to see. Finally he gave up the search and went to sleep, frustrated and exhausted.

The next morning, in the sunlight, he found the billfold in the yard exactly where he had looked the previous night. Although pleased, he was also exasperated that he had wasted so much time and energy looking without success the night before.

Some of us have experienced similar emotions when trying to find the knowledge, insight, and wisdom needed to grow and change. When light shines on a lost or confusing issue or problem, it is easier to see and understand. But when we remain in the dark, our frantic searching is futile.

Sometimes we need to step back, relax, and wait until God illumines our path with light and understanding.

Lord, all insight originates with you. You are the source of understanding, good judgment, and wisdom. Please turn on the light for me.

Read Genesis 1:1: "In the beginning God created the heavens and the earth."

God did not need to create the universe; he chose to create. God created light, the earth with its plants and animals, and finally human beings as his culminating masterpiece. God was and is intimately and lovingly involved in all he created.

Some of us feel as though we do not belong. We exist, but we do not really know why. Maybe someone in our past ignored or abused us or tried to make us into their own image. In the process we became alienated from our immediate world and even the entire universe.

Believing God chose to fashion us into being, that he takes pleasure in our existence, that he remains an active participant with us on planet Earth, and that we are an integral part of his universal plan lends meaning and dimension to our daily lives. The phrase "In the beginning God created the heavens and the earth" expands our capacity to hope in the future.

God, you created the vast universe. It is beyond my comprehension; yet I'm part of it all. I am both lifted up and humbled.

Read Ephesians 3:20: "... to him who is able to do immeasurably more than all we ask or imagine, according to his power that is at work within us..."

A recent article in our local newspaper included these instructions:

PRESERVE RESOURCES BY USING LESS ENERGY

REDUCE, REUSE, AND RECYCLE

CONSERVE WATER

Environmentalists warn that we are systematically depleting our natural resources. If we do not conserve, they say, we will not have enough to survive on this planet. Many people are genuinely anxious about our future environmental supplies. We need to be careful by reducing our consumption.

Sometimes I get a similar anxious feeling, when I believe I'm using up all God's available resources. When this happens, I notice I begin to ration out my prayer requests.

But I need not worry. I can ask God to save, help, guide, intercede, comfort, heal, forgive, direct, sustain, and protect me, my family, friends, neighbors, pastor, missionaries, local and national governments, and the world. I do not have to be concerned about conserving my prayers. His power cannot be depleted. God's resources are unlimited.

Lord, your wealth knows no boundaries. You can do far above what I can ask or imagine in my entire lifetime.

Read Matthew 9:9–13: "Jesus said, 'It is not the healthy who need a doctor, but the sick. But go and learn what this means: "I desire mercy, not sacrifice"'" (vv. 12–13).

Matthew was a tax collector and the people did not like or respect him. Yet Jesus made friends with Matthew and even ate at his house. The religious leaders were perturbed by this and asked why Jesus spent time with such a man. If we read between the lines, we can hear the men asking, "Why isn't Jesus eating with us instead of with that Matthew?" Jesus heard the comments and read their thoughts. He responded, "I came to befriend and help those who realize their need."

When we admit our neediness, Jesus is there. We do not have to try to impress him with our good thoughts, superior works, or lofty performances. He did not come only to those who have it all together. Jesus came to those of us who acknowledge and admit our lack. Jesus came for all.

Lord Jesus, I need you.

Read Psalm 16:5–6: "Lord, you have assigned me my portion and my cup; you have made my lot secure. The boundary lines have fallen for me in pleasant places; surely I have a delightful inheritance."

Years ago after I asked God to fill my cup, it seemed instead he ate my lunch. As I saw my dreams fade away, I worked harder to hold on and eventually burned out. I wondered where God was and why he let it happen.

Now as I reflect back, I wonder if he could not fill my cup because I already had it full with my personal agenda. I wanted to accomplish great things for God, but I had my own ideas. Perhaps he was waiting for me to empty the unusable contents so he could pour in his plan.

When we admit our need and ask God for help, it is like emptying our life cups. Emptiness, though uncomfortable, is a necessary prerequisite to filling.

Our overflowing cups yield anxiety. God's portion produces security. He draws healthy working and serving boundaries for us. And though not guaranteed earthly perfection, we are assured of a "delightful inheritance."

Lord, I come to you with an empty cup. My image of your will is not more important than what you want. I once grabbed for it all, now I want only what you plan to give me.

Read Isaiah 42:16: "'Along unfamiliar paths I will guide them.'"

"My daughter's life is such a mess right now," said the mother of a young adult. "I want to tell her what to do, but I think God wants me to allow her to make her own choices this time. It's hard for me to back off. I feel so lost, so uncomfortable!"

The middle-aged businessman sitting next to her nodded. "I think I understand," he said. "I was passed over for a promotion again today. I'm disappointed but also angry. I used to overwork or drink these feelings away. Now it all feels so funny, so strange, so unfamiliar!"

Changing destructive behavior patterns and the accompanying misconceptions lead us down a pathway that is unfamiliar, uncomfortable, and often frightening. We may have never tried to live without rescuing or controlling someone else. Some of us have never really experienced our own feelings. Perhaps we have never attempted to adjust to life without our ineffective methods of overworking, people pleasing, or alcohol abuse. In the unfamiliar changing process we may feel empty. But God is there even in the midst of the emptiness; we can walk through it with him.

Lord, I will put my hand in yours and let you direct me down this unfamiliar path. You know what is up ahead.

Read John 16:33: "'In this world you will have trouble. But take heart! I have overcome the world.'"

Several years ago I worked with a painting subcontractor on a large renovation job. At the end of one particularly stressful day, he stopped by my office to chat. "You know, I'm a Christian now, and I don't understand why God keeps allowing all these problems to invade my business. Delays, missed deadlines, broken equipment, injuries, trucking strikes, agitated clients, and disgruntled employees. What's the deal?"

Some of us think that when we face problems we must be doing something wrong. It is an uncomfortable predicament for those of us who are intent on doing everything right. So we renew our vow to work harder and longer and faster.

But Jesus said that problems are an inevitable part of life. The healthy way to approach our daily dilemmas is to admit that no one is exempt. Step-by-step we can face them, asking the appropriate questions and finding adequate answers. The unpleasant circumstances in our daily lives are normally not unbearable. Acknowledging this fact will help us face the discomfort, ask for God's help, work for a solution, and then move on.

Lord, I know the problems I face are not the end of the world. Yet even if they did bring the end, I would then see you face-to-face. Either way I win.

Read Matthew 10:29–31: "'Are not two sparrows sold
for a penny? Yet not one of them will fall to the ground
apart from the will of your Father. . . . So don't be
afraid; you are worth more than many sparrows.'"

After glancing at the dashboard clock, I looked up to
notice a sparrow flying straight toward my windshield.
The little bird hit the front window and then fell to the
ground. Remembering Jesus' words, I whispered, "God
saw the death of this tiny bird!"

God is intimately involved in all his creation. He
cares about the demise of a common bird. He cares about
us when we are hurt or suffer loss. According to Jesus,
we, his human creation, are worth more than many
flocks of prolific sparrows. Though we encounter disease
and death, he never leaves us alone. In the midst of our
busy and problematic days, the God who sees the sparrow fall also watches and cares for us. You and I are valuable to him.

*Lord, if you care about the fate of each sparrow, then
you are surely mindful of me. What a reassuring
thought! I don't have to parade like a peacock or soar
like the eagle to be important to you. You care about
me, an ordinary person facing the inevitable pain of
living in this world. Thanks for your attention and
concern. And thanks for the promise that I'll live
with you forever when I die.*

Read Psalm 78:39: "For [God] remembered that they were merely mortal men" (TLB).

God is not surprised by our inadequacies and imperfections. The human condition is no secret to him. We do not fool him with our noble attempts at self-righteousness and spiritual game playing. William Backus, an author and founder of the Center for Christian Psychological Services in St. Paul, Minnesota, lists several attitudes we form when we forget our humanness and believe we are indispensable:

Nobody else can do the job I do as well as I.

No matter what time of day or night it may be, I must always make myself available to meet all the needs of all others.

Jesus expects me to give up all my right to privacy, rest, and recreation if I am to serve fully.

These statements would be realistic only if we were superhuman. Although we may try to ignore our human needs and foibles, God doesn't. He never forgets who we are or how we were made. And still he loves us and treats us with dignity. We can learn to depend on someone bigger and mightier than ourselves.

Lord, I am your creation, formed of the dust of the earth, yet according to your incredible plan. I trust in your divine help and redemptive power.

Read Psalm 147:3: "He heals the brokenhearted and binds up their wounds."

"My husband tells me I'm not spiritual enough when I ask him to come home and spend time with the children and me," said the wife of a caring but overextended pastor. "I feel guilty for having this desire. My heart feels so heavy. I'm glad God doesn't treat me like my husband does."

In Mrs. Charles E. Cowman's book *Streams in the Desert Volume 2* are these words by Elizabeth Prentiss: "When your hearts will not fly, let them go, and if they will neither fly nor go be sorry for them and be patient with them, and take them to Christ as you would carry your little lame child to a tender-hearted, skillful surgeon. Does the surgeon, in such a care, upbraid the child for being lame?"

We are often hard on ourselves. When we fall while trying to walk on crippled legs, we scold. Others may demand that we run when we can barely limp. But God knows the truth. He sees our pain and does not reprimand us. He is the skillful surgeon, and his bedside manner includes compassion and understanding. He carries us when we cannot walk, he teaches us to use crutches when we get strong enough, and he encourages us until the healing is complete.

Lord, you are kind and gentle with me. Thanks.

Read Isaiah 30:15–17: "'In quietness and trust is your strength, but you would have none of it'" (v. 15).

Years ago God told Israel, "Stop striving to be just like your wayward neighbors. You do not necessarily need more horses, armies, and weapons. Cease your running around. Be quiet; trust me. I have a plan." But they would not listen. They were more comfortable with their own strategies. They wanted racing horses. It made more sense to them. In his book *Hope in the Fast Lane,* Keith Miller writes: "I don't know whether or not you . . . can know what it is like to be a driven person, . . . [to go] to bed, staring at the ceiling, feeling frantic about the fact that you have more to do the next day than you can possibly get done. . . . This compulsive working/committing has been a way of life for me. . . . So for me to be living a quiet, sane life, . . . instead of at a high-pressure, high-anxiety pace, is indeed like being born again."

Like the Israelites and Keith Miller, I am more familiar with racing horses. During the last few years God has encouraged me to be quiet, take a deep breath, and trust him. I do not show my godliness by racing and hopping and panting and running. My spiritual authenticity is not proved by racing to do and accomplish and give answers. I can be God's person while being quiet and still.

Thank you, God, for a more balanced living pattern.

Read Philippians 1:20–21: "For to me, to live is Christ" (v. 21).

Paul was not obsessed with his ministry. His main focus was Christ himself. Oswald Chambers wrote: "If I am devoted to the cause of humanity only, I will soon be exhausted and come to the place where my love will falter; but if I love Jesus Christ personally and passionately, I can serve humanity."

When obsessed with a ministry or cause, we may try to accomplish the impossible through superhuman strength. Frustration often results when others do not join our passionate campaigns. Eventually our inability to achieve impossible dreams leaves us with an acute sense of powerlessness. When devotion (or addiction) to a ministry or cause is carried to an unhealthy extreme, burnout will likely follow.

The desire to help and do good deeds for others does not have to squeeze the joy out of your relationship with God. Your ministry or mission in life need not dominate your life. Like Paul, we can turn our focus on the source of all good—Christ himself. There we find freedom.

Lord, sometimes I think I try to prove I'm worthy to be your child by allowing my service and good deeds to monopolize my time and thoughts. Help me to change my focus and allow you to work in and through me, dispelling my drivenness.

Read James 1:2–4: "Is your life full of difficulties and
temptations? Then be happy, for when the way is
rough, your patience has a chance to grow. So let it
grow. . . . For when your patience is finally in full
bloom, . . . you will be . . . strong in character" (TLB).

The jack pine and lodgepole pine trees produce seed-
filled pinecones that may cling to an overloaded tree for
twenty years. Yet germination never occurs until the
intense heat of a forest fire causes the cones to shed,
dropping seeds to the fertile cooled ashes below. Only
after the fire does new growth take place.

Can anything good result from our human burnout?
Out of the white heat of our burnout comes the opportunity for new growth. When we admit we cannot do it all,
we realize our need for help from others and from God.
We stop long enough to enjoy life and eventually learn to
be grateful. Burnout allows us the opportunity to reeval-
uate our priorities and develop greater effectiveness. It
make take a long while for us to appreciate the benefits,
but the blessings are there if we stop to recognize them.

*Lord, although you did not cause my burnout, you
loved me through it, and I am thankful. Help me
believe that I can be blessed through these difficulties.*

Read Galatians 5:1: "Do not let yourselves be burdened again by a yoke of slavery."

"I'm tired," said a friend of mine. "When my husband is gone, I don't go to sleep at a reasonable time."

"But he travels every week with his job," I said. "You must be tired a lot."

"Yeah, I guess I am," she admitted. "Recently I stopped long enough to ask myself why I don't go to bed at a decent time when he's gone."

"And what was your answer?" I asked.

"Well, if I go to bed and sleep, I'll be wasting time. I need to make good use of each minute."

My friend has an inner slave driver who gives her faulty messages. "Your value depends on how well you spend each second of the day or night. Keep busy, don't waste any precious moments, and make certain you account for every hour."

Many of us have faulty rules that control our thoughts and, consequently, our behavior. What can we do to change the defective messages and stop the self-destructive patterns?

Challenge the old rules with new, more respectful self-talk. My friend tried the following: "I am a valuable person even when I am not busy. I can go to sleep at a reasonable hour and still be a productive person."

Lord, you love and accept me whether I'm working or sleeping. Today I'll listen to you and be free.

Read Luke 9:18: "[Jesus] was alone, praying, with his disciples nearby" (TLB).

Some of us may think that we should wait to rest until everyone else is satisfied or preoccupied. When our spouse goes on a business trip, after the children are in bed, if no one in our Sunday school class needs us, when all the extra office work is done, then we consider taking time for ourselves.

Yet Jesus did not wait until his disciples were on the road or resting for the night or visiting relatives to take time to be alone. With his staff nearby he went off by himself. We are not being selfish, unhealthy, or imbalanced when we occasionally take time away from our friends and families to be refreshed.

We can give ourselves permission to take solitary mini-retreats—perhaps to watch a fire in the fireplace, to enjoy a sunset, to drive in the country, to kneel in prayer, or to write in our journal. We need not give to someone else twenty-four hours of every day. Sometimes we can give to ourselves.

Lord, please give me the courage to follow your lead and take some time to be alone.

Read Romans 1:11–12: "Your faith will help me, and
my faith will help you" (v. 12 NCV).

"I'll be praying for you as you recover from your dental
surgery," I promised my friend as she left our Bible study
and headed for the clinic. She was the working mother of
two preschoolers. I knew that the operation would
severely affect her schedule and energy level for the next
few days.

"Oh, you don't need to bother," she said with a smile.
"I'll be just fine. I don't need your prayers."

Some of us may believe that it is godly to give but not
to receive. When help, prayer, or love is offered to us, we
become uncomfortable. We know how to give, to meet
others' needs, to nurture; but we do not know how to
accept help. Learning to give and take is part of growing;
it allows us to live a more balanced life-style. In her book
Women Who Love Too Much, Robin Norwood writes,
"As we give up the role of supernurturer, we make space
for someone to nurture us."

Paul realized that he could learn and gain from the
people he loved and ministered to in the name of Christ.
He did not feel like he had to do all the giving. He
longed to visit them and receive help as well as give it.

*Lord, help me to let down my false guards and allow
others to give to me and nurture me.*

Read Matthew 12:14–15: "But the Pharisees went out and plotted how they might kill Jesus. Aware of this, Jesus withdrew from the place."

There was a plot to get rid of Jesus. He knew it and left the place of danger. But he did not withdraw from serving; he continued to minister wherever he went. He did not stop being the person God the Father wanted him to be. Later, when the time was right, Jesus died on the cross. But at this particular time, he removed himself from the source of danger.

Some of us do not take care of ourselves. We stay in situations that are dangerous, even though we have the option to leave. By staying we think we are showing our spirituality or moral character. In some circumstances we do need to stay and confront the issues. However, some of us may equate love and concern with allowing injustice and pain. We truly believe that we prove our loyalty and compassion by permitting others to threaten and harm us emotionally, mentally, spiritually, or physically. The question, What would Jesus do? may help us with the difficult decision to stay or leave.

Lord, please give me courage to act with wisdom and strength. Help me to know the difference between running away and taking care of myself.

Read John 6:28–29: "'What are the things God wants us to do?'" (v. 28, NCV).

When people asked, "What are the things God wants us to do?" Jesus said, "The work God wants you to do is this: to believe in the One that God sent."

You may be asking, "Lord, what do you want me to do?" This is a valid question, but some of us ask this to the exclusion of the more essential question, "Who or what do you want me to be?" Do! Perform! That is all many of us know. But Jesus says that God wants us to *be;* to be a believing person. Being is more basic than doing. After all, we are human *beings,* not human *doings.* Doing flows naturally out of being.

We do not have to do or perform to get God to love us. He just wants us to believe that he loves us. He wants us to believe that he sent Jesus to show us that love. Learning to be who we really are before God involves faith. We can learn to be first and then do.

> *Lord, today I will release my obsessive need to perform in order to win your favor. I will be quiet enough to acknowledge the growing faith within me.*

Read Isaiah 54:10: "'Though the mountains be shaken and the hills be removed, yet my unfailing love for you will not be shaken,' . . . says the Lord."

"I got mixed messages growing up," said a friend of mine. "I received the message that I was a perfect little girl, responsible for bringing pleasure to adults. Yet I felt bad, afraid I might not measure up."

I nodded with understanding. Perfect little people don't, in fact they can't, experience negative thoughts or feelings. They must not question or ask for what they need or desire. So when normal human needs surface in a perfect little person, shame is produced.

Perfect little people usually grow up to be perfectionistic adults. They are expected to know what to say; how to think, feel, and act; as well as who is upset and how to fix it. And they always make their family and friends look and feel happy. Yet perfect people are often depressed. They are mad that their needs and longings are unfulfilled, but since they must not express anger, they turn it inward and then try harder to be more perfect!

It's a vicious circle that can be broken by accepting the unconditional love of God. One day with great relief and joy I prayed, "I'm not perfect, Lord! I never was; and I never will be here on earth." I wanted to shout the news.

Lord, you are perfect and yet you love me. Thanks.

Read Psalm 115:1: "Not to us, O Lord, not to us but to your name be the glory, because of your love and faithfulness."

A friend said to me after weeks of ten- to twelve-hour workdays, "Please pray that I will not be resentful of all the things I have to do, of all the things that make demands on me."

"I'll pray for you," I responded. "What are the things that make demands on you?"

"Oh, you know," he replied. "My job and the overtime, my children, my wife, my ailing parents, the Sunday school class I teach, my Bible study group, and the hockey team I coach."

"Are you burned out, Tom?" I asked.

"Maybe," he said and changed the subject.

Inherent in my friend's thinking and behavior is the philosophy author Carmen Renee Berry calls the Messiah Trap. The trap includes these fallacies: "If I don't do it, it won't get done" and "Everyone else's needs take priority over mine." Those of us who adhere to these lies are on a journey into burnout. We have the mistaken idea that we must accomplish what only God can do. Acknowledging this begins our healing and the transfer of glory back to the God who deserves it. God's love and faithfulness will give us courage to change our burnout-prone life-styles.

O Lord, show me what to do next. I want to change.

Read Psalm 103:13–14: "For [God] knows how we are formed, he remembers that we are dust" (v. 14).

"Sometimes I feel so alone," revealed the wife of a busy executive and mother of three preschoolers. "I wish my husband would spend time with the children and me. But I guess I'm just being selfish. I shouldn't let my wants or needs get the best of me. God probably wants to teach me to be strong and forget about my selfish desires."

Human longings for intimacy and security are not wrong. God made us with basic needs to be loved and cared for. When we are neglected or ignored by those we love and trust, we may experience feelings of abandonment and loss. Those feelings are normal and understandable. God does not blame us for our ordinary and natural emotions. They are part of being human.

God is not surprised by the intensity of our needs or desires. He remembers how we were formed and where we came from. God never shames us for being human. We need not scold ourselves for what God accepts.

Lord God, in love you created me. You know my personality. You know my legitimate heart's desires, and you don't tell me they are wrong. Thank you for treating me with such acceptance and lovingkindness. Help me to accept my humanness.

Read Philippians 4:6–7: "Do not be anxious about anything" (v. 6).

Our anxiety level increases when we believe statements like, "Disappointing my parents would be terrible" or "If I make a mistake in front of others, it would be awful." The truth is, it would be distasteful, painful, annoying, inconvenient, even sad, but not the end of the world.

What if you do make a mistake delivering your next sales presentation? What if your mother is angry because you can't come to Sunday dinner? What if your spouse retreats in pouting silence when you say no?

The next time you feel anxiety in your stomach, ask yourself, "What is the worst thing that could happen to me?" Listen carefully for the answer and then ask another question: "Will that worst scenario ever cause God to withhold his love from me?"

Lord, if I made a mistake, I'd be embarrassed. If my mate got mad at me, it would be extremely unpleasant. If one of my parents died, I'd be grief-stricken. But with your help I would endure, knowing that one day I'll be with you and everything will be perfect.

Read 1 Chronicles 28:9: "'The Lord . . . understands every motive behind the thoughts.'"

"I often worry my family and boss will be disappointed and angry with me," admitted a busy and well-liked woman. "I do everything possible to control their responses and reactions. I get so anxious I want to run away, but I'm driven to stay around and repeat the process. How can I change?"

Like my friend, I've often felt like I'm on this merry-go-round. I've learned a helpful exercise called thought stopping and substitution. First I try to identify the stress-producing thought. For example: "My boss will be angry because I didn't get everything done. That would be terrible. There must be something wrong with me." Next, I imagine the anticipated scene. I let myself feel the negative emotions it causes—knot in the stomach, sweaty palms, nauseated sensation.

Then I interrupt the destructive thought and substitute it with a new one. Perhaps: "My value does not depend on my boss's opinion or mood. I finished all I could. I'm not a terrible person."

Learning to break the vicious circle perpetuated by negative thought patterns is like developing a new habit. It takes time. Be patient with yourself. God is.

Lord, you understand me. Help me identify and change the destructive thoughts that rob my peace.

Read Luke 6:1–11: "Jesus said, . . . 'Which is lawful on the Sabbath: . . . to save life or to destroy it?'" (v. 9).

Several years ago when I was in the throes of severe burnout, my husband and I concluded that I needed to get away alone. I was grateful my husband made the necessary plans since I was too charred to think straight. I longed to be healthy again and felt getting away was wise. Yet deep inside I questioned the decision. "What will others think?" I wondered. "I have responsibilities. The Bible study class is counting on me. My clients need me. A caring wife and mother does not abandon her duties and leave." The same rigid expectations that contributed to my burnout were limiting me again.

Jesus was not restricted by man-made rules and regulations. On one Sabbath day Jesus and his hungry friends picked a few heads of grain to eat. During another Sabbath Jesus healed a man's hand. Both times the religious leaders were appalled that Jesus would break the Sabbath rules merely to meet physical needs. But Jesus simply asked, "Is it right to do good or harm on the Sabbath; to save or destroy life?" People, including me, are more important than rigid rules and traditions.

Lord, the shoulds, oughts, and musts have stunted my ability to form compassionate relationships with myself, others, and you. Please help me to lighten up and live.

Read Isaiah 43:19: "'See, I am doing a new thing!'"

Are those of us who concentrate on work, service, or ministry to the exclusion of meaningful relationships missing out on something? Henry Cloud, Ph.D., codirector of Minirth-Meir Clinic West in Newport Beach, California, says we are. He writes, "The bonding relationship is a foundational need. . . . It is essential for our spiritual, psychological, and physical well-being. . . . We begin to break down when we are emotionally isolated."

An acquaintance of mine recently admitted, "I want a more balanced life-style, but I don't know if I can change. I'm just more comfortable working, organizing, and implementing strategies than interacting with people. Yet sometimes I feel alone, like I'm missing out on part of life. Do you think there's hope for me?"

The answer is a resounding "Yes!" God creates new behavior patterns in his willing children. He says, "Look, I am creating something new, it is now in the process. Don't you see it happening?" Where we have previously experienced the barrenness of isolation, God will bless us with healthy relationships. Feeling comfortable with the new ways will take time. We can decide to cooperate with God, daily practicing new attitudes and actions. There is hope.

Lord, thanks for the promise of new things to come.

Read Psalm 39:5–7: "Each man's life is but a breath. Man is a mere phantom as he goes to and fro: He bustles about, but only in vain. . . . But now Lord, what do I look for? My hope is in you."

Many of us believe that we must always put on a happy face so that others will think we are fine spiritual people. Even when we are sad or discouraged, we smile and attempt to prove to our world that all is right.

Although there is nothing wrong with maintaining a positive outlook, we need not pretend that we never hurt. God knows that our human battles include victories and defeats. He does not abandon us when we feel discouraged or depressed. The inclusion of "downer" psalms in the Bible indicates that God acknowledges our daily struggles and invites us to share them with caring friends and with him.

Some days life feels fine, and we are eager to face any challenge. Other days we feel gloomy, wondering about the futility of it all. God remains the same regardless of our vacillating moods. He is our constant hope even when everything we do and say seems to count for nothing. With him by our side we can walk through the ambivalent feelings that often accompany confusing and hectic circumstances.

Lord, I realize I'll never have perfectly consistent emotions or reactions to my daily difficulties. You're my hope for stability.

Read Matthew 23:5: "'Everything they do is done for men to see.'"

"Each day I feel compelled to show that I've done something of value; it has to be measurable," confessed a busy wife and mother. "I seem to need to prove to myself and my family that I'm not a loser, a failure, or a misfit."

We may identify with this woman's comments. Perhaps this is one reason why we experience inner frustration when we do not accomplish all we intended to do. It may explain the knotted stomach or the overpowering need to produce. We try so hard to prove that we are worthwhile human beings. Eventually we find out that we can never do enough, so we keep trying—over and over and over. Maybe the religious teachers of Jesus' day experienced similar thoughts. This verse says that everything they did was for men to see. Did they wish to prove that they were valuable and worthwhile? Perhaps they wanted to be seen as significant in the eyes of other people.

But God does not love us because we do more than our peers, siblings, or spouse. We are his children and valuable to him. We can cease our unnecessary striving and live in the joy of his acceptance.

Lord, I want to stop my striving and relax in your love. Please help me.

Read Matthew 16:5–12: "Then they understood that he was ... telling them to guard ... against the teaching of the Pharisees and Sadducees" (v. 12).

"Watch out for the 'yeast' of the church leaders," said Jesus. Initially his followers were confused, but after Jesus explained, they understood. He cautioned them about believing everything the religious leaders said.

Some of us have neglected to take responsibility for our own thoughts, perceptions, and beliefs. We swallow whole what someone in authority tells us. Perhaps a parent, spouse, or boss assured us that working hard and long would bring ultimate success. We may have been conditioned to believe the performance-renders-happiness creed. Perhaps church leaders have pushed us into overextending ourselves in the guise of "service" or "good works."

Jesus warned against blindly following those in authority. It is acceptable with God to ask questions, express our honest opinions, and explore the truth. We can learn to listen to our God-given insights, knowledge, and wisdom. Personal study of God's word will help us become discerning, wise, and confident.

Lord, help me not to fall for false teaching just because someone has authoritative influence over me. Help me to be perceptive in determining the truth.

Read 2 Corinthians 4:2: "We have turned away from secret and shameful ways. . . . This is how we show everyone who we are. And this is how they can know in their hearts what kind of people we are before God" (NCV).

Those of us who try to do and make everything just right live by many unspoken rules. These unspoken bylaws need to remain hidden, because if they were revealed, others might discover that our family, church, or organization is not perfect.

Lies will be exposed when we take the heavy lid off our boiling secret pots. We may risk being labeled disloyal or unspiritual or selfish. But the advantage to facing the risk is that we can move toward becoming the healthy people God intended us to be. With God-given courage and strength we can remove the lid to uncover the following lies:

It is best not to talk about perceptions or feelings.

You should keep all problems to yourself.

It is best to deny reality if it is less than perfect.

You should keep the peace at any cost.

People must agree if they genuinely care about one another.

Telling the truth about our feelings, beliefs, and actions allows others to know who we really are, thereby inviting growth, productivity, and intimacy.

Lord, please help me lift this awkward lid. The benefits of positive change are too great to ignore. I need and want your support.

Read Psalms 51:1–6: "Surely you desire truth in the inner parts" (v. 6).

My husband and I had worked all day installing a financial program in our home computer. Several hours earlier, when we thought we were finished, we discovered a large discrepancy in our checking account reconciliation. We followed the directions in the manual, but nothing worked. We were stumped, and tired.

As my husband walked out of the room, I scanned the screen for the umpteenth time. Then I saw it. "Honey, come quickly!" I shouted. We had informed the computer that we owned five thousand dollars more than we did. When we told the computer the truth, the checkbook balanced.

For years many of us have fed ourselves lies. We are perplexed and exhausted trying to understand why our lives don't work. Maybe we need to take the time to identify the lies and replace them with the truth. Then we can start changing destructive behavior that is the consequence of believing those lies. The change will not take place as instantly as with a computer, but it will happen.

Lord, please help me locate where I have accepted lies about myself and replace those lies with your truths.

Read Psalm 43:3: "Send forth your light and your truth, let them guide me."

When Samantha was a teenager, she often came home from school to find the family's furniture thrown on the front lawn and her father in a drunken rampage. This scene gave her an unspoken message: "Gather the younger children, keep them safely away, and go call the police." Samantha learned it was her responsibility to take control of fixing the problem, to keep a facade of peace at any cost, and always to protect the family secret. These pressing duties denied her the experience of feeling her own pain and fears.

Twenty years later, Samantha suffered severe anxiety attacks and complete burnout. The unrealistic expectations thrust on her young shoulders had contributed to the development of some serious misconceptions. With God's help, she identified some of the lies that governed her life. These misbeliefs included "I am responsible for everyone else's safety, happiness, and well-being," "I can't ever question my role," "To acknowledge my own desires or feelings would be selfish."

Like Samantha, we can locate our inner fallacies. God is truth, and he promises to teach us. He will direct us in identifying the lies that defeat us.

Lord, please give me insight and wisdom. I want to change my self-defeating habits.

Read Genesis 40:1–23: "[Pharaoh] restored the chief cupbearer to his position, . . . but he hanged the chief baker, just as Joseph had said to them in his interpretation" (vv. 21–22).

One day a fellow prisoner asked Joseph to help him understand a confusing dream. After admitting that God gave him discernment, Joseph interpreted the dream. "You will soon be released and have your job back," said Joseph.

When another prisoner heard the favorable outcome, he asked Joseph to interpret his dream as well. This time the news was not as pleasant. Joseph could have tried to fix up the news to be more palatable. But Joseph remained consistent with what he knew to be true. He did not try to manipulate the man's reaction. He simply told the truth.

God is always pleased with the truth. However, some of us have learned to modify or sugarcoat reality. We may believe we must keep the peace or should save someone from further disappointment or that we need to soften the blow so someone will feel better. Practicing integrity is learning to be and do on the outside exactly who and what we are on the inside. Practicing integrity allows us to become whole and complete persons.

Dear Lord, I want to say and do on the outside the same as I think, feel, and believe on the inside. Please help me.

Read Matthew 20:29–34: "Jesus stopped. . . . 'What do you want me to do for you?' he asked. . . . They answered, 'We want our sight'" (vv. 32–33).

The two blind men first caught Jesus' attention by putting themselves in a position to be heard. When Jesus posed the direct question: "What do you want?" the men replied honestly.

Some of us have been conditioned to avoid the words *I want.* We believe that it is selfish or unspiritual to make a direct request. Sometimes we fail to receive what we need because we refuse to ask. Many times our communication reflects the false idea that says, "I shouldn't have to ask. If I have to ask it ruins everything."

Relating our needs and desires is not unspiritual. God invites us to be up front with one another and with him.

Lord, I admit that I have sometimes withheld vital information about myself in the false belief that I am being considerate and spiritual. Please teach me the skills of honest communication. I really want to learn.

Read James 4:6: "But [God] gives us more grace."

God gives, we receive. God offers to us, we take. God transfers to us and we possess. We need not strive to control how, when, or where we receive, we have only to accept.

Why is it so difficult for some of us to receive? Could it be because when we are the givers we remain in control? Learning to give and receive helps us develop into balanced and healthy people. We reduce some of our anxiety when we loosen our grip and gratefully accept the daily gifts God offers us, many through our fellow human beings.

The following practical exercises may encourage you in the process of learning to acknowledge God's blessings and to receive without shame or obsession. For the next month, each time you hear a Bible verse, listen for examples of God's benevolent nature. Or starting today make a mental list of the gifts in your life. What brings you comfort? Who causes you to smile? What new insight have you gained lately?

It is God's generous and gracious nature to give. You and I are blessed to receive.

Lord God, today I will open my heart and hand to accept all that you have for me. Please sharpen my mind and spirit to be gratefully aware.

Read Proverbs 27:1: "Don't brag about what will happen tomorrow. You don't really know what will happen then" (NCV).

I had great expectations for the day. Before I could leave the house, however, I received several phone calls, delaying my start. It rained during my drive, slowing my traveling time. The motel where I had made reservations was filled with high school athletes, so I had to hunt for different accommodations. When I finally found a vacancy, they gave me an outside room in a dark alley. It was sub-zero weather, I was alone, and had requested an inside room, so I asked to be moved. I dropped the key to my new room down a crevice in my van and spent half an hour trying to retrieve it. Meanwhile my growling stomach reminded me I had not eaten. On the way to the restaurant, traffic snarled to a stop. Two police cars and an ambulance blocked the intersection. A wreck! Another delay! "This is not how I planned it!" I thought.

We can make plans, but we cannot guarantee the outcome. Learning to stay flexible reduces our anxiety when things don't go the way we expected. When we acknowledge our disappointment and adjust our expectations, the knot in our stomach relaxes. Then we are ready to enjoy ourselves and others.

Lord, sometimes things don't go the way I've planned. When that happens, help me learn to flex.

Read John 6:15–21: "They were terrified. But he said to them, 'It is I; don't be afraid'" (vv. 19–20).

Jesus' followers rowed the boat nearly four miles from shore when they saw a man walking toward them—on the water! The scene terrified them. How could a person defy nature and walk on water? It was beyond their comprehension. Then they learned that the man walking on the water was Jesus and their fear evaporated.

Like the disciples, you and I often fear what we do not understand. Do you tremble at the thought of coping with your spouse's disease? Are you confused about your child's choices, fearful of the ramifications of her or his decisions? Does the prospect of facing your past terrify you? We often run from the things we do not understand. Sometimes we mock what we cannot comprehend.

What do you have difficulty understanding and consequently fear? Take action today. Go to the library and read about the subject. Call an expert and ask responsible questions. Pray for insight. Becoming knowledgeable may not eradicate the fear, but gaining understanding will alleviate the anxiety.

Lord, I believe that you do not wish for me to remain terrified of what I don't understand. Please help me discover the facts, reduce my confusion, and release my fear.

Read John 11:1–6: "'Lord, the one you love is sick.'
. . . Yet . . . he stayed where he was two more days"
(vv. 3, 6).

Martha and Mary sent a message to Jesus that their
brother, Lazarus, was deathly ill. They wanted and
expected Jesus to come to his bedside. But Jesus in effect
said no. He had a sound reason for his decision.

On occasion we may decide that it is advantageous to
say no to a request, even a reasonable one. With Jesus as
our example, we can be assured that this is acceptable.
We are not obligated to say yes just to make someone else
feel good. Saying no may merely mean "In my opinion,
granting your request would not be beneficial at this
time." We can say no without rejecting the personhood
of the one making the request.

The statement "No, I don't care to go out to dinner
tonight" is not the same as "I don't like to be in your
company." If we say, "No, I will not teach first-grade
Sunday school this year," it does not mean that we do
not care about children's spiritual education. We can say
no and remain loving and caring people.

*Lord, help me to remember that no is not a naughty
word. Teach me the healthy benefits of saying yes* and
no.

Read Matthew 16:13–16: "'But what about you?' [Jesus] asked" (v. 15).

"How do you feel about God?" asked a concerned neighbor.

"Oh, I never think about it," replied the man. "My wife takes care of all that kind of thing for me."

Years ago someone related this true incident to me. It reminds me of the time Jesus asked his disciples who people said he was. "Some say you're a prophet," they answered. "Others say you're John the Baptist or Elijah."

"What about you?" asked Jesus. "Who do you say I am?"

Some of us, like the man who left matters of faith to his wife, find it difficult to accept responsibility for our own beliefs, moral values, or growth. "Someone else will do it for us," we may reason.

But in order for us to benefit and grow, we need to make some personal choices. It is not possible to live profitably through someone else's perceptions, beliefs, or prayers. As the disciples did, we have the privilege of deciding for ourselves. Genuine growth transpires when we admit our need, face our responsibilities before God, and deal with our own problems. Then the joy of positive change is ours to claim.

Lord, I really do want to grow and mature. Help me accept responsibility for my own development.

Read Psalm 39:2–3: "But when I was silent and still . . . my anguish increased. My heart grew hot within me, and as I meditated, the fire burned; then I spoke."

During a teacher-training session, the department head said, "Never talk about being afraid of the dark. It will give the children ideas."

Those of us who want to do everything just right sometimes obey an unspoken command we learned as children: the "No Talk" rule. We may have the mistaken notion that mentioning a problem, fear, weakness, or imperfection actually causes it. Experience shows, however, that admitting our fears and feelings may decrease their power over us and make the circumstances less ominous.

When an adult or child is prevented from talking about a feeling, perception, or problem, it grows inside. King David acknowledged that when he obeyed the "No Talk" rule, his anguish increased and his heart grew hot within him. His words are a vivid description of a threatening inner explosion. Admitting the dilemma, whatever it may be, allows us to ask for prayer and help. Go ahead. Face the fear. Uncover the problem. Talk to a caring friend. And turn it over to God.

Lord, it seems it should be easy, but it isn't. For so long I have kept silent about my real feelings. Please help me to have courage like David, to open my mouth and admit my problems.

Read Genesis 12:10–20: "'Say you are my sister, so
that I will be treated well for your sake and my life
will be spared because of you'" (v. 13).

Just as Abram predicted, Pharaoh's staff thought Sarai
would make a lovely addition to the king's harem. So they
paid Sarai's "brother," Abram, a dowry and included Sarai
with the other women. When the king discovered he had
been misled, however, he was not pleased. He released
Sarai and then ordered them all to leave the area. Abram
feared for his life, so he lied. Sometimes we, like Abram,
mince the truth to assuage our apprehension about our
jobs, relationships, and future. Perhaps we rationalize
our dishonesty by saying we are trying to keep the peace
or make it easier for others. At times it appears we value
another's reaction more than God's opinion. Yet once
we recognize our propensity for hiding the truth just to
make things look better, we are able to ask God for help
in facing our fears. Living in harmony with reality, even
though it means taking a risk, contributes to a healthy
sense of self-worth and personal dignity. God loves us at
all times, but his plan is that we learn to live honestly and
courageously.

*Lord, when I'm tempted to slant the truth to ease my
pain, give me courage to face reality and tackle each
unpleasant situation head-on.*

Read Proverbs 20:9: "Who can say, 'I have kept my heart pure; I am clean and without sin'?"

Recently I overheard a mother say to her young child, "I know Mommy got angry with you this morning. But it wasn't my fault, was it?"

Dutifully the little boy responded, "No."

"You forgot your lunch and left your bed unmade, so mommy had to get mad, right?"

Some of us try to maintain an inner equilibrium of thinking and reacting correctly. We dare not allow ourselves to feel guilt when we behave in a way that goes against our I-must-be-right code, so we transfer the shame to "willing" others. We usually are not aware that we do this, nor are we aware how our subtle blaming damages another.

We may admit our shortcomings, but only in safe areas, when it does not shake our precarious self-esteem. We do everything possible to keep our weaknesses a secret, even from ourselves. As long as we can blame others for our faults, we remain blind to our need for God's help. However, God can and will show us the truth about ourselves, others, and himself, if we ask him to. Living honestly before others and God will help us develop a sense of self-worth and strengthen our relationships.

Lord, remove my blinders and help me accept the truth about myself.

Read Mark 9:31–32: "But they did not understand what he meant and were afraid to ask him about it" (v. 32).

"Soon the Son of Man will be betrayed by a few men. They're going to kill him, but three days later he'll come back to life." When Jesus spoke these words to his disciples, he was referring to himself and his own fate.

Jesus' message confused the men. Yet none asked him to explain what he meant. They were too afraid. We are often like the frightened disciples. Instead of admitting our confusion or fear, we clam up, perhaps because we are bothered by our inadequacy or imperfection.

Frank noticed that his daughter continued to lose weight, but he refused to ask about her problem. Charles, chairman of the church elder board, learned about a questionable situation concerning his pastor but was afraid to confront the issue. Often our fear causes us to retreat and remain silent. Silence is not always golden. With God's help we can face our fear, admit our confusion and ask for clarification and help. Our honest confrontation with fear moves us toward growth and change.

Lord, too often I run away from reality. I admit I don't always understand. Help me have the courage to meet my fear directly.

Read 2 Timothy 1:7: "For God hath not given us the spirit of fear; but of power, and of love, and of a sound mind" (KJV).

"I didn't know it before, but I realize it now," said the middle-aged man who was recovering from work addiction. "I'm afraid of the disapproval of my dad, I'm afraid of the rejection of my wife, I'm afraid I will not perform well enough on my job. Every day I fear I might fail. Where did all this fear come from?"

We may have received this fear as a result of hurtful past experiences, but it did not come from God. God does not give us unhealthy fear, timidity, dread, or cowardice. God gives us power, the strength to be and do. He also gives us love that does the most beneficial thing, not just the easiest. This kind of love does not give in for the sake of peace at any cost. God also gives us minds that can think, perceive, and reason based on reality.

Unhealthy fear causes us to shrink from reality and to hide from honest and loving relationships. We can progressively replace our unhealthy fear with a new way of thinking based on faith in an unfailing God.

Lord, I believe that my irrational fear does not originate with you. Please help me release my fear and live by faith.

Read Psalm 56:11: "In God I trust, I will not be afraid. What can man do to me?"

"Are you mad at me?" I asked. Even when I didn't verbalize the question, I pondered it silently. As a child, I avoided doing anything that might cause my parents' disapproval. If they seemed irritated or unhappy, I assumed they were disappointed in me. When I married, I followed the same patterns. My "Are you mad at me?" question was not always a direct inquiry. Sometimes it was a martyrlike attitude that permeated my personality. I thought that to show my love I must assume and remedy another's sad or angry mood. Often I believed I was the cause of my loved one's unhappiness or distress.

But I am changing. I no longer want to be so afraid of other people and their reactions. When someone else has a bad day, negative thought, or contrary mood, it doesn't have to ruin my day; I don't have to forgo my sense of well-being.

We do not improve the world by adopting the negative mind-set of another human being. On the contrary, this only hinders individual peace and growth. When we honestly confront our fear of others, trusting God to take care of us, we can learn to say with the psalmist, "What can man do to me? I will rely on God and not be afraid."

God, I want to stop cowering in fear of another's reactions. I put my confidence in you. Help me.

Read Philippians 4:11: "I am not saying this because I am in need, for I have learned to be content whatever the circumstances."

"As a child I felt my father's daily ridicule and judgment. I desperately wanted to please him, but it was never enough. Pain and anger drove us apart, but honesty and forgiveness brought reconciliation. I have my father's support now; both verbally and emotionally. I feel his approval and respect. It's a new experience for me and has taken a long while to get used to. Sometimes the old insecurities threaten to raise their ugly heads, so I affirm myself regularly with the following words: I am a valuable and worthwhile person regardless of your reaction to me. I do not need your approval to be accepted by God." This is the testimony of someone in the process of changing an overextended and exacting life-style.

The apostle Paul did not need others' support in order to feel good about himself or his ministry. His value as a unique and gifted person did not come from what his family or friends said or how they acted. Paul, like the young man with the newfound peace, learned that other people are not responsible for his happiness or contentment.

Lord, I am a responsible (self-sufficient) person through your strength. You love and accept me regardless of the reactions of others around me. I am grateful and content.

Read Psalm 63:1–8: "Your love is better than life" (v. 3).

"Why is Psalm 63 special to so many people?" asked the Bible study leader.

From the corner of the room, a quiet voice responded, "It's a psalm for lovers. It's a psalm for me."

This answer surprised everyone. On the surface, it seemed unspiritual, but was it? For those of us whose loved ones (mothers, fathers, husbands, or wives) have not been there for us, emotionally or physically, feeling or experiencing love is often difficult. We may feel unloved, abandoned, unwanted, or loved conditionally. We long for the acceptance inherent in genuine love. Many of us can identify with David in this psalm. We are frustrated lovers. We are people longing for love. When human love is unavailable, God fills up our loneliness and longing.

O God, I agree with David. Experiencing your accep-
tance and understanding love is better than life itself.
In the midst of my starving human relationships, my
heart longs for you. You give my spirit a refreshing
drink of unconditional love. Alone at night, I think of
you. Your unshaming presence brings a song to my
lips. You never push me away, so my heart clings to
you. You are stronger and more stable than I. You ful-
fill my deep, insatiable longing for love. I am grateful.

Read 1 John 4:16–19: "There is no fear in love—dread does not exist; but full-grown (complete, perfect) love turns fear out of doors and expels every trace of terror!" (v. 18 Amplified).

The young bride snuggled close to her husband. The scene appeared serene. But deep inside the young woman wrestled with unsettling questions: "What should I say? What should I do to make him happy? How can I assure myself that he'll be pleased with me?" There was little relaxation, little safety in the security of the newlywed love.

That young bride was me. Although (more than twenty years later) I have learned to be less obsessed with my husband's response to me, I sometimes struggle with the same questions and insecurities. Instead of relaxing in the pledged love of our relationship, I strive to do and make it more. I think I do this out of fear. Sometimes I allow my anxiety to taint my love.

Fear keeps me from experiencing the joys of committed love. There is no fear in genuine love. I realize I'll not love perfectly here on earth, yet I want to cease striving and enjoy both the human and divine love offered me.

Lord, fear has held such terror for me. When this old fearful pattern threatens to rob my contentment, help me to open the door to love.

Read Mark 8:1–10: "And having sent them away, he
got in the boat with his disciples" (vv. 9–10).

"These people have been here listening to me for a long
time now," said Jesus to his disciples. "Some have traveled far. I feel for them. They may faint from hunger on
the way home. Let's give them something to eat."

So Jesus fed four thousand men and their families.
They ate till they were satisfied. Then Jesus sent them
away, and he left with his disciples. Perhaps some begged
him to stay and continue performing miracles. But Jesus
left. His loving, caring miracle did not preclude the firm
action of setting time limits.

"We don't have to be willing to lose everything for
love. . . . Sticking to reasonable, healthy limits is a prerequisite to love and relationships that work. We can
learn to make appropriate choices concerning what we're
willing to give in our relationships—of ourselves, time,
talents and money," writes Melody Beattie in her book
Beyond Codependency. Many of us think love is always
giving and fulfilling another's need. By observing Jesus'
example, we learn that we can love and still set limits.
This is the healthy and balanced way to live.

*Lord, teach me about both sides of genuine love. I
want to learn to give and take.*

Read Psalm 31:7–8: "I will be glad and rejoice in your love, for you saw my affliction and . . . the anguish of my soul. You have not handed me over to the enemy but have set my feet in a spacious place."

Our false ideas about work, service, and love restrict us. When we live only by the shoulds, oughts, and gottas, we confine ourselves to narrow boxes. There is not much breathing room in these cramped spaces—no room to develop our creativity, relationships, personality. We do what we gotta, we force others to act like we think they should, and we let others dictate who we ought to be.

After years of living this way we feel a deep anguish in our souls. If we keep busy enough, we don't have to deal with the disappointment or pain. But we do not have to stay in that box! God sees our distress, and when we let him, he opens the lid and invites us out into the wide open spaces. He releases us from the limitations of our misconceptions, lifts us up, and sets our feet in a spacious place.

Lord, you see me here. I'm hurting. Please deliver me from the confinement of my obsessions. Lead me to greater freedom. I will be glad and rejoice in your love.

Read Ecclesiastes 3:13: "That everyone may . . . find satisfaction in all his toil—this is the gift of God."

"Honey, you've had a busy day. Come sit beside me and watch the ball game," suggested my husband.

"In a minute," I responded.

Silently I concluded, "First I gotta clean the kitchen, wash a load of clothes, finish a report for tomorrow, and take my contacts out." My promised "in a minute" evolved into several hours.

"The Gotta's have become the primary conventional response for anyone trying to get ahead in today's fast-paced environment. . . . The Gotta's can run your life," writes Robert J. Kriegel in the book *If It Ain't Broke . . . Break It!*

"I gotta get an A on the test," "I gotta clean the house before company comes," "I gotta make another sale," "I gotta study my Bible lesson." These are a few of the daily demands we make on ourselves.

We need to accomplish certain tasks each day in order to lead healthy lives. But when we let the must dos, shoulds, and gottas control our lives, we lose our sense of inner peace. God is not the one who pressures us. He wants us to enjoy our life's work, not be controlled by it.

Lord, getting rid of the excessive gottas in my vocabulary won't be easy. Please help me.

Read Romans 12:11: "Never be lacking in zeal, but keep your spiritual fervor, serving the Lord."

Long ago I circled this verse in my Bible: "Never be lazy in your work, but serve the Lord enthusiastically." In the King James Version, this text is translated, "Not slothful in business, fervent in spirit . . . " We who want to do everything and do it right often use verses like these to condone our driven life-style. Perish the possibility anyone would ever call us lazy or slothful. And cherish the thought everyone might find us zealous, fervent, and hard working. But does this verse really encourage us to continue our obsessive behaviors?

A truly slothful or lazy person makes inactivity and idleness a daily habit. We need not be afraid of becoming lazy if we add balance to our work and service. Because we have the availability of God's energizing Spirit, we can learn to work and serve with enthusiasm and then rest at the appropriate times without feeling guilty. We make the best use of our time and abilities by focusing wholeheartedly on our current God-given opportunities before we leap into the next project.

Lord Jesus, while you were on earth you were enthusiastic, zealous, and diligent, though never obsessively demanding or unbalanced. Help me to release my fear of appearing lazy and learn to live as you did.

Read Ecclesiastes 9:2: "Both good and bad things happen to everyone" (NCV).

I was tired after an extra long workday, but my husband surprised me and had dinner on the table when I got home. We dined by candlelight. I rested on the sofa while he cleaned up. We watched a romantic movie. It was a relaxing, recuperative evening. But then it happened. The phone rang. In the rush to answer it, my husband knocked over a burning candle. It flew through the air, hitting the grand piano before it landed on the carpet. Huge globs of candle wax melted into the crevices of the piano and fibers of the plush carpet. We spent two hours cleaning up the mess. "How stupid!" he muttered.

But inside I smiled. "I don't buy that anymore," I thought. "It was an unfortunate accident, and no one or no thing is stupid because of it. Joy and fun can mix with mistakes and disappointment. A spilled candle mess need not wipe out the joy of the previous moments."

Sometimes we have all-or-nothing thinking. Either everything is wonderful and perfect or all is botched up and disastrous. But imperfection and excellence (or good enough) can coexist. Learning to live with that reality will result in a more peaceful and accepting life.

Lord, dissolve my all-or-nothing thinking. Help me to accept the realities of life's inconsistencies.

Read 1 Corinthians 2:5: ". . . that your faith might not rest on men's wisdom, but on God's power."

"Sometimes I'm afraid of 'faith,'" remarked a friend of mine. "Having faith means I 'let go.' 'Letting go' means not controlling the outcome. Releasing control means things might turn out differently than I had in mind."

When people, plans, and circumstances fail to fulfill our expectations, we may panic inside and deduce that something (or everything) is wrong. If things are wrong, they cannot be beneficial. Because they are not beneficial, they must be worthless. If the results are worthless, we must be, too. We cannot allow this to be true, so we conclude, "I need to stay in control." So goes the cycle of perfectionism, which when activated leaves little room for faith.

Once we acknowledge our controlling attitudes and actions, we are in a position to break the self-defeating cycle. We can use the shears of faith to cut the heavy cord of our everything-and-everyone-must-be-just-right creed.

Faith releases us to accept that God's wise plans are more beneficial than our own demands. God is powerful, and with his loving help we can break free from our perfectionistic patterns and live.

Lord, you are stronger than my perfectionism. I relinquish my control and turn my life over to you.

Read Luke 5:27–28: ". . . Jesus . . . saw a tax collector by the name of Levi sitting at this tax booth. 'Follow me,' Jesus said . . . and Levi . . . followed him."

"When I'm asked what my husband does, I change the subject," said a friend. "People just don't understand how anyone could be a tax auditor."

Long ago tax collectors had even less respect than they have today. People viewed tax collector Levi (also called Matthew) with contempt, yet Jesus chose him to be on his twelve-man team.

Sometimes we make judgments (aloud or silently) about who is or is not valuable. When people fail to meet our standards, we may write them off. But God doesn't. He is not as interested in an ideal performance as in our willing faith. Oswald Chambers, author of *My Utmost for His Highest,* wrote, "The men and women our Lord sends out on His enterprises are the ordinary human stuff."

Some of us think we could never be good enough for God to use us. Others of us believe that because we have proved ourselves to be extraordinary, God must utilize us. But God does not say, "You are superhuman; I'll call you" or "That woman is always right; I'll send her to do my job." God employs the ordinary imperfect people of this world, including you and me.

Lord, even though I'm not perfect, you choose to work in my life. Thank you.

Read Luke 5:1–11: "Simon Peter . . . said, 'Go away from me, Lord'; . . . Then Jesus said, . . . 'Don't be afraid.'" (vv. 8, 10).

Simon and his crew fished all night with no success. They were tired and discouraged, yet at Jesus' suggestion they tried one more time. Immediately the fish seemed to come from nowhere. The men threw the fish into the boat and it began to sink with the weight of the catch.

An amazed Simon begged, "Lord, please get out of here. I'm just not good enough for you."

"Don't worry," said Jesus. "From now on you'll be working with me."

Peter was afraid to be near Jesus because he felt he could not live up to Jesus' standards. Yet Jesus calmed his fears with words of assurance. Some of us, like Peter, see our own failures and become anxious about falling short of God's expectations. But Jesus says, "Don't be afraid to get to know me and trust me. I have a plan for you. We'll work together, and it'll be just fine."

Lord, I want to be close to you. Without you I'll never be all that God wants me to be.

Read Matthew 6:26: "'Look at the birds of the air;
they do not sow or reap or store away in barns, and
yet your heavenly Father feeds them. Are you not
much more valuable that they?'"

Many of us try to prove our value by working more than
anyone else. Hearing the coveted words "What a hard
worker you are!" spurs us to increase our work load.

Maybe we think we are worthwhile only if we remain
in total control of our bodies. We exercise and manage
our food intake. If the mirror or scales betray us, our
worth as a person drops. Perhaps we have become preoccupied with how our spouse thinks and reacts to us, so
that the slightest criticism or suggestion plummets us to
the depths of silent despair. Our self-worth comes not
from who we are in Christ but from the opinion of
another.

You and I are worthwhile regardless of how many
hours we work or whether we have a perfect body. We
are valuable individuals no matter what our mate says or
does. As Jesus said, we are much more valuable than the
soaring birds, yet they do not work, jog, count calories,
or try to win favor. God cares about the birds of the air,
but you and I mean much more to him.

*Lord, it helps to know the birds don't have to sow,
reap, or accumulate to be valuable to you; neither
do I.*

Read Psalm 18:35: "Your gentleness has made me great" (TLB).

"God has been so gentle with me," said the recovering anorexic. "It has given me permission to start being gentle with myself. I didn't panic when I gained a pound this week. When I got a B+ on my trigonometry exam, my heart didn't flip."

Some of us are so hard on ourselves. We set up unrealistic goals. When we wake up in the morning, we make a detailed list of what we must accomplish that day. There is much more on the to-do list than could be completed in a week. We set ourselves up for defeat.

But God does not frown on us when we get only a portion of the to-do list completed. He does not reject us when we gain a pound. God does not look at a person's reflection in the mirror to see the inside of a heart. He knows our heartfelt desires and genuine willingness to grow.

God is gentle when we fall short of our own unreasonable goals. His gentleness encourages us to gather inner courage and to change in healthy ways.

Lord, thank you for your gentle acceptance. Help me to learn to be as reasonable with myself as you are with me.

Read Job 38:1, 35: "Then the Lord answered Job . . .
'Do you send the lightning bolts on their way? Do
they report to you, "Here we are"?'"

"Go for it! The sky is the limit!" We heard this "encour-agement" when we were growing up. Perhaps we accepted the creed that if we just worked hard, long, and fast enough, we would get ahead and fulfill all our dreams. Could this sky's-the-limit philosophy contribute to our anxiety?

The California Workers' Compensation Institute figured the cost to industry of stress-related work losses at $460 million in 1988. A major Japanese bank estimated that careless mistakes due to rushing added 25 percent to its budget. Is this progress?

Maybe we can help reduce this epidemic of stress-related disorders by readjusting our expectations. Admitting there are limitations to our productivity or achievements may decrease our stress levels.

A recent personal example of lowering expectations included reducing my goal of working with four clients per day to two. When I lowered my expectations, the knot in my stomach untied, and I was able to focus my attention on the job at hand. We begin to relax and enjoy ourselves, others, and our jobs when expectations become more realistic.

*Lord, you can do anything. All nature reports to you.
I, on the other hand, can't reach to the sky. There is
relief in admitting this.*

Read Isaiah 5:20: "They say that what is right is wrong, and what is wrong is right; that black is white and white is black, bitter is sweet and sweet is bitter" (TLB).

"What do you mean I'm addicted to working and doing?" countered a friend. "I don't think so."

She had worked a sixty-five-hour week, accepted additional projects at the office, and agreed to chair a new task force at church. But we had not had time just as friends for months. The Bible study time we once enjoyed together was now nonexistent. Similar to the situation in Isaiah, my friend insisted that black was white and sour was sweet. She was an expert at convincing herself that all was well. Loved ones stood by and wondered how this previously rational woman could be so confused.

We hurt ourselves and others when we pretend that our obsessive performance behavior and work addiction is healthy. This socially accepted life-style hinders our physical, mental, social, and spiritual growth.

Life will be more rewarding and balanced when we admit that black cannot appear white, sour will never taste sweet, wrong can never be right, and tranquillity cannot exist with drivenness and work addiction. Sometimes we have to admit the bad news before the good news can emerge. We can change.

Lord, show me where I'm insisting black is white.

Read 2 Chronicles 33:1–13: "In his distress he sought
. . . the Lord" (v. 12).

"My son will never change," the concerned father said.
"He seems obsessed with proving he can be the youngest
man in his company to make it big. But then he's always
been obsessed with something."

Many years ago another young man made it big
before the age of twenty. Arrogance and ruthlessness
characterized his leadership. He mocked the values he
learned as a child. But one day he woke up in prison—
old and alone, humiliated and desperate. "Lord God, I
need you," he prayed. "I'm powerless to undo the mess
I've made of my life. Please help me!" God heard and
renewed his life.

Some of us have pasts we would rather forget. We
may have laughed in the face of a loving and just God
while we pursued our power obsessions and eventually
burned out. Or perhaps in the endeavor to do everything just right we lost sight of our priorities, hurting
ourselves and others. Manasseh had an amazing change
of heart and mind. We can, too. When we admit our
dire need, God listens—every time.

*Positive change is possible, Lord. Thank you for that
affirmation.*

Read Proverbs 12:15: "A wise man listens to advice."

"Almost every time I talk with my boss, Margaret," confided my friend, "she sounds like she's just run up three flights of stairs. 'I've only got a minute,' she pants, 'but I want to touch bases with you.' Then she launches into a confusing reason for her visit or call. Afterward I know I have a task to complete but no idea what direction to take. Talking with Margaret about this is a lost cause, because she's usually preoccupied and rushed."

When a friend shared this experience with me, I identified—with her boss. Pushing too hard, working long hours, neglecting to pause and relax caused me to be less effective. I wanted to produce and make a significant contribution, but what I did hindered me from achieving these goals.

Perhaps you identify with this dilemma. The next time an employee, associate, family member, or friend attempts to discuss the confusion they experience when dealing with you, stop for a moment. Listen without trying to come up with a retort. Does the criticism have a ring of truth to it? Have you sensed that you've been working harder and longer with fewer results? Listening to the input and advice of others may be a step in the direction of positive change.

Lord, help me be willing to accept the insight of others. Then give me wisdom to act responsibly.

Read Ecclesiastes 7:16: "Don't try to be too right all the time. Don't try to be too wise, either. Why should you destroy yourself this way?" (NCV).

Although we may not exhibit all the symptoms of work addiction, some of us are driven to a related self-destructive pattern of rigidity and perfectionism. We get physically sick when our well-orchestrated plans or dreams do not go according to our expectations. We think in terms of polarities, adhering to the following mottoes: It's now or never—a success or a complete failure. I must do everything or nothing at all. There is no in-between for us. This all-or-nothing thinking propels us to keep striving. To cease striving would mean we are worthless.

But we don't have to be right all the time. Sometimes our mistakes help us learn, enhancing our future endeavors. Although it isn't necessary for us to do it all, neither must we retreat and do nothing. We can do our part. Others can do their part, and we can leave the results to God. When things do not go the way we planned, we can step back and try again. Learning to accept the good and bad, the bright and the dark, is a less stressful way to live.

Lord, I realize that I don't have to be all-knowing or all-wise all the time. Teach me balance and tolerance with myself and others.

Read Ecclesiastes 10:4: "Calmness can lay great errors to rest."

As I left the store I noticed a blinking red light in the parking lot. Soon I realized the police were prying into my car with a coat hanger. I raced to the scene. "What's the problem?" I asked.

"This your car?" responded one policeman, ignoring my question. "You didn't put your car in park," accused the other officer loudly. "It rolled back and creamed this van. Besides that, you left your lights on!"

"Shame on you," I scolded myself silently. "How stupid! I didn't want to run this errand for my husband anyway." But then I caught myself. "OK. It isn't my husband's fault. I made a mistake. I wish I had put the car in park and turned off the lights, but I'm human and I goofed."

Following the officer's directions, I drove my car forward. Thanks to adequate safety bumpers, there was no damage to either car. The policemen smiled sheepishly.

Some of us panic and resort to shaming (ourselves or others) when we first face a problem or crisis. With practice we can learn to respond in new ways.

Lord, help me break my old habit of shaming and blaming. May I learn to face calmly each new day's diverse situations and unique problems.

Read Proverbs 31:25: "'She shall rejoice in time to come'" (KJV).

"To love life is to love time. Time is the stuff life is made of." This quote from Benjamin Franklin intrigues me. Living in harmony with time. Agreeing not to compete against time. Becoming friends with time. What a hopeful possibility!

A colleague surprised me when she recently said, "I'm in the process of changing my philosophy about time and work. I'm beginning to think that maybe fulfillment and success are not found in keeping my nose to the grindstone each and every minute. I've decided to try to be a bit easier on myself, to take breaks, to pause and talk with fellow workers, and to rest when appropriate. But, I admit this is extremely uncomfortable behavior for me. Am I doing the right thing?"

Perhaps God allows finite human beings to live within the confines of time to protect us from anxiety overload and burnout. Changing our concept of time as a slave driver or tyrant to that of a friend can help us become more peaceful and content. Then, like the woman mentioned in Proverbs, we may learn to rejoice in each moment that comes our way.

Lord, thank you for the safety of time limitations. Although I realize that one day time restrictions will not be necessary, help me to be content with my now.

Read Jeremiah 17:14: "Heal me, O Lord, and I will be healed; . . . for you are the one I praise."

"You really love this, don't you, Joan?" said my customer. "You just seem to come alive when you're working." This comment came from the first client I took after my burnout necessitated a sabbatical. As she said it, I felt my stomach tighten. I had tried hard to leave this workaholic life-style behind. Yet any statement or situation that reminded me of my excessive behavior sickened me.

It's true, I do get a certain high when rushing, working, and finding solutions. I am what someone has called an adrenaline junkie. Experts say the "busy" disease is both a process and a substance addiction. The chemical is adrenaline. As long as the chemical keeps flowing, we medicate the pain and distress of life.

However, as God helps us develop a new, less driven and more honest life-style, we learn to cope with life's inevitable disappointments and cultivate a healthy association with our work. Healing and positive change in this area of our lives is possible.

Lord God, you are the master healer. I believe your intervention in my life can restore me to health. Please come and heal me. I'll cooperate with your treatment.

Read Luke 10:38–42: "'Martha . . . ,' the Lord answered, 'you are worried and upset about many things, but only one thing is needed. Mary has chosen what is better, and it will not be taken away from her'" (vv. 41–42).

Martha was the original servaholic. Although she was genuinely concerned with helping others, her serving controlled her. Her guests may have felt that she cared more about her good deeds than spending time with them.

Martha lived many years ago, yet her workaholic lifestyle is prevalent today. Those of us who try hard to do and make everything around us just right are often distracted from the most important things in life.

Like Martha, we get dragged around by our work addiction, perfectionism, and people pleasing. If we cut the leash on our habitual doing and working, we can relax, like Mary, and learn to sit at Jesus' feet.

It is at Jesus' feet that we begin to understand who we are and how we can be the person God created us to be. In his presence we find help for dealing with life's dilemmas and disappointments and gain firsthand knowledge of God's unconditional love and acceptance.

Lord, I get so tired. Sometimes life seems to control me, instead of my controlling it. Please help me to balance my doing with quiet listening.

Read Daniel 6:26–27: "He is the living God and he endures forever. . . . He rescues and he saves."

This week I read the true stories of a lifeguard who saved a toddler from drowning, a nurse who performed CPR on a heart attack patient, and a passing motorist who interceded for an elderly mugging victim. These rescuers stepped in to save another person from danger or death. There is a good kind of rescuing.

But some of us are unhealthy rescuers. We believe lies that include the following:

Other people are incapable of helping themselves adequately, so I must do it for them.

I should try to fix or change someone when he or she is sad, disappointed, or angry.

It is my personal responsibility to keep all things on an even keel for my family and friends.

I am responsible for my family members' happiness and satisfaction. My contentment depends on theirs.

Unnecessary rescuing causes exhaustion and propels us to the edge of burnout. We can learn to change the way we help others, leaving the saving to a tireless and compassionate God.

Lord, teach me the difference between healthy and unhealthy helping. I'm bone tired.

Read Hosea 6:6: "For I desire mercy, not sacrifice, and acknowledgment of God rather than burnt offerings."

Those of us in service-related pursuits and careers want to help others. And we do. But sometimes we work, serve, and help when we could be spending quality time developing relationships with our families, ourselves, or God. We become involved in additional worthwhile programs and meetings even though our agendas are already full. Our fixing, helping, and serving may be thwarting our personal growth. Perhaps it hinders others' development as well.

God prefers compassion that overflows in merciful daily action over planned good deeds wrought out of a persistent need to prove something. God loves us no matter what we do. We can offer him our hearts first and then our relaxed good deeds.

Lord, why am I compelled to do and give? Help me step back from the passion of my sacrificial service to allow you to produce your compassion within me.

Read Proverbs 23:23: "Buy the truth and do not sell it."

"Last year I took a job caring for seven to nine children each weekday morning," said a friend of mine. "But fifteen to twenty kids showed up every day. It was frustrating and exhausting, but I tolerated it in silence for weeks. When I casually mentioned the overcrowded conditions to the management, they seemed not to hear me. They acted unconcerned. So I coped as long as I could. Finally one day I gathered my courage and resigned. On my last day, I overheard the boss tell my replacement, 'There will never be more than seven to nine children each morning.' I couldn't believe that he would lie so deliberately, but I said nothing.

"Later I learned that within two days the new employee insisted on additional help. My former boss said he wasn't aware there were so many children in the day-care room and immediately hired help. Can you believe that?" exclaimed my friend.

Sometimes our overworking and rescuing contributes to misunderstandings about the truth. Once we comprehend this, perhaps we will grant ourselves permission to change our habits. It is all right with God to speak up and state the facts. He is pleased when we buy the truth and never forfeit it.

Lord, my I-must-endure-and-do-it-all thinking is exhausting to me and confusing to others. Give me courage to admit the truth and not back down.

Read Galatians 6:2–5: "Carry each other's burdens and . . . you will fulfill the law of Christ. . . . For each one should carry his own load" (vv. 2,5).

When I memorized these verses as a teenager, I was confused by the seeming incongruity. "I can and will carry others' burdens," I agreed, "but how could I be so selfish as to be concerned with my own problems? My major consideration should be for other people and their troubles."

The way I understood these verses contributed to my I-must-do-everything thinking and eventual burnout. I believed I was obeying God by helping others while neglecting myself.

What I am learning now is what Paul knew all along. I rob myself and others if I assume their daily problems or needs. By trying to carry all the burdens, I play God.

Most people need assistance during times of excessive difficulty. We are privileged to help. Yet when we take on the responsibility for another person's day-to-day dilemmas, we are headed for disappointment. And chronic disappointment often leads to disillusionment and then burnout. This is not the way to fulfill the law of Christ. We need not carry more than our share of everyday loads. This is good news.

Lord, please help me make this difficult life-style switch to healthy and beneficial load-carrying.

Read Psalm 118:8: "It is better to take refuge in the Lord than to trust in man."

One day while talking to an associate, he shared a portion of his recent counseling session with me. "People always expect me to fix everything," he told his counselor. "I'm tired of trying to be right all the time. When will this all end?"

"When you decide you don't want to live this way anymore," said his counselor. "Do you want to stop pretending you're superman with all the answers?"

"But no one will want to be with me if I admit I have needs and problems of my own," he responded.

"Have I kicked you out yet?" joked the counselor.

My friend chuckled. "No, but I'm paying you."

"The decision is yours," repeated his counselor. "Think about your choices. We'll discuss it later."

My friend left with a heavy heart. If he changed his behavior, others would be upset. But one issue bothered him more: "If I stop helping everyone, will it be all right with God?" During the next week he studied his options and prayed. Then it dawned on him: "If I continue to play the superhero, I encourage others to trust in me instead of God. Perhaps if I back off, their faith will have an opportunity to grow." That day the weight of the world began to roll off his tired shoulders.

Lord, please forgive me for trying to play God.

Read Luke 13:18–19: "Then Jesus asked, 'What is the kingdom of God like? . . . It is like a mustard seed, which a man took and planted in his garden.'"

Many years ago a brilliant missionary doctor named Albert Schweitzer said, "There can be no Kingdom of God in the world without the Kingdom of God in our hearts."

But what is the Kingdom of God like?

Jesus answered this question by painting a word picture of a mustard seed that grew and became a tree in which birds perched. The Kingdom of God begins within us when a minuscule seed of faith is planted. It takes faith to work toward changing our obsessive attitudes and behaviors. Sometimes our faith seems very small. But as this seed of faith is watered and nourished it grows first into a shrub and eventually into a strong tree. Our faith grows as we cooperate with God and his kingdom.

During church on Sundays many of us pray, "Our Father in heaven, hallowed be your name, your kingdom come, your will be done on earth as it is in heaven." The next time we pray for God's kingdom to come change the world, let us also ask that the Kingdom of God come and change our individual hearts.

Lord, may your will be done in my heart as it is in heaven. Grow the miracle seed of healing within me.

Read Jeremiah 29:11: "'For I know the plans I have for you,' declares the Lord, 'plans to prosper you and not to harm you, plans to give you hope and a future.'"

"I need to declare a major so I can plan my schedule, but I'm confused," admitted a college student. "I want to be an engineer, but maybe God wants me to do something else."

"I have an offer for a great position," said a middle-aged executive and father. "My present job is fine, but I don't want to turn down this new opportunity. Would God care if I accept?"

"Tony asked me to be his wife," confided the young woman. "I love him, and we share the same goals. Yet I've been thinking, maybe God doesn't want me to marry him."

Sometimes we think we need to be unhappy or unfulfilled in order to learn and grow spiritually. But God has good plans for us. He does not want to deprive us or keep us forever guessing. His plans are usually in harmony with our God-given insights and talents. God is in charge of everything. He has all the resources in the world at his disposal. He will not look down on us if we make decisions that seem favorable to us. He is a good God, and he wants us to have a hopeful future.

Lord, I believe you want only what is best for me, and I will trust you.

Read Romans 11:35: "And who could ever offer to the Lord enough to induce him to act?" (TLB).

"I should have had a longer quiet time this morning," said the young mother in my Bible study. "Then my day would have gone better."

Some of us, like this busy young woman, may believe we can pray, study, read, or serve enough to induce God to bless us. However, God will not be manipulated. His love or support does not fluctuate in proportion to how many minutes we put into our quiet time each day.

We are God's children. He loves, blesses, and acts on our behalf regardless of how many spiritual gymnastics we perform. Although when we spend quiet time in his presence we are enriched and blessed, this does not alter the reality of his grace.

We can learn to relax and enjoy God's company. His love is unconditional.

Lord, I want to spend time with you. I long to know you and understand your words. You are God. I know I could never do enough to make you love me more. In this reality I feel secure and blessed.

Read Romans 4:18–21: "But [Abraham] was strengthened in his faith, . . . being fully persuaded that God had power to do what he had promised" (vv. 20–21).

Faith is confidence in God's ability (and willingness) to fulfill and complete what he started. It is trusting that God is in charge; that he can and will do what we cannot see or figure out.

Although Abraham had previously tried to control his own future, when faced with the confusing circumstances concerning Issac, Abraham had faith that God would see him through.

Though we try with all the discernment and understanding we can muster, we will never know exactly what tomorrow holds. We wish we could. We want desperately to make our plans or dreams come true. When we are thwarted in our attempts to control the weather, the environment, the economy, the government, our mate, parents, children, or boss, we often become frustrated. Faith is loosening our grip on people, things, and circumstances. Faith is not resignation but active release. There is a difference. Resignation brings defeat and joylessness; faith produces freedom and life.

Lord, strengthen my faith. Like Abraham, may I be persuaded that you have power to do all that you've promised to do.

Read John 18:10–11: "Peter, who had a sword, drew it and struck the high priest's servant" (v. 10).

"I hear you're leaving the Christian college to go to the university," said Betty's aunt. "I think you're making a big mistake, honey."

"I don't think so, Aunt Sue," said Betty. "I prayed about it, and I think it's the right decision."

"I just want to keep you from unnecessary problems and pain," said Aunt Sue.

Counselor Carmen Berry calls individuals like Aunt Sue "Protectors." These caring people are bent on protecting others from themselves. They try to judge what is and is not hurtful to someone else. Sometimes those of us who want to do and make everything right go to incredible lengths to protect another, as Peter did when he cut off the soldier's ear. But we may hinder rather than help. Had Peter been successful in protecting Jesus, the entire world would have been robbed of a savior. If Aunt Sue had successfully changed her niece's mind, Betty might never have met her husband or become acquainted with the ministry that led to the couple's career.

We can care about others without making decisions for them. Peace and calm enter our hearts as we accept God's plan for ourselves as well as others.

Lord, I'm relieved that I'm not anyone's ultimate protector. That is your job, and I'll let you do it.

Read Luke 6:41–42: "'Why do you look at the speck of sawdust in your brother's eye and pay no attention to the plank in your own eye?'" (v. 41).

"Why didn't you tell me the contractor called to change an installation date?" a harried product manager asked her secretary. "Now I've missed the deadline and will probably lose some business."

"Well, you were so busy and all," explained the secretary. "I was trying to help. I wanted to save you from having any more stress."

Protectors, like this secretary, are expert at hiding the unpleasant truth from others (for their own good, of course). However, they often hide the truth from themselves as well.

Those of us who want to make everything right often easily discern the problems in another's life but may remain unaware of the troubling behavior in our own. Jesus addressed this situation when he said, "First, deal with your own needs, difficulties, and issues. Then you will be able to help another." We genuinely help others when we learn to face the truth about ourselves and let others deal with their own problems and reactions.

This is a reasonable and compassionate way to live.

Lord, this is difficult to admit or even understand. Help me to see myself clearly and move on to experience growth in my life.

Read Matthew 16:21–23: "Peter took him aside and began to rebuke him. 'Never, Lord!' he said. 'This shall never happen to you!'" (v. 22).

"I want you to be aware that in a few days I'm going to be killed," said Jesus.

Upon hearing these words, Peter decided he'd better have a talk with Jesus. "There's just no way we can let this happen to you," he said.

Jesus' response was immediate. "Peter, you think you're helping, but you're actually hindering me. Stop trying to be bigger than God."

Some of us are like Peter. We attempt to step in and protect or rescue another from upcoming pain, confusion, or hurt. But to do so may be hindering God's plan for insight and growth in our loved one's life. We cannot always know God's agenda for another's spiritual maturity. Peter's interference could have blocked God's beneficial plan for Jesus—and us.

Sometimes we try so hard to make everything right for someone else that it completely wears us out—physically, emotionally, mentally, and spiritually. What a relief to learn that we do not have to be the protector in every situation.

Lord, please help me to step aside and watch you work. I know you have a plan, and I am grateful.

Read Psalm 99:4: "The King is mighty, he loves justice—you have established equity; in Jacob you have done what is just and right."

Some of us try to "fix" another's feelings, assuming we know what the other wants, needs, or deserves. Sometimes while we are busy attending to the unfair problems (actual or presumed) of others, we ignore our own needs and growth. Our personal boundaries are all wrapped up in someone else. Although we genuinely wish to help, we may become so burdened to do and make everything right for others that our attention is diverted from what God has for us to learn.

Recently a friend told me that she feels sorry for the other church staff members when one specific pastor is commended. She then feels personally obligated to do or say something to make the additional staff feel good, too. She admitted she is exhausted looking out for everyone's well-being.

God is the one who makes all things fair and right. It is a welcome relief to realize that we do not have to assume his responsibility. We can relax, grow quiet enough within to gain our own insight, and joyfully trust God to work in the lives of those we care about.

Lord, you are powerful and fair. I'll allow you to do your job. Please give me understanding and wisdom in knowing when and how to help others.

Read 2 Chronicles 19:11: "Act with courage, and may the Lord be with those who do well."

"I'm tired of trying to be all things to all people. It's an impossible task!" admitted a friend. "But everyone is accustomed to my doing for them. They appreciate this way of life. They don't have to find their own solutions, pray their own prayers, or deal with their own dilemmas, because I take care of anything I see is needed.

"Other people's pleasures, demands, and beliefs always come first, even before what God wants me to be and do. I've always thought God wanted me to go back to school and pursue my music, but I abandoned the idea because it was so different from what my family wanted. I thought that was the loving and unselfish thing to do. Now I'm not so sure."

God does not expect us to do for others what they can do for themselves. When we spend our God-given time attempting to be all things to everyone else, we rob ourselves of the creative role he planned for us. God only asks that we be who he created us to be. And he gives us power and courage to complete this reasonable goal.

Lord, if I decide to be the person you made me to be, it may rock the boat. Please grant me continued courage to change.

Read Matthew 6:1: "'Be careful not to do your "acts of righteousness" before men, to be seen by them.'"

"I think I'm getting sick. I have a sore throat and chills," said an overworked pastor. "I'm so tired."

"You've been under a lot of stress lately. Why don't you take off for a while and recuperate?" I suggested.

"Oh, I can't do that," he responded. "It'd put too much pressure on my staff. They couldn't handle it all. Besides that, I promised to host a support group all this next week. They'd be disappointed if I didn't follow through."

Some of us want everything to be just right, and when it isn't, we think it is up to us to remedy the situation. The fear that we might disappoint others often causes us to neglect our own health. Although unaware of it, we may perform our deeds of kindness to win acceptance and escape feelings of inadequacy. Like this pastor, sometimes we may be extra nice so that others will see and approve. We become liberated people when we begin genuinely to believe that we can give, help, be nice, and still take care of ourselves. God will see that others are taken care of when we cannot do it. We can trust him.

Lord, please help me identify the motive for my "acts of righteousness." I want to be a kind yet healthy child of God.

Read John 21:15–25: "'Lord, what about him?'" (v. 21).

"Peter, do you care about me more than all the other important things in your life?" asked Jesus.

"Oh, yes, Lord," answered Peter. "You know I do."

"I have a plan for you, Peter," responded Jesus.

"I'm calling you to supervise, guide and nurture those who choose to believe in me after I'm gone."

"Lord, what's your plan for *him?*" Peter pointed toward his friend John.

Peter's inquiry marred the intimacy of the moment. Perhaps he had not fully sensed the magnitude of Jesus' forgiving and compassionate words. Did Peter feel responsible for his colleague's present and future state before God?

Some of us, like Peter, may be so concerned with someone else's response to God's call that we neglect to deal honestly with our own. You and I are individually responsible for who we are and what we decide before God. We do not have to make spiritual decisions for other people. Allowing others to develop their own spiritual relationships frees us to relax and enjoy serving God.

Lord, I always believed it was more godly for me to be concerned with my loved ones' spiritual welfare than my own. Now I'm beginning to see that being honest and straight before you offers us all more freedom. I want to serve you. Please help me.

Read Psalm 118:27: "The Lord is God."

"Sometimes I feel good trying to do everything for everyone," I said, "but other times I feel bad. I'm confused. I don't want to live this way anymore."

Carmen Renee Berry calls this the Messiah Trap. She writes: "The Messiah Trap is an odd combination of feeling grandiose yet worthless, of being needed and yet abandoned, of playing God while groveling." Those of us caught in this trap adhere to two basic rules, she says. The first rule is, If I don't do it, it won't get done. Messiah Trap people are doers, helpers, genuinely nice people. We keep homes and offices running smoothly. But we are often tired and overwhelmed because we think other people's happiness is our responsibility. Rule number two is, Everyone else's needs should take priority over mine. Because we don't want to be selfish, we often neglect our own needs. People depend on us for answers and unending support. It makes us feel important and worthwhile. However, when inevitable humanness breaks through our facade, we have no one to help *us.* We then feel isolated and lonely.

But there is a way out of this trap. We can change how we think and live. Learning to let God be God in our own lives and the lives of those we love will result in a more balanced and peaceful life.

Lord, you alone are God. I'll let you take over.

Read 1 Corinthians 2:10–16: "No one can really know what anyone else is thinking, or what he is really like, except that person himself. And no one can know God's thoughts except God's own spirit" (v. 11 TLB).

The chairman of the deacon board stood up and said, "I'm thankful for my wife. She keeps me on the straight and narrow path. Actually, she acts as a holy spirit in my life. When God has something to say to me, I rely on her to make it clear."

Unfortunately the hidden message in this testimony perpetuates the rescuing and fixing role that many perfectionists play. On the surface this thinking and behavior may sound considerate and noble. However, we don't have to speak for God in another's life. When we try to do so, the other person does not have the privilege of learning his own lessons or changing his own behavior.

By drawing clear boundaries concerning our mental and spiritual lives, we experience less stress within our relationships. We learn to respect and appreciate one another when we accept personal responsibility for our own growth.

Lord, I'm tired of playing God in others' lives. It's a relief to find out I do not need to try to read another's thoughts or decipher your plan for them. Please help me as I step aside and allow you to work directly.

Read 1 John 1:8–10: "If we confess our sins, he is faithful and just and will forgive us our sins and purify us from all unrighteousness" (v. 9).

"With God's help I'm learning to love again," said my Bible study partner. "Somewhere along the line I learned that loving another person meant getting inside his skin, trying to make him a better person, attempting to influence his decisions, pushing him toward maturity. Now I'm realizing that true love means standing beside, supporting, accepting, and encouraging. This new, less demanding way of life is unfamiliar. I need daily help."

Trying to get inside another's thoughts or feelings in order to alter reactions and behavior is breaking and entering. It's against God's moral and spiritual law. When we attempt to climb inside and change another's beliefs, emotions, or perceptions to match our own, we are impersonating the Holy Spirit.

These are sobering thoughts. Once we realize that our helping is actually hindering, we may feel humiliated and sad. What can we do?

We can ask God to help us. He is an understanding Father. When we go to him with our shortcomings and sins, he forgives and assists us in changing our defeating habits. This is the best news of all.

Lord, I've committed crimes against you and others. Please forgive me and aid me in forgiving myself.

Read Joshua 24:15: "'Then choose for yourselves this day whom you will serve.'"

"God has made it a rule for Himself that He won't alter people's character by force. . . . He would rather have a world of free beings, with all its risks, than a world of people who did right like machines because they couldn't do anything else." C. S. Lewis wrote these words, in *God in the Dock,* about our freedom of choice. God will not force us to love him. He does not manipulate our feelings, thoughts, or decisions, even though he knows what is best for us. God's unconditional love allows us freedom to choose.

Some of us want to make certain that those we love make the "right" choices. We may try to push them into decisions concerning career, spouse, church, and even daily activities. But pressing others to be who we want them to be eventually wears us out and often keeps us from developing our own God-given gifts.

God does not try to change us by using force. He tells us the truth and then allows us to make our own decisions. With his help we can learn to treat our loved ones in the same way. Freedom and acceptance flow into our relationships when we relax our grip.

Lord, I'm grateful for the gift of free choice. I wish to let my friends and family make their own decisions as you allow me to do. Please help me.

Read Psalm 119:130: "The unfolding of your words gives light; it gives understanding to the simple."

When our children were born, my husband and I lovingly cared for them daily. We held them close, rocked them to sleep, and fed them. As they were able, we encouraged them to learn to walk, dress themselves, and communicate. We watched excitedly as they grew.

Likewise our heavenly Father is actively involved in our growth; he encourages us according to our capabilities and understanding at the time. He does not push us; he waits until we are ready. If God told us everything about ourselves and life all at once, we would be confused and crushed. Instead he teaches us based on our spiritual and emotional age level. God's gentle unfolding plan increases our insight and encourages our consistent growth.

Lord, you are a compassionate and caring Father. Thank you for nurturing my development step-by-step and giving me understanding just as I need it. Help me to be as patient as you are with my simple and imperfect attempts at gaining maturity.

Read Nehemiah 9:17: "But you are a forgiving God, gracious and compassionate, slow to anger and abounding in love."

Some of us will do almost anything to make others feel better. We may have learned this in childhood and carried it over into our adult relationships. When someone else is sad, angry, or guilty, we believe it is our responsibility to make that person feel happy, calm, and forgiven. However, this practice usually enables the one we are trying to help to continue negative or harmful behavior. It also often depletes our energy and stunts personal growth.

God is the one who grants ultimate comfort, peace, and forgiveness. It is not our job to take away another's grief, indignation, or shame. We allow God to help our loved ones when we stop trying to make everything right for them. God alone can touch human hearts and restore them to health.

Lord, I wish I could make everything right for all the people I love. It feels so strange to stand aside and watch others hurt. I feel like I need to do something. Please help me as I change and grow in this area of my life.

Read Romans 12:18: "If it is possible, as far as it depends on you, live at peace with everyone."

In high school I hung a copy of this Bible verse inside my locker. I wanted to be a peacemaker. Over the ensuing years, becoming a peacemaker came to mean being a person who avoided conflicts. I didn't want anyone to be upset with me or with the situation. This desire translated into a don't-rock-the-boat mentality. If a bill was due and we had no money to pay it, I hid the truth, taking on responsibility to work it out. When someone else asked me to do something I didn't believe was right, I often did it anyway to maintain peace. If others wanted me to ignore my personal interests, because it was inconvenient for them, I complied so everyone would be happy—everyone but me.

I thought I was obeying God. I was a peacemaker, wasn't I? I had interpreted Paul's advice to mean, "With all the zeal, drive, and power you can muster, keep the peace." This attitude sabotaged my relationships and contributed to burnout.

Paul's words suggest there are times when peace is not possible or does not depend on us. With God's help we can become peacemakers without selling our souls to a philosophy of peace at any cost.

Lord, please give me courage to be a truthful peacemaker. Like Paul I will work toward peaceful solutions within human limitations.

Read Luke 22:31–38: "Jesus answered, '. . . Peter, before the rooster crows today, you will deny three times that you know me.' Then Jesus asked them. . . " (vv. 34–35).

Although Jesus was fully aware of Peter's upcoming failure, he did not dwell on it. Neither did Jesus spend time trying to manipulate another response. He told the facts, listened to Peter's reaction, and continued with his teaching plans. Had I been in charge and experienced Peter's unconcerned response, I probably would have sent Peter on an errand to remove him from the place of temptation. But Jesus allowed Peter to take responsibility for his own actions.

Jesus sets a healthy example for us. We need not try to control the way others respond to unpleasant information or situations. If the boss is angry when told of a lost account, if a spouse sulks on learning the car needs repair, if a child doesn't study and fails a class, we need not panic. Allowing others to experience the consequences of their own attitudes and behavior may be unfamiliar territory for us. We may have tried to do and make everything right, attempting to control the responses and actions of others. With God's help we can cease this exhausting practice.

Lord, I relinquish my hold on others. Please help me as I commit to a new, less tiring life-style.

Read Psalm 131:1–2: "Lord, . . . I don't pretend to 'know it all.' I am quiet now before the Lord. . . . Yes, my begging has been stilled" (TLB).

Once a month Maggie and I met to have breakfast and talk. This particular morning Maggie was tearful. "My son-in-law finally walked out on my daughter and grandchildren," she said. "Must be a midlife crisis. He doesn't make any sense. I've been trying to figure it out, but it's so confusing."

Maggie was stressed out and I was concerned about her health. "You OK?" I asked.

"He's driving me crazy," Maggie responded. "He's making a mistake. I need to get through to him."

Maggie could not admit her own pain because she was obsessed with fixing him. Detaching from her son-in-law's erratic behavior might have helped her deal with the loss, but it was hard for her to let go.

Some of us may need to realize we cannot change the motives or actions of someone else. As we give up our preoccupation with fixing everyone and everything, we make room for God to heal. Stepping aside and letting God take over can renew our peace of mind.

Lord, detaching from someone else's problems does not mean I don't care anymore. I care a great deal, but I know I can't fix what another has broken. You are the master repairman. I'll let you do your job.

Read Mark 9:38–41: "'Do not stop him,' Jesus said"
(v. 39).

"The other day we saw a man we didn't know performing miracles. He said he did these good things in your
name, Jesus," explained John. "But he doesn't do it like
we do, so we told him to stop. After all, he isn't part of
our group."

"It isn't necessary to stop him," responded Jesus. "If
he says that he believes in me, and does these miracles in
my name, believe him."

Sometimes we think that we are the only ones with
the right way to worship or serve God. We become preoccupied with getting others to minister just like we do.
We may even attempt to manipulate their response to
Jesus.

Jesus reminds us, as he did John, that we need not
attempt to control another person's relationship with
God. When we let go of responsibilities that are God's
alone, we experience reduced stress. We are then able to
focus on the insight God wants to give us.

*Lord, when I try to manipulate someone else to
respond to you just like I do, please remind me to
step back and allow you to work unhindered.*

Read Philippians 1:15–18: "But what does it matter?"
(v. 18).

"But what does it matter?" This may be a puzzling question for some of us, because everything has mattered to
us—intensely. What other people said, believed, and did
mattered so much that we felt it our spiritual duty to
change or persuade them. Paul posed this question when
explaining his response to others who were preaching
with questionable motives. Paul recognized it was not his
place to change another's preaching methods or attitudes, yet he did not ignore the truth. Some undoubt-
edly preached out of envy and egotism. But Paul was
primarily concerned with his own responsibilities and
attitudes before God. He knew it was not his job to fix
each situation.

One day during my recovery from burnout and
workaholism I read the words *It does not matter!* It does
not matter! It does not matter! Slowly this reality permeated my thinking. Much of what I believed mattered the
most paled in the light of God's eternal plan. What matters is my own response to God. I begin to relax when I
allow others to make their own decisions.

*Lord, you are in charge, not me. Please help me
learn to take responsibility for only my own matters.
I cannot change someone else.*

Read Matthew 23:1–4 and 12: "'They tie up heavy loads and put them on men's shoulders, but they themselves are not willing to lift a finger to move them. . . . For whoever . . . humbles himself will be exalted'" (vv. 4, 12).

Perhaps we think that by persuading others to fit into our perfect images we will finally be satisfied with our lives. Like the religious leaders of Jesus' time, we sometimes tie up heavy loads of shoulds, oughts, and musts, and then place them on others' shoulders. This practice falsely promises to alleviate our own painful inadequacies. If we can coax another to perform so we look good, then our own imperfection will not bother us so much.

"Whoever humbles himself will be exalted," said Jesus. What paradoxical thinking, opposite to the lifestyle philosophy practiced by these religious leaders. Humbling oneself includes admitting need, feeling the private sorrow and contrition associated with that need, and asking and trusting God for positive help. It doesn't seem like the way to the exalted life, but Jesus says it is. In this gracious way of life we find freedom, respect, and dignity.

Lord, this concept is unfamiliar to me. Relinquishing control of those around me leaves me feeling vulnerable and alone. I definitely need your help.

Read Exodus 14:13–14: "Moses answered the people, 'Do not be afraid. . . . The Lord will fight for you; you need only to be still.'"

"I'm worried about my husband," a middle-aged woman told me. "I think his boss is involved in shady business deals. I lie awake nights trying to figure it all out. I don't know what to do."

Staying awake at night will not alter the way her husband's boss conducts business. Although she may want to express her concerns to her husband, she is not responsible for the situation's outcome.

Like this woman, we may sometimes feel the need to control what is not ours to oversee. Occasionally we shout; other times we quietly hint. Perhaps we withhold our approval, hide the unpleasant truth, or try to fix what we perceive is wrong with someone else. When we attempt to make all things right, we try to do more than we are capable of handling. It wears us out. As we stop trying to figure it all out, we can let God take over. Moses instructed the Israelites to release their anxiety concerning the Egyptians to God. "The Lord will fight for you," he said. When we give the situation to God, we can stop our inner thrashing and watch him work.

Lord, it takes faith to cease trying to remedy my loved ones' dilemmas. I know it's not my battle to fight. I'll be still and let you take over.

Read James 3:2: "We all make many mistakes. If there were a person who never said anything wrong, he would be perfect" (NCV).

As we change, we may begin to understand and feel how much our life-must-be-just-so attitudes and behavior have harmed others. Shaming our family or friends into becoming our idea of the best may have not only embarrassed them but damaged their souls as well.

We now realize we will never be able to change our spouse, friends, boss, parents, or children. Our efforts to alter another's thoughts, beliefs, and actions (so our lives would be less stressful) kept the focus away from our own need and contributed to our burnout.

It takes courage to acknowledge perfectionistic thinking and one-upmanship behavior, feel the shame and guilt, ask for forgiveness, and move on. The freedom we find in this less exacting way of life is worth the long and painful changing process.

Lord, I will never be perfect and neither will my family or friends. I've hurt others with my former attitudes. Thank you for forgiving and changing me.

Read Ezekiel 11:19–20: "'I will remove . . . their heart of stone and give them a heart of flesh'" (v. 19).

"I stopped feeling years ago," the old man confided in a rare truthful moment. "I built a wall around my heart so I'd never hurt again."

The phrase "heart of stone" could refer to the brick walls many of us, like the sad old man, build around our inner being and personality so that nothing or no one can get in. We believe these sturdy walls will protect us from additional hurt, shame, and disappointment. But the resulting isolation only increases our pain and distress. Locked inside these stone walls we may think we are safe, but we are vulnerable to loneliness and depression. In order to avoid feeling the ache, we often work harder and do more.

God wants to soften our stony heart. We can start by dismantling a portion of the wall and letting a breath of fresh air into the musty house. Once we start the demolition, by admitting our need to God, ourselves, and someone who cares about us, God rushes to help.

Lord, help me punch holes in the walls. I want a new heart—sensitive enough to hear and understand your voice and alive enough to enjoy intimate interaction with those who care about me.

Read 1 Peter 5:3: "Not lording it over those entrusted to you, but being examples to the flock."

In a rare and unmasked moment, a talented, strong-willed, and deeply caring father commented, "I see the pained way my children and others relate to me. I guess I need help. But I'm not going to get it. Changing now would hurt too many people."

This man failed to realize that the most beneficial thing we can do for our children, colleagues, and friends is to deal honestly with our own unresolved issues. We may have unfinished business such as resentment, self-image problems, anxiety, unhealthy relationships, or work addictions. Acknowledging our problems is not easy. It is painful to risk revealing our secrets, so we often turn our energy away from dealing with our own growth and concentrate instead on controlling others. It's an exhausting life-style.

If we wish to influence our family and friends favorably, we can decide to confront our own perfectionistic problems and commit to positive personal change. It is a unique privilege to accept personal responsibility before God. Coming to God with expectancy and faith will help us understand his love and experience self-worth.

God, sometimes I've tried to lord it over others by pushing them to complete changes I need to make. Help me offer the greater gift—a healthy example.

Read Psalm 40:4: "How blessed is the man who has made the Lord his trust; and has not turned . . . to those who lapse into falsehood" (NASB).

"You shouldn't feel that way." "You're not really tired." "You couldn't be hungry!" "We don't have time to stop and let you go to the restroom. You don't have to go that bad anyway!"

Comments like these may sound sadly familiar to us. Perhaps other people shamed us into doubting our emotions, perceptions, desires, or needs. As a result, we may have lost our individuality and become victims of another's distorted expectations. It is not profitable, wise, or spiritual to sacrifice who we are for the sake of someone else's whims or our own desire for protection from negative reaction. God wants us to be the people he created us to be, not to stifle our uniqueness for another person who has a "better idea."

God has absolute power and yet he does not victimize his children to prove it. On the contrary, God treats us with respect. The choice is ours. We can trust our lives to a confused or power-hungry human or a loving and almighty God.

Lord, I sometimes feel unimportant and used. I've allowed others to make my decisions for me. I don't want to do that anymore. Please help me have the courage to give up my victim mentality so I can walk with my head high and my heart focused on you.

> *Read Genesis 50:15–17:* "'I ask you to forgive your brothers the . . . wrongs they committed in treating you so badly'" (v. 17).

What if the person we need to forgive is one we are supposed to respect? What if the one who harmed us is a parent, teacher, spouse, or minister? Forgiving may seem like an impossible task.

Smoldering anger and resentment at someone who hurt me contributed to my workaholism and burnout. I wanted to forgive, but it was difficult. In the book *Forgive and Forget: Healing the Hurts We Don't Deserve,* Lewis B. Smedes's insight helped me: "The highest respect you can show people is to let them take responsibility for their own actions. Love has . . . the power to let people be responsible for hurting us. Love does *not* forever find excuses for them, or protect them."

We may find acknowledging another's abuse difficult, because it contradicts all we were taught. The admonition "Honor those in authority" may have contained the hidden meaning "Always do what you are told, keep the peace, and hide the truth if it hurts or looks bad." But God is pleased when we admit the truth, even about our hurts. Facing reality releases us to begin forgiving.

> *Lord, Joseph didn't excuse his brothers' wrongs. But he did forgive. Please help me do the same.*

Read Matthew 18:21–35: "'How many times shall I forgive?'" (v. 21).

"I'll never forgive my father," the young man said. His father had abused him emotionally and verbally, demanding that he think and behave like an adult. Extreme pressure to be an ideal child contributed to a life of perfectionism and obsessive work habits. His childhood experiences were unfair. The young man was understandably angry. He was robbed of the love and security due every little boy. As a young adult the man relived the pain of this wrong each time he vowed "never to forgive that man."

When we refuse to receive and extend forgiveness, we commit ourselves to a personal prison. Extending forgiveness does not mean that we deny the wrong done to us. We admit and face the reality of the injustice. Although we cannot undo the past, we can choose to forgive and be willing to renew this decision every time unforgiveness rears its head. Feeling the effects of forgiveness may take a long time; it is a process. But deciding to forgive is a step to freedom out of a spiritual and emotional prison. God promises to help us every step along this painful yet liberating path toward forgiveness.

Lord, this forgiveness journey is difficult and distressing. But with you I'm finding that it isn't impossible. That's wonderful news, and I'm thankful.

Read Genesis 4:6–7 and 16: "Then the Lord said. . . ,
'Why are you angry?'" (v. 6).

"Cain, why are you angry?" God asked. God did not
want Cain to pretend that he was not angry at his circumstances. Instead God gave Cain the opportunity to
admit and talk about his anger and resentment, but Cain
chose to ignore God's offer of help.

In his book *Codependency,* Pat Springle discusses the
biblical basis for acknowledging and admitting our
anger: "In the unconditional love and acceptance of
God, we have an environment in which we can be honest
and vulnerable. We not only can acknowledge our present hurt and anger, but we can be objective about the
cumulative hurts of the past—and the resulting anger
that has been stored inside us."

God is ready and willing to listen. Admitting our
anger is the first step in learning to deal constructively
with this emotion.

*Dear God, I admit that I have been angry. Even
feeling the emotion of anger is a new experience for
me. Please help me as I learn to talk about my anger
and deal with it in healthy ways.*

Read Ephesians 4:26: "When you are angry, do not sin. And do not go on being angry all day" (NCV).

Anger is a normal reaction to inequity, injustice, and wrong. Some of us have been robbed of our uniqueness and individuality, and it is not fair. Feeling angry is an understandable response. As a result of the past, we may be afraid of our own anger. We may believe that if we admit our anger, even to ourselves, we will act inappropriately. It is possible that our repressed anger has come out as depression.

"I don't want to live the rest of my life with this boiling resentment and bitterness. But what can I do?" asked a friend of mine. I've asked the question myself.

The following suggestions may help: Admit the legitimate anger to yourself, to God, and to another person. If possible, go to the person with whom you are angry and share how you are feeling. Face the negative effects the anger has had on your life. Ask others for prayer and listening support. Tell God you are committed to the process and then give yourself time to heal. Walk daily toward the freedom that is waiting for you.

Lord, my anger scares me. Help me be truthful about it, willing to confront and willing to release.

Read Ephesians 4:15: "...speaking the truth in love..."

"If you don't have something nice to say, say nothing at all." We may have heard this adage since childhood. We believed it and made it our creed. Yet the fallout of this logic can be disastrous. Sometimes we need to tell our children what they do not wish to hear. The messages "Don't play in the street" or "Wear your boots" or "Be home by midnight" may not make us popular. It may be even harder to speak the painful truth to a spouse. "No, I won't lie to your boss" or "I didn't like it when you yelled at me in front of our guests" or "I don't agree with your choice" may be met with rejection.

In *Telling Each Other the Truth,* William Backus writes, "We cannot measure love solely by whether or not what we say hurts someone's feelings. The fact that another person may not like what we have spoken does not automatically mean we have done wrong."

It is often difficult for those of us who always try to think, do, and say the "right" thing to speak the truth in love. But God promises us courage. He will help us through the rough spots.

Lord, help me not to say merely what people want to hear or to try to "help" others by telling lies. Even though it may feel uncomfortable, I want to be lovingly honest in my relationships.

Read Psalm 18:29: "With your help I can advance against a troop; with my God I can scale a wall."

We sat around the table during a morning break. Included were male and female employees as well as managers. We bantered easily until the conversation turned to a serious topic—fear.

"If the truth were known, I suspect we'd all admit to being afraid of something," said one woman.

"I've never been afraid in my life," declared an outspoken man. "What *are* people afraid of?"

"I'll tell you," said a new employee. "Although I'm not fearful of airplane rides, being alone, or even dying, I am afraid of being rejected by others. I'm afraid I'll make a gross mistake and disappoint my parents and spouse. I can't stand their rejection and ridicule. Fear paralyzes me and keeps me from doing what I want to do and being who I want to be. It's like a brick wall I can't jump over."

Some of us are immobilized by silent fear. We long to run free but find ourselves staring at a menacing barricade. With God's help and consistent practice we can learn to confront and scale this wall of fear.

Lord, my self-defeating actions are based on fear of failure in the eyes of another. Today help me remember I don't have to win another's approval to be valuable. My fear wall is looming large in front of me, but with your help I'll scale it. Thanks.

Read Matthew 26:20–30: "And while they were eating, [Jesus] said, 'I tell you the truth, one of you will
betray me.' . . . When they had sung a hymn, they
went out" (vv. 21, 30).

Jesus knew that Judas, one of his close associates, had
chosen to turn against him. This reality must have saddened him, as it did the other disciples, yet Jesus continued to be and do what God wanted. After announcing
the distressing news, Jesus prayed, shared the bread and
the cup, talked of forgiveness and his Father's kingdom,
and then sang a song with the others. He did not allow
the twisted actions of Judas to hinder him from proceed-
ing with his plans.

Some of us have permitted the negative thoughts and
improper behavior of others to keep us from fulfilling
our God-given roles. We may allow other people's ideas
to dictate our decisions. Sometimes this means we
overextend ourselves at work, church, or home because
we do not say no. It is not necessary to do this in order to
be compassionate and kind.

With Jesus as our example, we gain strength to carry
on with our lives regardless of the attitudes or behavior of
others.

*Lord, help me to live my own life based on your
input, and not be sidetracked by the decisions of
those around me.*

Read Exodus 14:1–4: "'But I will gain glory for myself through Pharaoh and all his army, and the Egyptians will know that I am the Lord'" (v. 4).

"I want to believe God works all things for good in my life. But when the bad choices of those I love negatively affect me—and my family—how can good come from that?" asked a friend.

Similar questions have plagued God's people for centuries. Power-hungry Pharaoh abused the Israelites and ignored God. When he reneged on his promise and chased after the Israelites, Moses discussed the dilemma with God. "Moses, follow my directions," said God. "I'm going to be glorified through Pharaoh." Could God be honored through a tyrant?

Some of us may secretly fear that the sinful actions of a loved one will halt the fulfillment of God's will in our own lives. Consequently we try to change the other person. We may overwork, overdo, or overhelp only to become disillusioned when change does not take place the way we planned. However, the truth that God is in charge can help relieve our anxiety. God will gain glory in any way he wishes, even though we may not understand. Like Moses, we can trust him to do his mighty work.

Lord, I realize I'm not responsible for the impure motives or actions of another. I wonder how you can be glorified in my unlikely circumstances, but I will stand back and trust you.

Read John 9:1–3: "'Who sinned, this man or his parents, that he was born blind?' 'Neither this man nor his parents sinned,' said Jesus, 'but this happened that the work of God might be displayed in his life'" (vv. 2–3).

The disciples' question mirrored the assumption of the time: Pain, disease, and suffering are the consequences of sin. Jesus confronted this fallacy. Although a wrong/sin may contribute to an illness, Jesus knew that is not always the case.

If something goes wrong in our lives, it doesn't automatically mean that God is punishing us. We often long for our lives to be free from hurt or injustice. But this is an impossibility in an imperfect world. God knows and understands our pain. His son, Jesus, experienced rejection and heartache. The unfair and hurtful things that happen to us even when we try so hard to cause everything to be just right will never separate us from a loving and comforting God. We can trust him even when we are confused, hurt, and disappointed.

Lord, I don't understand why hurtful things have happened to me. Sometimes I've wondered if I've done something wrong. Yet I know you love me no matter how much inequity and imperfection surround me. I'm reassured by that. I ask you to work in my life and bring glory to yourself.

Read John 11:33–38: "When Jesus saw her weeping
and the Jewish leaders wailing with her, he was moved
with indignation and deeply troubled. 'Where is he
buried?' he asked them. They told him, 'Come and
see.' Tears came to Jesus' eyes" (vv. 33–35 TLB).

When one of his best friends died, Jesus arrived in town
several days after the funeral. At the grave Jesus wept
tears of sorrow and anger—sorrow at the death of his
friend and anger at the unbelief and wrong so prevalent
in an imperfect and decaying world.

Like Jesus, we feel angry when we see the devastating
effects of sin and unbelief. Sickness, death, abuse, injustice, and pain are the natural results of living in a world
that ignores its Creator.

Both anger and grief are normal responses to death,
sin, and injustice. As long as we live on this damaged
planet, we will experience these and other disturbing
emotions. One day we who have chosen to follow Jesus
will join him in a sorrow-free place. Until then, like
Jesus, we can allow ourselves to grieve.

*Lord, teach me to be honest with my human emo-
tions while I dream of a better day.*

Read Lamentations 3:48–57: "My eyes will flow unceasingly, without relief.... What I see brings grief to my soul" (vv. 49, 51).

"It's nine months now, yet I still feel like my heart is torn," said a young divorcée. "My friends tell me to get on with life. I know I should, but I can't."

This woman grieved alone or buried her feelings because her pain annoyed friends and family. Sometimes she tried to medicate her pain by working harder or longer.

Mourning our losses is uncomfortable and distressing. During the process we may doubt our sanity and God's compassion. The author of the Book of Lamentations wrote heart-wrenching poems expressing his pain. God did not say, "Your book is too depressing to be included in the Bible." God allows us the time we need to heal from our losses. He does not require us to hurry up and get on with it. If we insist on racing through the mourning process, we do ourselves and others an injustice. Ignoring, denying, or hiding from our grief is not healthy or biblical. When we acknowledge our loss, feel the depth of our ache, and freely admit our need, we give God an opportunity to comfort and restore.

Lord, I'm tired of trying to grieve perfectly. Please help me.

Read Proverbs 14:8–10: "The folly of fools is deception" (v. 8).

"Our situation really isn't as bad as it seems," said Doris with a half smile. "I'm too sensitive. My husband, Bill, promised to quit drinking and get a job. If I make it easier for him now, it will get better in a few weeks. I can keep working overtime till everything is better." Doris confided to her pastor that she felt confused and afraid most of the time. Yet she remained reluctant to admit her need and the severity of her husband's problem.

"Honesty means acceptance. We must begin by accepting the fact of our addictedness. To accept this is not to affirm it, but to admit it, to acknowledge that it really exists." Gerald May, M.D., wrote these words in his book *Addiction and Grace.* We may have a difficult time accepting that the way we deal with problems and disappointments is defeating and destructive. We deceive ourselves. Some of us, like Bill, are addicted to substances. Many of us, like Doris, burn out because we are addicted to other people and their problems. All of us need to uncover the deception that permits the addiction to continue. God will meet us in our honesty.

Lord, this is difficult to admit, but I can't handle it alone. Help me accept the truth.

Read Ezekiel 45:10: "You must have honest scales, an honest dry measurement and an honest liquid measurement" (NCV).

Centuries ago in Judah it was a common practice to use inaccurate scales and weights in the marketplace. Although God warned against such business tactics, the people continued to cheat their friends and clients.

Those of us who want to do and make everything right may shake our heads, believing ourselves to be more honest than this. Yet the very nature of our performance addiction, perfectionism, or people pleasing often evokes dishonesty.

"The promise of perfectionism is basically a lie," writes David Stoop in his book *Living with a Perfectionist.* Absolute perfection is not possible in this life, but some of us keep trying. We may lie to make situations and relationships look better, stretch the truth to placate others, hide any evidence that our work addiction is harmful, and deny the pain in our hearts.

Admitting that our "perfect" ways may be measured with deceitful scales is difficult. We need God's patient and powerful intervention to help us change our ineffective methods of working and relating.

Lord, I'm in the process of throwing out all the inaccurate weights I formerly used. Please help me not to dig them out of the trash again.

Read Proverbs 28:13: "He who conceals his sins does not prosper, but whoever confesses and renounces them finds mercy."

"If I claim that I am not a workaholic, that I am not a type-A personality, not sick, not angry, not hurt, not disappointed at my losses, and not burned out, then I continue to live in denial." This is an excerpt from my journal several years ago. Facing my denial meant admitting I had lived a lie. When I discovered the extent of the lies I told myself, others, and God, I was shocked and hurt. I confessed the sin of my untruthfulness and found God's mercy and unconditional acceptance.

In his book *Inside Out,* Larry Crabb writes: "To look honestly at those parts of our experience we naturally deny is painful business. . . . But to change according to Christ's instructions requires us to face all we prefer to deny." When we refuse to continue the denial, we open the way to admit our need to God.

Learning to be honest opens the door to allow God to work toward growth and healthy change in our lives and relationships.

Lord, I know you love and accept me yet hate it when I hide, pretend, and lie. I now believe that in order to grow and heal inside I need to be truthful with myself and you. Please help me face the pain and sin inside me.

Read 1 Kings 18:1–2, 15–18: "The word of the Lord came to Elijah: 'Go and present yourself to Ahab'" (v. 1).

When King Ahab saw Elijah, he shouted, "Is it really you, the biggest troublemaker ever?"

"I'm not the cause of your troubles," said Elijah. Ahab blamed Elijah for Israel's problems. He refused to take responsibility for the results of his own poor choices.

Some of us, like Ahab, blame others for our self-made problems. We delude ourselves into believing we are not responsible, perhaps to assuage our own pain and guilt.

When we begin to accept responsibility for our own actions and choices, we breathe hope back into our suffocating lives. We gain a sense of self-worth by becoming accountable for our decisions and growth. Then we are able to fulfill our God-given roles with integrity. Positive personal change becomes an exciting possibility when we stop passing the buck.

Lord, would you please make me aware of the behavior patterns in my life that are destructive? I'm ready to stop blaming others and take responsibility for my own thoughts and actions. Please heal me from the inside out.

Read John 1:16: "From the fullness of his grace we
have all received one blessing after another."

Many of us feel compelled to do and make everything
right so that others will respect, approve, and love us. We
have a difficult time accepting love that is unconditional.
Our society has honed obsessive perfectionism to a sci-
ence. Perhaps this is why the entire concept of grace
seems so foreign.

I long to understand God's grace and become a grace-
ful person. Grace means considerateness; goodwill;
favor; extra time to meet an obligation; and the unmerited love and favor of God toward us. Grace is characterized by gratitude and joy. As I become a grace-ful person,
the judgmental, perfectionistic attitudes shrink. I'm
beginning to appropriate the idea of "unmerited favor."

One thing I know: Only God's grace is perfect. And
he offers me grace upon grace, blessing after blessing.

*Lord, I'll never perfectly understand grace, but I
accept it.*

Read Acts 11:26: "The disciples were called Christians first at Antioch."

"When I was a child," said a friend, "the aunt who raised me used the word *Christian* as a whip to keep me in line. She often said, 'This is the Christian way to act,' when she wanted me to do something or make her look good. Then when she didn't agree with someone else's decision or idea she said, 'That's not the Christian thing to do!' Because of my aunt's attitude, I vowed I would never allow myself to be labeled Christian."

Some of us may associate the word *Christian* with a set of dos and don'ts or a system of shame and blame. Like my friend, we need to reprogram our childhood tapes to accept the true meaning of this word. Being a Christian is not merely something we do, it is something we are. In fact the word was first coined as a noun, not an adjective. People were called Christians because they followed God's Son, Jesus Christ. The word means Christ's follower. Becoming a Christian is a free choice, with a liberating result.

Lord Jesus, I am saddened when anyone defines my relationship with you as if it were a set of shoulds and musts. Bearing the title of Christian is a graceful privilege. Help me pass to others the mercy and benevolence of your name.

Read Luke 6:36–37: "'Be merciful, just as your Father is merciful. Do not judge.'"

"How we are with ourselves is exactly how we are with others. To the degree that we are gentle with ourselves, we are gentle with others. To the degree that we forgive ourselves, we forgive others. And to the degree that we love ourselves, we love others."

After reading these words by seminar leader and writer Louisa Rogers, I wrote in my journal, "Perhaps this is the way to be less critical, judgmental, or picky." I had prayed that God would show me how to be less exacting in my silent attitude toward others. While on a writing retreat I noticed within me a growing tolerance toward God's people who looked, thought, or behaved differently than I. I was also nicer to myself, refusing to be a slave driver. Yet I accomplished even more than usual. It seemed like a paradox to me. Imagine relaxed attitudes producing greater effectiveness! If we practice Jesus' gentle but firm teaching of love and forgiveness with ourselves first, we will be delivered from a deceptive web of self-preoccupation and free to extend this tolerance to others.

Lord, even in the face of my obsessive behavior, you are full of mercy. May your compassionate and forbearing nature flow through me to others.

Read Ezra 3:12–13: "But many ... wept aloud ...
while many others shouted for joy" (v. 12).

The day construction began on the temple foundation
some cried, others shouted and laughed. Although no
one responded exactly the same way, each accepted the
other and celebrated.

Those of us who want to do things just right may have
the idea that we must fit our emotions into identically
wrapped boxes. When our responses differ, we panic.
David Kiersey and Marilyn Bates, authors of the book
Please Understand Me, advise, "If my emotion is less
than yours, or more, given the same circumstances, try
not to ask me to feel more strongly or weakly."

God created us as individuals with differences. He
accepts, and welcomes, our varied emotional expressions.
We can learn to do the same.

*Lord, sometimes I've tried to cram my family mem-
bers, friends, and associates into neatly packaged
boxes of my perceived perfection. Help me as I change
and allow others to respond in their own way.*

Read Romans 15:7: "Accept one another, . . . just as Christ accepted you, in order to bring praise to God."

Many of us are not aware that we harbor the silent attitude that if others don't feel, believe, or behave as we do, they're wrong. The following are examples of this kind of thinking:

If someone cleans house differently than I do, she is lazy.

If somebody doesn't like to read or study, he is not intelligent.

If someone attends a different church than I do, she has poor judgment and is unspiritual.

If another enjoys different sports than I, he is a wimp.

When someone makes a career choice contrary to my interests, she is a loser.

If another enjoys being alone more than with a crowd, he is antisocial.

God accepts us whether we are introverts or extroverts, whether we choose structured or flexible life-styles, and regardless of our career or denomination choice. When we accept one another's God-given uniqueness, we are released to live together with freedom, respect, and joy.

Lord, you accept me. Help me accept others.

Read 1 Corinthians 12:4, 5, 11: "There are different kinds of gifts, . . . [and] service. . . . All these are the work of one and the same Spirit, and he gives them to each one, just as he determines."

Earlier this year the college my daughter attends asked her to sing and me to accompany her on the piano in the parents' weekend final service. On the designated Sunday morning hundreds of visiting parents, students, and faculty filled the beautiful chapel. Glancing at the printed program, I noticed the special music included music majors and accomplished musicians. Doubts about our musical contribution pushed at the corners of my mind.

Prior to the service, all who were on the program met backstage to pray together. One student prayed, "Thanks, God, that we each have different talents, yet it all fits into the balance of the total program." Hearing those words, I relaxed.

While walking back to our seat my daughter asked, "Did you hear what the pianist prayed?"

"Certainly did," I replied.

"That's it!" she whispered. "Even though I don't have the same type voice as the senior music major, I can sing my song. And God will speak through both of us." She smiled and squeezed my hand.

We each have different gifts, talents, and sounds. God planned it that way. When we do our individual part, the variety of God's creation shines through.

Lord, I don't look, sound, or think exactly like my peers. That's OK. It adds variety to life.

Read John 9:1–34: "Then they hurled insults at him. . . . The man answered, 'Now this is remarkable! You don't know where he comes from, yet he opened my eyes'" (vv. 28, 30).

Some of us have a hard time rejoicing when good, useful, or profitable things happen to someone else. We are similar to the religious leaders of Jesus' day. When Jesus healed a man who had been blind all his life, the man was happy with his newfound sight, but the religious leaders were not. Instead of accepting the good, they changed the subject and tried to find an issue to complain about. They were angry with Jesus for doing the beneficial deed.

Sometimes we who want to make everything right secretly believe that another's good fortune might decrease our opportunities. But this is not true. We do not have to think or act like these religious leaders of old. We can learn to rejoice genuinely when favorable or advantageous things happen to others. God has enough good for all of us.

Lord, sometimes I think that someone else's benefits will result in less for me. This misconception causes me to feel "grabby" and anxious inside. Help me to relax and celebrate another's joy.

Read Mark 10:17–18: "'No one is good—except God alone'" (v. 18).

Some of us are confused about the meaning of the word *good.* We may think that the good people we know will always give us what we want. This philosophy may transfer over to our belief about a good God. Because God is good and he gives us good things, we assume we will never be hurt. But life is not like that. The sun and the rain produce good results, because the flowers need both to grow and blossom.

One day a man ran up to Jesus, calling, "Good teacher." Jesus' response was revealing. He said, "No one but God is good." What did Jesus mean? God is good. He is not good because he supplies us with everything we want but because all that he is and does is beneficial in the total picture. He is constitutionally good. Good dwells in God. There is no one like him. Jesus performed on earth all the inherent goodness of his Father, God. Knowing and experiencing Jesus helps us understand the balanced goodness of the Almighty God.

Father, you are good. I do not fully comprehend this. All goodness dwells in you, now and forever. Thank you for sharing that goodness with me.

Read Exodus 14:15–20: "Then the angel of God, who had been traveling in front of Israel's army, withdrew and went behind them. The pillar of cloud also moved from in front and stood behind them, coming between the armies of Egypt and Israel" (vv. 19–20).

With the Egyptians hot on the heels of the Israelite people, God changed his protective plan. For days God's angel effectively led them from the front of the ranks. But then God decided to move the angel to the rear. As a result, the approaching Egyptians could not see the Israelites. Then Moses guided the people across the Red Sea. God carried out his purposes by changing his way of working.

Sometimes we may put God in a box, saying statements such as, "God healed me this way. He'll do it the same way for you" or "Here is how he helped me choose a partner and career. Just wait, God will work this way for you, too."

God does not use a cookie-cutter method to produce his will in people's lives. He has all the diverse resources in the universe at his command. God knows what each individual needs to mature and works in each specific situation. We can trust him.

Lord, sometimes you work as you have before, other times you surprise me. I don't have every answer, so I'll step aside. Do your job in your way.

Read Luke 22:31–35: "But he replied, 'Lord, I am ready to go with you to prison and to death'" (v. 33).

"Don't worry, Lord," said Peter. "I'll always stand by you. I'm ready to go to jail for you. Why, I'd even die for you."

"Peter, this very day you will pretend you don't even know me," Jesus replied.

Peter could have responded, "Oh, my! Lord, if this is going to happen, please help me. I don't want to act this way. I need courage to go through what's ahead." Instead Peter said, "There may be trouble ahead, but I can handle it. I'll never stop trusting you, Lord. Whatever happens, I know my faith will see me through."

Like Peter, I sometimes bite off huge chunks of faith at a time. "Lord, there will never come a time when I won't totally trust you," I whisper. But then my overconfidence becomes more than I can handle.

I'm learning I don't need to guarantee the future. Instead I can live each day by faith. Faith is a gift from God, and I gratefully accept it one day at a time.

Lord, release me from the burden of tomorrow's faith. It's too heavy for me. I willingly give you my "now" and trust you to take care of my "forever."

Read Matthew 6:34: "'Therefore do not worry about tomorrow.'"

According to the National Headache Foundation, more than forty-five million Americans suffer from various types of recurring headaches. The majority of these headaches are tension related. The NHF suggests that "learning to live one day at a time" may relieve anxiety that contributes to the pain and inconvenience of muscle-contraction headaches.

Long before this admonition appeared on the NHF's "52 Ways to Reduce Stress" list, Jesus said, "Don't worry about tomorrow. Today has enough dilemmas. Learn to face life one day at a time."

This advice is difficult for some of us to follow. After spending our today making big plans for our tomorrow, we then worry that something might go wrong. We may pray for direction and then worry we made a wrong decision. We instruct and then worry that others won't heed our advice.

But with God's help we can learn to cease concentrating on tomorrow's what-ifs. Then our muscles can relax, and we will experience less worry-related pain and tension. The elimination of all stress is impossible in this imperfect world. But it is encouraging to learn that living one day at a time can alleviate unnecessary anxiety.

Lord, please help me to incorporate this tension-releasing philosophy into my belief system.

Read Ecclesiastes 6:10: "Everything that happens was planned long ago. . . . It is useless to argue with God about it. This is because God is more powerful than man is" (NCV).

"I just don't have enough time," lamented a working mother of three. "I feel pulled in different directions. I wish God would make twenty-nine hours in a day. Then I might be able to do it all."

Career demands, family problems (including children and elderly parents), financial obligations, and society's emphasis on competition and performance have caused us to be stretched to the limit. Is it possible to ease the tension caused by time limitations as well as job and family stress so life is more enjoyable?

We *can* do some things to prevent stress from building up to a dangerous level. Becoming aware of our own needs and implementing plans to fulfill those needs are positive approaches.

There are twenty-four hours in one day, seven days in one week, twelve months in a year. This fact will not change. It is useless for us to dream about twenty-nine-hour days. God, who is bigger and more powerful than we, planned the twenty-four-hour system, and he is in charge. Learning to live sensibly and prayerfully within the existing limitations will help relieve our stress.

Lord, what steps can I take to live more appropriately within the twenty-four-hour day you give me?

Read 1 Peter 5:5–6: "Clothe yourselves with humility toward one another . . . that [God] may lift you up."

Some of us know others we would characterize as selfish or self-serving. We are determined not to be like them, so we run as fast as we can in the opposite direction. We help everyone. We do more than our share at work, home, school, or church. We may even neglect our own bodies, minds, and souls in order to fulfill others' needs.

Although other people may need to learn to care, love, and serve, some of us do too much. Perhaps we believe that our overworking, excessive service and peace-at-any cost creed are humility in action. But are they?

Humility is seeing ourselves as God sees us. We recognize our humanity and lack of faith. Honestly facing the truth that we are created beings is a humbling experience. We are imperfect and needy but forgiven, valued, and lifted up by God's unconditional love and acceptance.

Lord, I realize I am not perfect. Yet in your presence I find freedom, mercy, and the strength to go on. Please teach me more about who you are and who I am in your sight. I want to serve you.

Read 1 Peter 3:15: "Always be prepared to give an answer to everyone who asks you to give the reason for the hope that you have. But do this with gentleness and respect."

Some of us believe we must have a solution to every crisis, a remedy for each dilemma, a reason for all questionable behavior, the rationale for every emotion, and the answer to every spiritual inquiry. We feel we owe it to God and his reputation. With so much tragedy and pain in the world, we long to be part of the solution. Yet the strain of trying always to have all the answers is often overwhelming.

Maybe a fresh look at Peter's words would help us. We are personally responsible for what we choose to believe. It is our privilege to share our experiences or opinions and how God has helped us. Yet Peter did not indicate we should have an answer for everyone else's hope, only our own. Only God knows everything about everyone. We need not have all the answers. Understanding this can produce peace within us.

Lord, I'm grateful for the hope you've given me. You give others a reason to hope, as well. However, it must be their own choice. Please release me from the pressure of having all the answers.

Read Psalm 23:3: "He restores my soul."

"Whenever I say I need to rest or take a nap, I get dirty looks from my family," said an overworked mother and wife. "This pushes my button and keeps me moving. Recently I realized that I let their reactions control me. Should I stop and rest even if they don't approve of it?"

We do not have to wait to rest until someone else notices our exhaustion and suggests we take a break. We have probably taught others that we are indispensable and indestructible. If this is the case, it is unlikely they will suggest we relax. God grants us permission to take responsibility for ourselves and rest. He encourages us to return to a balanced life of doing, trusting, and resting. God wants to refresh and replenish our souls. We can learn to cooperate with him regardless of what others say or do.

Lord, if I quietly and consistently admit my honest need for rest and recuperation, is it possible my friends and family will understand and stop seeing me as a superperson? Please give me courage to try it. I really need to be restored.

Read Ecclesiastes 11:8: "However many years a man may live, let him enjoy them all."

"I'm going now," said my secretary. "Thank you for everything."

"All the best to you in your new career," I said. As she walked out the door, she handed me an envelope. Once back in my office, I opened it. Inside was a bon voyage card with the following hand-written message: "Joan, I hope someday you can stop and smell the roses."

Today as I work in my home office a lovely lily plant sits on my desk. The fragrance fills the room. I am enjoying it as I write. Back then I was so busy, so rushed, so preoccupied, so driven. Now I am less obsessed. I did stop to smell the flowers. And I'm grateful.

The wisest man in the world once said, "Enjoy every day of your life." We can learn to stop racing through our tomorrows and start relishing our todays.

Lord, I don't know how long I will live. May I enjoy each day that is mine—now.

Read 1 Samuel 15:22: "To obey is better than sacrifice."

Some of us sacrifice our own social, mental, physical, and spiritual essentials and desires for the sake of another's advancement and happiness. We believe this is right and noble. Years later the recipients of our sacrificial giving may resent what we did in the guise of love.

One man admitted, "I'm sad and angry that my mother gave up her health and life for us kids. Now, as I start my own family, I'm without a mother. I feel robbed. Yet I'm helpless to do a thing about it."

Of course normal caring and parenting always requires some sacrifices. Most loving parents experience late-night feedings, car pools, and lost private hours. In the same way, many healthy adult relationships involve making adjustments and finding the middle ground on important issues. But some of us have the mistaken idea that we are expected to forfeit living a balanced and healthy life for the sake of another.

Personal dedication and obedience to God is preferable to overcommited and excessive sacrifices. When we accept responsibility for our own growth and spirituality, we free those who love us to do the same.

Lord, help me to take care of my own business and work before you. I don't want to "live" my life by sacrificing who you made me to be.

Read Psalm 116:1–9: "I was frightened and sad. . . . I was facing death and then he saved me. Now I can relax. For the Lord has done this wonderful miracle for me" (vv. 3, 6–7, TLB).

Several years ago after I had experienced chronic heart fibrillations and palpitations, my doctor sent me to a physical therapist. His goal was to teach me how to alleviate the symptoms associated with the stress in my life.

One day the therapist suggested I try biofeedback to help me learn how to relax. He attached me to a device, showed me how to monitor my responses, and then left the room. Immediately my pulse quickened and my mind tightened up. Within minutes the meter on the machine flipped out of control. "Someone must be messing with the controls from the next room," I concluded. How I wanted out of the room! When the doctor returned, he calmly said, "I guess we'll just forget using this again." I had a hard time relaxing. I thought it was wrong. When forced to go against my beliefs, my mind and body sent out negative impulses and almost broke the machine.

Gradually I have changed my beliefs about the value of practicing relaxation techniques. God is not opposed to taking it easy. He is pleased when I relax.

Lord, I was frightened and sad, but you saved me. Now I can relax. Thank you very much.

Read Psalm 54:4: "Surely God is my help; the Lord is the one who sustains me."

God is our helper and Lord. He alone is worthy to be our master or controller. Yet some of us have allowed someone other than God to become the lord of our lives. Still others of us may have become the controller.

When a human being is master of someone else's thoughts, beliefs, words, or actions, God's rightful place is usurped. When we strive to please a person instead of God, the burden becomes unbearable, often leading to overserving or overworking.

God, not other people, is the one who sustains us on a continuing basis. He keeps us going when we feel like giving up. When we are so exhausted that we cannot feel or even cry, he holds us up and waits for us to regain our strength. Others may push and lord it over, but the Lord God compassionately helps, nurtures, and sustains us.

Lord, I have allowed another person to be more important to me than you. Please forgive me. I want you to be my Lord. Thank you for helping and sustaining me as I change my ineffective attitudes and actions. This process is difficult, but with your support I can make it.

Read Proverbs 29:25: "Being afraid of people can get you into trouble" (NCV).

During a seminar I heard speaker Carol Travilla comment that some people "play to the grandstand instead of playing the game."

"I think that's what I've done," I responded silently. I visualized myself up to bat with the game tied in the ninth. "If I do this right, everyone will love and appreciate me," I thought. In my daydream as I searched the crowd for my family's and friends' reaction, I consistently missed each pitch.

Then I realized that by concentrating primarily on others' responses to me I had thwarted God's efforts to coach me into becoming the life player he had in mind for me to be. I genuinely wanted to stop playing this defeating game. This insight about myself gave me courage to move ahead—out of the workaholism, people pleasing, and burnout. Focusing solely on another's opinion can get us into trouble. We are responsible for playing our own game of life. God will help us meet this reasonable responsibility.

Lord, I'm often so afraid of what someone else thinks about me that I fail to be who you created me to be. I'm sorry. I want to stop living this way. Please help me.

Read Jeremiah 17:5–6: "'Cursed is the one who trusts
in man, who depends on flesh for his strength. . . .
He will be like a bush in the wastelands. . . . He will
dwell in the parched places of the desert.'"

Perhaps some of us are addicted to performance and
work because we are driven to please another human
being—a spouse, parent, child, pastor, or boss. When
this person is happy, we enjoy life. But if this individual
becomes displeased with us, our own outlook takes a
nosedive. So we increase our efforts, work harder and
longer to please. We put our full trust in another human
being's opinion. This is a painful way to live. In fact this
life-style often feels cursed. If our faith centers on
another human being, we can become depressed,
exhausted, and finally burned out when our dreams concerning this person fail to come true.

It was difficult for me to admit I trusted another person
for my sense of well-being and self-esteem, because I had
loved deeply and been so concerned. But I felt parched
inside. Relief came when I shifted my ultimate trust from
man to God. Gradually we can learn to care, give, and love
out of the freedom and joy of God's acceptance.

*God, I'm hurting. Admitting my misplaced trust, I
ache even more. I know you love me and don't want
me to feel cursed. Take me out of the desert into the
lushness of your freedom. I trust you.*

Read Psalm 146:1–4: "Do not put your trust in . . . mortal man, who cannot save" (v. 3).

We may not be aware that sometimes we care more about someone else's reaction than we do God's response. "Idolatry means basing your sense of life, value, and acceptance on something other than God." These words of Jeff VanVonderen in his book *Tired of Trying to Measure Up* reflect a pattern of misplaced trust. If the source of our trust does not laugh at a joke or respond to a sermon, we don't either. We may hide our desire to pray or study the Bible if our human idol thinks it is a waste of time. Perhaps we deny our own need for rest and recuperation if this person finds it inconvenient for us to be tired or ill. Fear of this person's ridicule or rejection causes us to doubt our value. We may become overextended in an attempt to lessen the pain of that fear.

But our lives can change. We can choose to place our trust in the one who offers us freedom from anxiety and drivenness. With his help we can learn to respect the opinions and feelings of others and still be true to our own. When we trust our days and future to God, we are free to become the people he created us to be.

Lord, forgive me for putting another ahead of you.
You alone can save me. Help me change this pattern
and live in freedom with myself and others.

Read Psalm 18:36: "You broaden the path beneath me,
so that my ankles do not turn."

Some of us have been crushed by the abuse or shaming of
other people. We may have learned to cope by hiding our
desires, neglecting our God-given talents, and squelch-
ing our personality.

The dictionary defines the word *personality* as "those
qualities that distinguish the individual as a unique person." When a person is not permitted or encouraged to
express his or her own desires, perceptions, feelings, gifts,
or personality, individuality is crushed.

When we are afraid of the people who ridicule and
hurt us, we walk a tightrope trying to placate them. We
attempt to do everything just right, and it wears us out.
We secretly long to be free, to be our own person.

God does not restrict or shame us. He invites us out
into a wide open space where we can express our gifts and
uniqueness. We do not turn our ankles walking a tightrope trying to make him happy. He gives us freedom to
create and become a healthy personality.

*Lord, thank you for releasing me to freedom. Please help
me discover the true personality you have given me.*

Read John 8:1–12: "'Neither do I condemn you'" (v. 11).

"Look here, Jesus," the religious leaders said. "We caught this shameful woman in the act of adultery. Now what are you going to do about it?"

Unlike them, Jesus did not use shaming techniques. Although he spoke of the woman's sin, he did not deny her value as a human being. With a simple question from Jesus, the religious leaders became silent and walked away.

Jesus then turned to the hurting woman. "I forgive your behavior, but I do not shame or condemn you. Go and live in the freedom of your forgiveness."

Some of us have lived with shame for many years. We operate from the underlying belief that who we are and what we do isn't OK. The unhealthy shame we feel camouflages who we really are and destroys our opportunity to grow.

On the other hand, healthy guilt, the consequence of going against our moral code, helps us to know who we are. We can then seek true forgiveness, resulting in growth and change.

Lord, help me learn not to accept the unhealthy shame that others want to lay on me. Thank you for forgiving me. May the freedom I have found in your forgiveness help me with my relationships.

Read Isaiah 54:4–5: "Do not be afraid. . . . You will forget the shame of your youth" (v. 4).

"We think that by 'doing it right,' we will get rid of the shame," observed psychologist Carol Travilla.

Some of us may be motivated to perfectionism by our toxic shame—the shame of making a mistake; saying the wrong thing; having an unproductive day; mispronouncing a word; gaining weight; not understanding directions; experiencing fatigue; wearing an inappropriate outfit; adding up the checkbook incorrectly; expressing a differing opinion; feeling disappointment; praying the wrong words; wanting to be alone; wanting to be with someone; needing to feel secure.

The inner message we hear is, "Shame on you! You are needy. You are human." It's fake guilt; and it's poisonous. We may attempt to avoid feeling the ache of the shame by denying it matters, working longer hours, or trying to do everything right. But we don't have to be hooked into listening to these self-defeating messages. God wants to release us from the overwhelming burden of perfectionism. We can forget the false shame and relax. God knows our human needs, and he accepts and likes us anyway.

Lord, teach me the difference between healthy guilt and toxic shame.

Read Romans 12:6: "And since we have gifts that differ according to the grace given to us, let each exercise them accordingly" (NASB).

"If shame causes a person to hide who she really is, then I must be ashamed of myself," commented a woman getting over the breakup of an unhealthy relationship. "I hide the books I read for fear of being ridiculed. I practice the music I love only when no one is around. I refrain from sharing my thoughts, especially when they differ from someone else's. I'm afraid no one will like me if I let them know who I really am."

Sometimes we are ashamed of healthy behaviors such as talking about feelings, making choices, taking care of ourselves, being successful, or even having fun. We may feel shame being ourselves.

Just because a friend or relative is not a musician does not mean you cannot be. You may enjoy reading, studying, and teaching while your friend would rather do a hands-on helping project. If you participate in sports and another does not, that's all right. You can use the gifts God gave you and pursue the activities and ministries you enjoy. God wants us to celebrate our differences.

Lord, please help me to accept my personality characteristics and talents as gifts from you. And when someone else doesn't understand who and what I am, give me courage to smile and not hide.

Read 1 Corinthians 12:29: "Are all apostles? Are all prophets? Are all teachers? Do all work miracles?"

Ducks swim, eagles soar, rabbits run, kangaroos jump, and monkeys climb. If the duck were forced to climb, the monkey to swim, the rabbit to fly, the kangaroo to walk, and the eagle to be earthbound, they would not survive.

Similarly, when human beings are coerced to do what we were not created to do, we do not thrive. We may become frustrated, ineffective, and depressed. Some of us were created to organize, others to initiate and dream; some to study, teach, and think; others to implement; some to empathize; others to advise. One may encourage by doing, another by listening. Some work well in a structured environment, others flourish with flexibility. Some find energy when alone, others need lots of people around them.

Although a duck can waddle, an eagle will fly to earth, the rabbit can slow down, and the monkey does not always climb, each works best when doing what comes naturally. Likewise each of us feel less stressed and most productive when our doing fits our temperament, talents, and personality. We can relax and be who we are. This is God's plan for us.

Lord, help me to be comfortable with the person you made me to be.

Read James 3:14–16: "If you harbor bitter envy and selfish ambitions in your hearts, do not . . . deny the truth. For where you have envy . . . there you find disorder."

If I become the person God created me to be, being true to my own personality, and serving out of my own gift-edness and calling, I no longer have to envy anyone else's career, marriage, ministry, or talents.

Believing this truth has gradually changed my life. Although I rarely voiced envy, I was secretly hurt and disappointed that others had fulfilled their dreams but I had not. As I learn that it is not selfish to nurture my God-given talents and personality, I am released to free-dom.

There is only one you. There is only one me. God cre-ated us both. We need not give away our uniqueness in quest of becoming what we admire in someone else. When we yearn for the gifts of another, we foster envy and self-preoccupation. By cherishing the person God made us to be, however, we bring order out of an other-wise chaotic and frantic life-style.

Lord, I want to break down the walls of bitter envy and disorder that come between us when I try to look, sound, and act like someone else. I know that when I remain committed to doing and being me, I honor you. That's really what I want to do.

Read John 3:22–29: "To this John replied, 'A man can receive only what is given him from heaven. . . . That joy is mine, and it is now complete'" (vv. 27, 29).

My friend Donna dreamed of being a recording artist. She longed to travel and give concerts. But her voice never developed enough to sustain a successful singing career. Each time she attended a concert she felt gnawing disappointment. This situation robbed her peace and joy.

In desperation Donna asked God to help her deal with the lost dream. One day she read how John's followers came to tattle on Jesus. "He is baptizing, and people are following him instead of you," they said. They assumed John would be jealous and hurt. But John said, "It's OK. I did my God-ordained job. Now Jesus is fulfilling his purpose." Donna shared her response with me. "If I do what God wants me to do, and be who God wants me to be, then I need not envy anyone else," she said. "No longer will I let lost dreams rob me of the joy of being me."

We can learn from John the Baptist and Donna. Becoming the person God planned for us to be frees us from longing for someone else's life, family, job, or ministry. In this freedom-producing life-style we find peace and joy.

Lord, release me from the energy-draining power of envy, and show me who you created me to be.

Read Matthew 22:37–40: "'Love your neighbor as yourself'" (v.39).

Loving my neighbor as myself does not mean loving someone else instead of myself or even ahead of myself. As a healthy child of God, I will love myself. But I will not be obsessively absorbed in self to the point of leaving others out of my life; nor will I live my life through or for others. To live primarily through or for another person means that I feel, think, decide, and hurt for that person. I try my best to fix all situations so he does not have to be sad or disappointed or angry or hurt. This may look like love, but it really is not. "Fixing" may actually rob him of living his own life before God. It may even deny him a sense of accomplishment and self-worth because I give the impression "You are not capable of doing this, so I'll do it for you." In this process, I may deprive myself of the time and energy I need to discover and nurture the real me.

But I can learn to be me. I can learn to appreciate, esteem, and respect the person God created to live inside my own body. I can learn to love myself and my neighbor.

Dear God, I know that you made me to be "me." I want to learn to love and accept the person inside me. I want to genuinely love others as well. Please help me.

Read Genesis 17:1–4: "The Lord appeared to [Abraham] and said, . . . 'I am God Almighty'" (v. 1).

In Genesis 17 God revealed himself to Abraham in a new and special way. "I am El Shaddai," God said. This Hebrew name has great significance. It is as if God said, "I am the all-sufficient one to whom nothing is impossible."

God had promised Abraham and Sarah a son. When Abraham was ninety-nine years old and Sarah not much younger, they were still childless. But El Shaddai came to Abraham and said, "I remember my covenant promise to you. It will happen just as I said it would. You and Sarah tried to do what only I can do. I am the all-sufficient one."

Some of us have the idea that we are sufficient to meet our own needs plus those of our spouse, children, clients, or church members. It's as if we say, "Come to me. I'm always here with answers to your dilemmas and supplies for your wants."

What a setup for idolatry! We can never perfectly meet another's needs. Only El Shaddai can do that. When we try to be the authority or rescuer in another's life, we encourage misplaced trust. Letting God be God is a more reasonable and peaceful way to live.

El Shaddai, I need you in my life. Others need you, too. I'm exhausted trying to play your role. Help me stop trying to accomplish what only you can do.

Read 1 Thessalonians 4:11: "Do all you can to live a peaceful life. Take care of your own business. Do your own work" (NCV).

"Don't tie yourself down yet, honey," said my friend to her daughter. "Have fun. See the world. This is the time in your life when you should be free. Don't get into a marriage with someone who dictates your every decision." I saw my friend's daughter shrug and walk away.

"I only want to help," my friend explained to me. But as we chatted she acknowledged that focusing on her daughter's fiancé kept her from seeing her own demanding habits. Once she began to stop formulating advice for her child, she admitted how much it hurt when her own mother lectured and chided.

Some of us attempt to solve our own past mistakes or disappointments by coercing and "helping" others. Although we may want to tell our loved ones about our honest perceptions, they have the right to choose not to alter their plans or behavior. Our main responsibility as adults is to do our own growth work. When we let go of trying to make everything right for someone else, God can work toward healing our own personal pain. Then we can be freed from being "the one with all the answers."

Lord, I'm beginning to see how my attitudes may sabotage the emotional and spiritual growth of us all. I need your help learning to do my own work.

Read 1 John 5:14: "This is the confidence we have in approaching God: that if we ask anything according to his will, he hears us."

A friend of mine prayed fervently over the years that her husband would read more. Eventually she realized God created her spouse with different learning preferences than she had. Although she loved to read and he did not, he was not a less valuable person. She stopped telling God what to do.

In *Hope in the Fast Lane,* Keith Miller reflects a similar sentiment: "For years I prayed specifically about everything, feeling I was helping the doing of God's will by the things I prayed for. . . . I know now that my prayers were often attempts to get God to do my will for a person or situation—as if I knew and was informing him of the 'best plan.'"

This does not mean we should quit praying for our family, but it does suggest that God's will might be accomplished best if we cease telling God specifically what to do in others' lives. When we really believe that God's ways are superior, we can let go of our need to manipulate and control with our prayers.

Lord, I love my family. Today I hold each one up before you. Please work unhindered in our lives.

Read 1 Thessalonians 5:17: "Pray without ceasing" (KJV).

This morning I overheard a minister say, "The only time I don't feel any stress is when I pray." Perhaps Paul realized that the simple act of honest prayer was stress reducing. Maybe he wrote the words "Pray without ceasing" to encourage us to have a less tension-filled life.

But what does this verse really mean? Did Paul think we ought to spend our entire days kneeling at a prayer altar or locked in our closet? Is this admonition merely another anxiety-producing "ought" to fulfill?

Possibly we could liken our praying to eating or sleeping. We sleep nearly every day, but at the appropriate times. We do not always have a mouth full of food, yet we eat on a regular or continual basis. To stop eating or sleeping would bring disastrous results. And if we cease praying, we dry up spiritually.

When we pray on a continual basis, sharing our joys and needs, our anxiety level drops. We are no longer forced to cope in negative ways. Talking with God nourishes our soul and helps us face life's daily surprises.

Lord, thank you for the privilege of talking to you. Teach me to practice your presence so I can pray "without ceasing."

Read Matthew 18:10: "'See that you do not look down on one of these little ones. For I tell you that their angels in heaven always see the face of my Father in heaven.'"

We human beings, especially perfectionists and over-achievers, sometimes grade the significance and value of others just as we grade ourselves. "Will he make a worth-while contribution to society?" "Does she have what it takes to finish school?" "Is his potential worth cultivat-ing?" "Can she make it in this competitive world?" We may ask these or similar questions in determining whether we will become winners or losers.

God is not discriminatory about who he helps or loves. Every child is worthy of protection, compassion, and encouragement. We are all just grown-up children. Each of us has a God-given right to develop personal potential. We can learn to value each individual human being, ourselves included, because every person is impor-tant to God.

Lord, each child is born equal in your eyes. Help me to assimilate this truth. May it make a positive differ-ence in my daily attitudes and interactions with other people.

Read Psalm 37:5: "Commit your way to the Lord, trust also in Him, and He will do it" (NASB).

"Sorry I'm late," my young employee said as she ran past me to the time clock. Over her shoulder she yelled, "Transmission fell out of my car!" She caught her breath. "Mom's drinking again. I had another fight with my boyfriend. Neither one would bring me to work. I can't afford to fix my car, 'cause my credit cards are filled up to the limit again. I don't know what to do." Suddenly she whirled around and blurted, "I wish God would give me a break."

Perhaps if we were honest, many of us would admit having a similar request. "Give me a break, God." But God doesn't walk into our lives and change everything just because we complain.

Once we give our lives to God, he becomes our manager. He works for our ultimate good. He coaches us on how to heal past damage, overcome self-destructive habits, and experience contentment as we trust him for the future. We benefit when we accept life on God's terms.

Lord, I've decided to give you my life and circumstances. I need you.

Read Matthew 18:1–4: "'Who is the greatest in the kingdom of heaven?'" (v. 1).

"Who is the greatest in God's world?" the disciples asked Jesus. This question suggests that the disciples were concerned with status, performance, and success. Did they want to become great in God's eyes, or in the eyes of others, or in their own eyes—or perhaps all three?

All of us long to be significant, to make a difference, to be considered "great." Like the disciples, we may ask, "Just what does it mean to be really great in God's eyes?

Jesus did not ignore the probing question, nor did he reprimand the men for asking. He answered directly using a visual aid. "See this little child?" he said. "Unless you exhibit the qualities of a trusting, teachable child you will never be great." Genuine greatness is not achieved by rushing or by pushing past others on our way to the top. We make lasting life contributions when we admit our need for God, acknowledge our interdependence on other human beings, and remain committed to continued growth.

Lord, you are the great one. I am your child. I come to you completely willing to have you teach and guide me.

Read Ephesians 4:16: "From him the whole body, . . . held together by every supporting ligament, . . . builds itself up in love, as each part does its work."

My son often works out at the local fitness center. Recently while spotting a friend lifting weights, he saw the man lose control. They both heard a pop and witnessed the man's massive pectoral muscle detach. This man pushed one specific part of his body too far.

Every Christian represents a unique part of Christ's body. There are arm muscles, shoulders muscles, leg muscles and ligaments, each with particular functions. When each exercises his unique job, the entire body is able to work out together. Yet when one person overworks, the entire body is in danger of dysfunction.

Some of us do our own tasks plus several other people's jobs as well. This creates unhealthy reliance on one body part to the detriment of the whole. While a few succumb to burnout, others remain underdeveloped.

But God has a good plan. He has designed us to work together, supporting one another, and building one another up in love. God's plan helps us avoid individual burnout while promoting healthy interdependence.

Lord, what is my part? May I exercise it with love and balance.

Read Acts 6:1–7: "'We will turn this responsibility over to them'" (v. 3).

Overwhelmed by too much work, the apostles decided they needed to concentrate on preaching and teaching and turn other ministry tasks over to specifically chosen laypeople. In so doing they had to risk giving up some control.

Some of us are afraid to share leadership control because we think others might not do the job the "right" way—the way we want it done. So we do it all, and when we cannot keep up, everyone becomes agitated.

The apostles' plan was a safeguard against neglect, disillusionment, and leadership burnout. Delegating some of the organizational responsibilities to other competent people ensured that everyone would be cared for, the apostles had adequate time for the ministry God called them to, and no one would be taken advantage of.

Perhaps a similar arrangement would benefit your church, home, organization, or business. Those of us who want to do and make everything right can relax our tight grip on the reins of leadership and learn to delegate.

Lord, I can't do it all and still be effective. Give me wisdom and courage to relinquish control.

Read 1 Corinthians 2:11: "No one can really know what anyone else is thinking, or what he is really like, except that person himself" (TLB).

In the movie *Driving Miss Daisy,* the wealthy Miss Daisy and her longtime chauffeur have both aged considerably. As they discuss their predicaments, Miss Daisy accuses the chauffeur of continuing to drive even though his eyesight is failing. "How do you know how I can see, 'lessen you look out my eyes?" is his response.

Those of us who try to make everything all right often assume we know what others think or need. "If you'd eat better, you would not get sick" or "You'll be sorry if you take that job in Europe" or "I bet you think I made a bad decision" or "You're cranky; you must be getting a cold."

What we do not realize is that our sick friend was bitten by a deer tick and diagnosed with Lyme disease, the European job would be a beneficial career choice, the person is actually proud of our decision, and the bad mood was due to job loss. When we assume we know another's thoughts or needs, we get dangerously close to playing God. By giving this responsibility back to God, we release ourselves to relax and enjoy life.

Lord, forgive me for thinking I'm powerful enough to know another's thoughts or needs. I want to learn to treat others with respect. Please help me.

Read Psalm 33:13–15: "From heaven the Lord looks down and sees all mankind" (v. 13).

During an afternoon walk, as I was trying to solve my world's problems, the following insight hit me: "I think I always know what is best for my parents, husband, children, and neighbors. But I do not! When I presume to see and understand people's motives and thoughts, I'm trying to play God."

Many of us have a warped sense of responsibility. We mistakenly think it is our duty to see into another person's mind and heart. Because we think we know others' thoughts and feelings, we assume we can handle or solve their dilemmas. "You definitely should take this job, it's just right for you" or "You'd better not marry this guy; you'll be sorry." These are two examples of our presumptuous thinking.

We don't have to have the knowledge of God on all these matters. No wonder we get exhausted attempting to do God's work. When we refrain from assuming God's all-seeing position, we allow him to work unhindered in the life of those we love.

Dear God, I want to learn to allow you to do your work. If I can be your instrument, I'm willing.

Read Romans 11:33–36: "Oh, the depth of the riches both of the wisdom and knowledge of God! How . . . unfathomable His ways!" (v. 33 NASB).

"Why did she do that?" "Is he mad at me?" "What did I do wrong now?" "What can I do to make her feel happy?" Many of us who focus our attention on fixing other people become obsessed with questions like these. We attempt to figure out how to solve another's problem, meet the need, or supply a desire, even before we are asked. We don't feel safe in a relationship because we always try to figure out why the other person is sad, angry, or disappointed. We often assume it is our fault.

Sometimes we transfer how we act and react in human relationships to our relationship with God. We try to figure out God. But the truth is we cannot figure God out. His ways are past finding out.

As we practice letting other people be instead of trying desperately to figure them out, we can also cease trying to be one step ahead of God. We can learn to feel safe in his love. We can learn to trust God even when we don't understand him fully. He is God. He is good and he is powerful. We can let go and depend on him.

My heavenly Father, just this moment I will relinquish my obsession to figure you out. I know I can't do it anyway. I am amazed at your awesomeness. You are worthy of my faith.

Read Psalm 37:7: "Be still before the Lord and wait patiently for him."

"While I was on retreat, trying to rest and recuperate, I heard an inner voice chiding, 'Don't just sit there. Do something. Pray, write in your journal, read the Bible," admitted my colleague. "Instead, I ignored the interior slave driver. I sat alone with my thoughts and God for several hours. This is new behavior for me."

Some of us attempt to pull down God's presence. Perhaps it's because we think we should make the most of our time. Maybe it's our way to prove our spirituality. We want perfectly inspiring times, and we panic when the experience does not meet our preconceived expectations.

"We are making a fetish of the moments when God did come and speak, and insisting that He must do it again; whereas what God wants us to do is 'walk by faith,'" wrote Oswald Chambers in *My Utmost for His Highest.*

Although we may choose to spend organized time studying and praying, we need not do so in order for God to love and speak with us. We can relax and walk by faith daily, even when the insight or inspiration does not flow freely. God is there, even in the silence.

Lord, I miss the mountaintop experiences. But it's OK, I'll walk the valleys with you as well.

Read Hebrews 4:16: "Let us then approach the throne of grace with confidence, so that we may receive mercy and find grace to help us in our time of need."

"What if I say it wrong?" mumbled my Bible study partner. "What will I do if he misunderstands?" This young wife and working mother planned to tell her husband that she felt sad, overworked, and exhausted. She wanted to ask her husband for help, but she was obsessed with doing it the right way. As we talked about it, her jaw and shoulders tensed.

Some of us may be like this young woman when we prepare to talk with God. We feel driven to say the right words, in the right place, and in the right way. We try to fit our prayers into a rigidly calculated formula. Then we worry whether we followed the rules correctly.

God is not concerned with our exact words or posture or methods. He wants our genuine faith. He loves and accepts us with open arms. We can speak freely to God through Jesus, even when we do not have it all figured out. We can tell him how we feel, how confused we are, and what we think at the moment. God listens patiently and then guides us through our needy times.

Lord, I'm throwing out the bogus rules and man-made regulations I've had about prayer. This new way of approaching you is going to take some practice. Thanks for understanding and bearing with me.

Read Matthew 26:69–75: "Then Peter remembered ..." (v. 75).

"I swear I don't even know what you're talking about," said Peter. "It's all in your imagination." This was Peter's repeated response to inquiries concerning his relationship to Jesus. Three people confronted him, while only yards away members of the Jewish council falsely accused his friend. Although he may not have realized it at the time, Peter was trying to protect himself. If he admitted the truth, even to himself, he ran the risk of exposing his true identity. That frightened him.

Many of us have used similar tactics to avoid risking exposure. When confronted with our excessive work habits and everything-must-be-just-right philosophies, we may reply, "You don't know what you're talking about. It's your problem!" We may genuinely believe what we say, although facts point to the contrary.

Peter's wall of disavowal tumbled when the rooster crowed. Jesus' words broke through his defenses. Though it was painful for him to face his denial, it was ultimately productive. After Peter recognized his need and accepted Jesus' love and forgiveness, he became a changed person. We, too, can allow our defensive walls to crumble, and face the uncomfortable changing process. Then we can become courageous and teachable people.

Lord, walk with me. Admitting the truth is scary.

Read 2 Timothy 3:16–17: "All Scripture is God-breathed and is useful for teaching, rebuking, correcting and training in righteousness, so that the man of God may be thoroughly equipped for every good work."

Many of us will do anything to keep from either making, or admitting that we made, a mistake. We have learned that making mistakes is unproductive and must be avoided. But we can learn from our errors. In a study by the National Academy of Sciences on effective learning techniques, psychologist Robert Bjork concluded, "People learn by making and correcting mistakes." Sometimes fumbling or botching up is the most effective way to master skills and grow.

One of the benefits of Scripture study is learning to recognize and admit our mistakes, thus enabling us to correct them and live more effective lives. Positive growth will occur when we refuse to accept the unhealthy shame that accompanies our human mistakes, and receive forgiveness for the genuine guilt of breaking God's moral and spiritual laws. As we allow ourselves to learn from mistakes, we are freed to fulfill our God-given roles.

Lord, help me to see my mistakes as opportunities to learn and develop into the person you created me to be. Thanks for your acceptance and forgiveness.

CONDUCTING GOD'S BUSINESS

Read Luke 2:41–51: "'Did you not know that I must be about my Father's business?'" (v. 49 NKJV).

Jesus' reply to his mother's question was surprising, yet we are not told that he apologized. He loved his parents, and after simply explaining that he was committed to doing God the Father's business, he rejoined them and remained obedient. What his family and friends thought he should do was not Jesus' major concern. He was committed to doing God's will.

We, too, are responsible for our commitments to God's plan for us. If someone else does not have the same spiritual focus, that is all right. In *Telling Yourself the Truth*, William Backus writes, "Other people have the right *not* to share my burden for my ministry." This truth releases us to fulfill our God-given gifts and call without trying to impose them on anyone else. Like the young Jesus, we can live harmoniously with others and yet remain true to who and what God has called us to be.

Lord, regardless of the reaction of my family and friends, I am committed to the business you have for me. Please give me the courage of that twelve-year-old child.

Read John 13:13: "'You call me "Teacher" and "Lord," and rightly so, for that is what I am.'"

The Jewish leaders were outraged by Jesus' claims to be Lord. He taught what they thought was heresy. In this verse Jesus admits he is not only the master instructor but the Lord himself. Jesus is an exact representation of the loving and almighty God. He is ultimate authority.

Human authority or power is temporary, although often necessary and helpful. We do not owe ultimate allegiance to any human being. Some of us have allowed another to tell us how to live. This practice has robbed us of our unique personality and gifts. Perhaps this is one of the reasons for our excessive doing, helping, and working. When we continue to give in to the unreasonable demands of another, we grant them ultimate power over us. Why do we permit this to happen? Carol Travilla, a Christian psychologist and author, suggests we render another person power over us when we are afraid of them—of their ridicule, rejection, or abandonment.

With God's understanding and compassionate help, however, we can gain courage to face this truth about ourselves. Only Jesus is worthy to be our Lord.

God, please forgive me for putting another in your Son's rightful place. With Jesus as my Lord I'm released to be myself and live in freedom.

Read Isaiah 44:6–21: "Some of [the wood] he takes and warms himself, he . . . bakes bread. But he also fashions a god and worships it" (v. 15).

Some of us try to control our future by overworking, excessive exercising, over- or undereating, disproportionate helping or fixing, or being overly nice. When confronted with the imbalance we may say, "But I like and need to work, exercise, eat, serve, be in control, and fix things."

Sometimes we use what we enjoy or need for existence to medicate our pain and drown our disappointment. Eventually the good, or necessary, becomes the most important thing—an idol. The man Isaiah described did precisely this—took his useful wood and abused it by making an idol to worship.

There is only one true God. He alone is worthy of our worship and dedication. We find genuine relief, refuge, and redemption when we trust our compassionate Father, instead of our man-made idols, to fill up our empty spaces and give life meaning.

Lord, I think I've crafted an idol from my work, achievements, and service. Returning this idol to its appropriate use is difficult to do. Please help as I focus my worship toward you and learn to adjust my priorities.

Read Ephesians 1:7: "So overflowing is his kindness
towards us that he took away all our sins through the
blood of his Son, ... and he has showered down
upon us the richness of his grace" (TLB).

Our Bible study group sat in a circle facing one another.
The discussion lesson for the evening was from the Book
of Ephesians.

"The words *rich* or *riches* are mentioned six times in
these verses," observed one woman. "Isn't that exciting?"

"To tell you the truth, I don't feel rich," I said. "I feel
like I'm walking around in darkness."

Silence filled the room. No one knew how to
respond. I no longer remember how our study group
resumed conversation that evening. What I do recall is
that my surprising revelation broke open a crack in the
"everything's fine" wall I built around myself. It was a
positive step out of my depression and burnout.

When we risk sharing our real feelings and thoughts
with a safe and caring person, we allow a little light to
shine through our darkness. We begin to move away
from isolation and pain toward forgiveness and healing.

*Lord, as a result of your kindness and grace, may I
learn to be vulnerable with the caring people you
put into my life.*

Read Genesis 13:1–4: "[Abram] went from place to place until he come to . . . where his tent had been earlier and where he had first built an altar. There Abram called on the name of the Lord" (vv. 3–4).

Abram's self-protective lies concerning his marital status got him into trouble. His dishonesty forced the Egyptian officials to ask him to leave. Having gone to Egypt to escape the famine, he and his family now wandered from one area to another until they came to Bethel. This place he knew. It was here that Abram had previously responded in faith to God's promises.

Much had happened since that time in Abram's life. Sometime during his travels, he must have decided that he wanted to enrich the spiritual side of his life. So he called on God.

Some of us have gotten off the track spiritually. We did not plan to do so. Perhaps we neglected our relationship with God while trying to keep busy and look good. We may have been disappointed by other people or disillusioned with life after trying so hard to do everything just right. But we're tired. Like Abram, we can go back to the place where we left our spiritual integrity. We can pray again, not to impress anyone but just talk to God. He is waiting.

Lord, I'm back. I need you. Please travel with me.

Read Psalm 143:10: "Teach me to do your will, . . . lead me on level ground."

"How can I help you?" I asked.

As his companion turned to look at the merchandise behind us, my customer responded, "I need a gift for my five-year-old daughter, who is in the hospital."

"How about a shirt?" I asked. "Here's a cute one."

"Hmmm. Maybe I should check with her mother. Would you hold this while I make a phone call?" He glanced at his friend, who joined him by the door. "We'll be right back," they promised.

When I walked back to the counter, the cash register was open. We had been robbed. The men's plan worked. The noble gift-buying story diverted my attention from the real issue—a robbery.

We may not be aware that our obsessive work and people-pleasing habits divert our attention from the real issues of life. While appearing noble, they often keep us from experiencing intimate and fulfilling relationships with others and God. Once we acknowledge that our excessive helping and doing actually hinders us and others, we can begin to change. God will give us insight about ourselves, as we ask him to. Then we can learn to practice new and healthful life skills.

Lord, help me to learn how to work and serve in ways that enhance my relationships.

Read Proverbs 14:25: "A truthful witness saves lives, but a false witness is deceitful."

For years Peggy tried to smooth things out between her husband and son. When disagreements surfaced, she was the peacemaker. As explosions erupted between the domineering father and rebellious son, she intervened. She lied to keep the family secret of verbal and emotional abuse. Now that her son is a teenager, she can no longer keep the peace.

Some of us believe it is within our power to smooth out volatile situations. In so doing we often unconsciously enable injustice and wrong to thrive. We may cling to this philosophy to show how much we care or to win acceptance and gain intimacy. Instead it brings resentment, rejection, and barriers. While we try to keep everyone and everything calm and right, we become personally exhausted and eventually burned out.

Learning to accept the truth about our situation, no matter how painful it may be, is the first step in removing ourselves from the practice of these ineffective and tiring habits. Difficult though it may be, admitting the truth will save lives—ours as well as others'.

Lord, I've kept an insidious secret. Please give me courage to tell the truth. I can no longer keep everything under wraps. I want to be free. You take over.

Read Hebrews 13:8: "Jesus Christ is the same yesterday and today and forever."

"I grew up thinking that if I wanted to show my mother that I loved her, I needed to be sad when she was depressed, mad when she was angry, happy when she was cheerful, upset when she was irritated, and elated when she was excited. I adapted to her moods and feelings while ignoring my own." The young bride shook her head. "The way I learned to relate to others is wrecking our marriage. My husband says he feels smothered, and I feel lost."

Some of us have the idea that if we have a thought, opinion, emotion, or conviction that differs from a loved one's, we must adapt or change it for the sake of unity.

But Jesus did not change his thoughts, goals, or commitments just because he loved someone. He showed genuine love and concern while remaining true to himself, his Father, and his mission. Jesus is the same today as he was yesterday. His words will mean the same tomorrow as they mean today. Jesus' mood does not fluctuate with our emotions. His character does not depend on whether we believe or obey him. Appropriating this concept will open up our relationships to a new-found freedom.

Lord, thank you for Jesus' consistent example. Help me learn how to love and show concern without altering my own God-given convictions and beliefs.

Read Mark 10:13–16: "People were bringing little children to Jesus to have him touch them, but the disciples rebuked them. When Jesus saw this, he was indignant" (vv. 13–14).

Jesus expressed love to the children and anger toward his disciples. How could this be? Jesus was angry, but that did not mean he quit loving. A person can be displeased with another and still love. We do not have to deny or repress our indignation because we think it's a sin. Jesus was displeased yet never sinned.

Jesus did not yell, flail, or scream when expressing his anger. Nor did he say, "For the sake of peace and my disciples' feelings, I will not express my displeasure." When he expressed the truth, everyone benefited. The disciples learned, the children were blessed, and Jesus did not bury resentment.

We, like Jesus, can learn to be honest and direct with our emotions, expressing them openly and moving on with blessing and acceptance.

Lord, knowing that you occasionally felt indignation and yet did not sin helps me to be more honest with my own feelings.

Read Luke 11:9–10: "'Ask and it will be given to you'" (v. 9).

"I'm leaving in the morning on a business trip," said a busy friend. "I hope my daughter has my clothes ironed when I get home tonight."

"That would be nice," I responded. "Did you ask her to help you get things ready?"

"No, but I'm praying that she'll think of it on her own and do it," she answered as she hurried away.

Some of us harbor the misconception that it is wrong or selfish to ask directly for what we expect, need, or desire. Sometimes, like this parent, we may unconsciously try to manipulate another's response with silent prayer. These practices may encourage us to try to do everything on our own or to play God in someone else's life. If we refuse to ask for help and try to hide our needs, we will eventually burn out.

Jesus says, "Ask and it will be given you." We may find it difficult to ask directly for what we want or need, because we fear the answer. But another's response is not our responsibility. With daily practice this communication skill can become a new, healthful habit.

Lord, help me learn to ask for what I need or expect with directness and common sense.

Read Exodus 18:1–27: "'The work is too heavy for you; you cannot handle it alone'" (v. 18).

Every morning Moses went to work managing the two million or so people in his care. The people stood in line from dawn until late at night to talk with Moses. When Jethro, Moses' father-in-law, came to visit, he said, "Moses, you're doing too much. You'll soon burn out at this pace."

Some of us, like Moses, are overcommitted. But we can admit our limitations, seek advice in establishing a plan, and learn to delegate the work load. There are limits to what we can accomplish on our own. One of the clues in Moses' situation was that the people were waiting all day to get an appointment with him. Although Moses was responsible and caring, his organization was not running efficiently.

When we are engrossed in our working, serving, and helping, it may be difficult to step aside, assess our needs, and develop alternative methods. But we can ask for advice. Another person may be able to see the situation more clearly and offer help. Jethro suggested that Moses appoint capable men to share his duties. We can develop a similar plan. Delegating our work load is acceptable with God.

Lord, I can't do it all. I know I need to relinquish being in control of every detail. Please help me establish a workable plan.

Read 1 Corinthians 6:12: "'Everything is permissible for me'—but not everything is beneficial. 'Everything is permissible for me'—but I will not be mastered by anything."

Once we discover the misconceptions that cause us to overdo, we may need practical tools to help us stay committed to the process of behavioral change. One simple yet effective strategy is, Always subtract an activity or obligation each time you add a new one.

Those of us who want to do everything and do it just right are usually dependable and competent people. As others recognize this fact, they ask us to organize, help, and accomplish—more. Although we care deeply about the many legitimate and worthwhile causes, we need to remind ourselves that when we do too much, we often become less productive. Using discretion and doing less may actually help us be more effective and healthy. Completing an existing time-consuming project before starting another may be an unfamiliar practice for us. But learning to say no to one activity because we have already committed to another is a wise habit to develop. This is a more relaxed and beneficial way to live. And it is acceptable to God.

Lord, help me become more comfortable with cutting back. I want to be an effective servant of yours.

Read Luke 8:26–38: "The man from whom the demons had gone out begged to go with him, but Jesus sent him away" (v. 38).

At first it may seem callous of Jesus to refuse the man's request. Wanting to go with Jesus seems like such a good idea. How could Jesus leave him on his own to deal with this new life-style? But Jesus knew it would be best for the man to remain where he was.

Sometimes we need to say no to others' requests. We may feel sorry for the person making the request, yet if we conclude it is not beneficial for one or both people, we need to set a boundary and turn them down.

Perhaps it is not in our friend's best interests to loan her money. The appropriate response may be to refuse her request. When asked to head a new committee, and we are already overcommitted, we would be wise to decline.

Like Jesus, we can learn to take responsibility for our own decisions whether we say yes or no. Doing so will help us live balanced lives.

Lord, give me the courage to say no when it is advantageous to do so. Grant me strength when the answer is yes and wisdom when I'm struggling with which response is most appropriate.

Read Isaiah 7:4: "'Be careful, keep calm and don't be afraid.'"

"Mom, I'm afraid of that dog," said a client's little boy. "He might get me."

"We'll be careful, Timmy," his mom replied. "Walk with Joan and me." We continued past the dog to my office.

"Good morning," said the dog's owner, who was a friend of mine. He and his dog were playing catch with a small ball. Timmy watched cautiously.

"They're having fun," said Timmy as he relaxed his grip on his mom's arm.

"Do you want to throw the ball?" asked my friend. Soon the boy joined in the fun, playing with the dog he had previously feared.

Some of our fears are legitimate. Others are irrational and rob us of the joy of living. Like my client's son, sometimes we need to confront our fear to learn that it is illogical.

If we're afraid of someone else's reaction because we think we might make a mistake, sound foolish, or say something wrong, we may back off. This behavior often keeps us from enjoying others' company. Yet when we challenge our fear, staying true to our own personality, beliefs, and thoughts, we usually find that we were safe all along.

Read Psalm 19:14: "May the words of my mouth and
the meditation of my heart be pleasing in your sight,
O Lord, my Rock and my Redeemer."

"Betty, do you know what this is?" an elderly friend of
mine asked while cleaning the kitchen with her daughter. She held up the tiny antique fork she had given her
daughter years before.

"Of course," mumbled Betty. "I'm not ignorant."

"Rejected again," my friend said to me later with a
sigh. She had wanted her daughter to acknowledge the
gift and reminisce. But her indirect question about the
fork's purpose produced irritation, not intimacy.

Some of us, like my friend, "code" when we try to communicate. We believe it is not OK to express needs or
desires, so we say things indirectly. We may try to make
others do the right thing, the thing we want them to do,
without asking precisely. Although it may feel uncomfortable, we can change the way we relate to others. Our lives
will be less stressful and our relationships more rewarding
when we learn to speak without hiding our genuine
thoughts and feelings. We may never be completely consistent in our communication skills, but God will help us
as we commit to positive growth in this area.

*Lord, help me communicate directly and without
manipulation.*

Read Mark 5:18–20: "The man . . . begged to go with him. Jesus did not let him" (vv. 18–19).

For most of my life I avoided using the word *no.* Sometimes it meant I participated in situations I knew were contrary to God's will for me. Often it meant I hid my opinions or feelings when they differed from someone else's. I neglected my own physical and spiritual needs for rest, because I could not refuse the request to work late "just one more time." I felt used and burned up.

Eventually I realized I could no longer function effectively by always giving in. I began to say no at appropriate times. At first it felt extremely unfamiliar and uncomfortable, but in time I developed a healthy habit.

One of my journal entries indicates my progress. I wrote: "No, no, no, no, no. No, no, no, no, no. No, no, no, no . . . " No's filled the page. The last line read: "And it's OK!" Musical notes lined the margins.

I am singing a new song.

Lord, help me to have the courage to say no when I believe it is sensible to do so. I want to follow your example.

Read 2 Timothy 2:24: "And the Lord's servant must . . . be kind . . . not resentful."

Anger is a normal human response to a real or supposed wrong, yet it need not automatically erupt in uncontrollable rage. Neither is it wise to deny or suppress displeasure, since unresolved anger often turns into resentment. Built-up resentment can rob us of peace with ourselves, others, and God. However, there are ways to decrease susceptibility to anger. We can

make our own choices, taking control of our own time schedule as much as possible;

learn to say no as well as yes;

stay true to our own beliefs, values, and opinions regardless of those who differ with us;

set and accept reasonable limits;

stop trying to direct what is not ours to direct;

change the misconceptions we have about anger;

ask questions when we do not understand;

respectfully confront the injustice or wrong;

pray and trust God before, during, and after we've done all we can do;

remember that only God is flawless and admit that nothing else is absolutely perfect.

Lord, my anger rattles me. Help me learn effective ways to handle it before bitterness sets in. I want to serve you and others without resentment.

Read Habakkuk 3:2: "Even when you are angry, remember to be gentle with us" (NCV).

Habakkuk assumed that the same God who does great and mighty works can become angry and yet be gentle. That was a new concept to me. "Can I learn to handle my anger in a similar way?" I wondered.

Human beings can never respond as perfectly as God does, yet we can learn positive approaches to our anger. Gayle Roselini and Mark Worden, authors of the book *Of Course You're Angry,* suggest asking ourselves the following questions: What am I feeling? Why am I feeling this way? What can I do about it? What am I going to do about it?

Those of us who want to do everything right are often hesitant to admit or express our anger because we believe it would be wrong. Dealing with our displeasure is uncomfortable and unfamiliar. Gradually we can change the way we think about this issue. The next time we notice anger welling within we can stop to ask the four questions. Becoming more comfortable with our own feelings will help us answer the questions. We can learn to own our anger and express it with gentleness before it becomes resentment or hostility.

Lord, sometimes I'm not sure why I'm angry. Help me to understand my feelings and decide what I can do about them.

Read Psalm 4:4: "In your anger do not sin."

"Expressing my anger in wholesome ways is difficult for me," explained a friend of mine, "maybe because I've seen anger displayed only in outbursts of rage. When I was ten years old, my father came home one day and asked Mom what we were having for dinner. I guess he didn't want hamburgers, because he got mad and threw the uncooked meat against the living room wall. It made a mess, and he didn't even bother to clean it up. Right then I decided I would never get angry at the people I was supposed to love. But I am angry. It just doesn't seem fair."

"Perhaps it isn't," I agreed.

We need not be afraid of our anger. The emotion of anger is merely a normal reaction to injustice and injury. Anger itself is not bad. God does not thwart our honest expression of the injustice done to and around us. When we begin to believe this truth, we open ourselves to learning wholesome ways to express our indignation.

Lord, I acknowledge that I am angry. Help me learn to deal honestly with this reality.

Read Psalm 66:20: "Praise be to God, who has not rejected my prayer or withheld his love from me!"

"One way to discipline a child is to withdraw from him," said a teacher friend of mine. "He'll get the picture and shape up. Try it. It works!" She taught a room full of preschoolers each day and then went home to two daughters of her own. Something about her philosophy did not ring true to me.

Years later I thought of this conversation as I interacted with others about our mutual perfectionism. In his book *Living with a Perfectionist,* psychologist David Stoop writes: "When a parent is unavailable, the child may experience this as a feeling of helplessness, as shame at needing someone else.... The way a child handles this anxiety early in life can be one of the major roots of perfectionism in adulthood."

When we were children, we needed specific direction, but we also needed acceptance and understanding. As adults we still need to know that we are accepted for who we are and not for what we do or don't do. God does not withhold his acceptance in order for us to learn. He is readily available when we call. God always listens to our heartfelt prayers.

Father, I'm grateful that you never reject me or withhold your love. Your positive parenting style helps me accept myself and grants me permission to change my perfectionistic behavior.

Read Luke 6:12–16: "Jesus . . . spent the night praying to God. When morning came, he called his disciples" (vv. 12–13).

The night before Jesus announced the names of his discipleship team, he prayed all night. Perhaps he felt the heavy responsibility of choosing these twelve men and wanted God's guidance. Maybe since he knew what was ahead, he needed his Father's reassurance.

Jesus chose his team with care. What they said and how they behaved would reflect on his ministry. He planned to spend a great deal of time with them, teaching and preparing them to take over his ministry. Still, Judas, one of the men he chose to carry on his work, betrayed him.

Even though we pray fervently for direction, our lives do not always look perfect or feel great. The most meticulously prepared plans may not come to fruition. At times other people will let us down. This is the reality of living in an imperfect world. Jesus knows our pain and disappointment. He has been there and he understands.

Lord Jesus, sometimes I forget that you experienced many of the same hurtful things I do. Thank you for your example of prayer. Thank you, too, for walking through the pain to the cross, so I could have hope in this imperfect world.

Read Isaiah 29:16: "You turn things upside down, as if the potter were thought to be like the clay! Shall what is formed say to him who formed it, 'He did not make me'? . . . 'He knows nothing'?"

"I had a dream last night," said an artist friend. "I finally succeeded in painting the ultimate picture. Peers awarded me my profession's highest honors. I was pleased with my work. The colors blended perfectly, the characters showed depth, and the total effect seemed to come alive on canvas. But then my dream turned into a nightmare. The figures I lovingly and painstakingly painted walked to the edge of the canvas demanding freedom. They jumped into my workshop, walked among my works, stopping to stare at the piece. 'No,' said the male figure. 'It's wrong. Colors aren't credible.' The woman added, 'Lacks imagination.' Both strongly suggested I improve what I had already completed."

What an absurd dream, you say? The artwork cannot tell the artist how to craft the masterpiece. Neither can we as created human beings try to tell our Creator how to design our future. Learning to cooperate with God and live in harmony with his plan for all creation produces balance in our lives and makes good sense.

Master Creator, no longer will I turn things upside down and tell you how to paint your masterpieces.

Read Exodus 16:1–5: "Then the Lord said to Moses, 'I will rain down bread from heaven for you'" (v. 4).

"Moses, did you and your brother bring us here to starve?" grumbled the Israelite people. "We should have stayed in Egypt. At least there we had food!" God saw the brothers' predicament and said, "I'm going to drop breadlike rain from heaven. Everyone will have enough food to eat."

As he did for Moses, Aaron, and the people, God can and will provide for us. The question is, Will we accept the provisions, or do we believe we should hold out for a better idea, a more appropriate solution? Perhaps we are afraid that if we give in to God's plan, we'll be disappointed.

When we refuse to accept God's blueprint, for whatever reason, we forfeit the blessings. Then we may grow anxious, confused, and exhausted trying to figure out a superior way.

God's provisions are available. We can learn to cease striving, obsessing, or manipulating and enjoy what God has placed in front of us. Even if the provisions change tomorrow or next week or in a year, it doesn't matter. We can be grateful today and leave tomorrow's supply in God's hands.

Lord, you provide for my needs daily. Please help me to be aware of your gifts and to accept them graciously.

Read Mark 9:24: "'I do believe, help me overcome my unbelief.'"

"I'm worried about my future, my present, my choices—everything," admitted a student in my class. "I so want to make the right decisions. But what if I don't? What then?"

Some of us are paranoid that we might make a big-time mistake, that we will misinterpret God's plan for us. We become so preoccupied with making certain our future is perfect that we often miss contentment today. Gradually we may lose the ability to enjoy our jobs, our relationships, our recreation, our faith, ourselves.

We long to relax and give it all to God, but we can't. Why? Who or what taught us that a situation or friendship must be just right or it is worthless? Perhaps it is time to risk uncovering our misconceptions about living a successful life. Let us take the initial precarious step toward peaceful living by talking with a caring friend or knowledgeable professional. With help we can begin to discover the perfectionistic thinking that binds us. While holding on to our shaky faith, we can ask God to increase our confidence and courage. We can move toward positive change.

Lord, increase my faith. Please teach me what is keeping me from letting go and allowing you to work in my life.

Read Philippians 3:12–14: "Forgetting what is behind and straining toward what is ahead . . . " (v. 13).

"I'm committed to forgiving," I confided to my counselor, "but I can't seem to manage to forget. This really confuses me."

My counselor directed me to the experience of the apostle Paul. Before his conversion Paul had persecuted Christians, attempting to stamp out the faith he later professed. Paul acknowledged his former activities, admitted his wrong, and still said, "I forget what is behind." He chose to focus on his redeemed future, even though he remembered the actions of his painful past.

Past experiences become a part of us. These may include the events from childhood that contributed to our perfectionistic life-styles or the times we hurt our family, friends, and associates with the everything-must-be-just-right philosophy. We may never totally forget, but these memories do not have to remain our primary focus. Like Paul, we can remain committed to living in the present, trusting God for each new day.

Dear God, when circumstances remind me of the past, help me to be committed to moving ahead. I want to live in the freedom of your forgiveness.

Read Proverbs 27:5: "Better is open rebuke than hidden love."

Repressing our anger appears to be safer than dealing with it. And initially it may be. It is certainly less stressful than confronting the issue and facing an uncomfortable conversation. But burying the displeasure is ineffective, because it does not improve things. We may believe that "stuffing" our anger is noble, because we look like the peacemaker. But stuffing may be self-protective. Author Richard P. Walters, in his book *Anger, Yours and Mine and What to Do About It,* writes: "If we let other people continue to do wrong by taking advantage of us, we have wronged them by failing to confront them. If we are silent in the face of injustice, we share the guilt." When we stuff our anger in the name of love and spirituality, it usually leads to resentment. Resentment left to seethe inside is self-destructive.

We can choose to deal with our anger. At first we may want to talk with a safe and caring person to let out some of the rage. Eventually we may decide to confront the person who is the object of our anger. This will probably take courage and self-discipline. But God will help us. He wants us to be free from seething resentment.

Lord, this boiling resentment threatens to destroy me. I need your help in facing and confronting it.

Read Psalm 25:5: "Guide me in your truth."

"For years I believed that if I loved unselfishly, I would never get angry," explained a depressed friend of mine. "So I consistently refused to be mad. Of course I was angry when I was treated poorly, but I called it by another name and pushed it down."

In her book *Codependent No More,* Melody Beattie lists several myths about the confusing emotion called anger:

Good, nice people don't feel angry.

Anger is a waste of time and energy.

If we feel angry at someone, it means we don't love that
    person anymore.

My friend believed these lies. Repressed anger contributed to her depression. Admitting her anger set in motion the possibility for inner healing. "If the anger exists, why is it there?" she asked. That caused her to seek the truth about the injustices she had experienced and subsequently denied. When she realized that acknowledging the wrongs committed against her was acceptable to God, she saw a light at the end of her long, dark tunnel.

Are you hiding anger under a mask of determined service or obsessive work habits? Is it worth the anxiety and depression to keep up the facade? If not, start by admitting the truth of your anger. God will help you in finding the truth.

Lord, this is a scary process. Please guide me.

Read Psalm 7:11: "God is a righteous judge, and a God who has indignation every day" (NASB).

"Is anything wrong?" I asked.

"No!" retorted a friend. "See you later. 'Bye."

Five minutes later, the phone rang again. "Yes, there is something wrong." I recognized my friend's voice. "I'm angry with you!" she admitted. "I've felt your disapproval lately, and I don't like it."

"Did I do anything when we were together?" I asked.

"No," she answered. "But in the last week I've sensed you don't agree with my recent decisions. Your letters and telephone calls make me feel bad."

At the end of our talk I asked her to tell me when I do anything that makes her feel uncomfortable.

We can love and yet be angry. This is a new concept for many of us. We may think that in order to manifest "perfect" love, we have to hide or thwart any feelings of displeasure.

The Bible says God expresses his indignation every day. He is understandably angry at the injustice and disbelief in this world. He becomes angry while still loving us. We human beings do not love or express anger perfectly; yet God gives us the freedom to experience both emotions. We can learn to express our anger truthfully while continuing to love.

God, help me to admit and express anger and to love in healthy ways.

Read Matthew 7:12: "'So in everything, do to others what you would have them do to you.'"

As a child I was intrigued by the Golden Rule. I asked myself, "What do I want others to do to me?" The answer: I wanted others to be nice to me, to listen, help, care, support my ideas and dreams, approve of me, compliment, and love me.

So I determined to do to and for others what I wanted (and needed) for myself. I suppose I believed if I did to others what I thought they wanted, they would reciprocate. It worked! People frequently treated me well. I had found the secret to satisfying relationships (or so I thought).

As an adult, however, my concept was incomplete. Because I must "be nice," I couldn't be honest about my feelings. Sometimes others took advantage. The strengths we learn in childhood help us become self-productive adults. But a strength pushed to excess is a weakness. For example, the ability to listen is a favorable attribute. But if we neglect to share who we are, then only listening becomes a hindrance to developing balanced relationships.

I have redefined an inadequate childhood concept with the following: "Do for and to others with the same respect, dignity, and honesty you wish shown to and for you."

Lord, help me treat others in an equal and caring manner.

Read Exodus 14:10–12: "They were terrified and cried unto the Lord. They said to Moses, '. . . What have you done to us?'" (vv. 10–11).

As Pharaoh's army approached, the frightened Israelites blamed Moses. "Look what you've done! It's your fault that we're in this mess!"

Perhaps some of us have made similar charges—if not aloud, then silently. Confusion and anger about past or present circumstances and fear about the future may cause us to point at another. "He's the reason I'm not happy or fulfilled in my work" or "She's to blame for my perfectionistic habits." Ellen Sue Stern, author of the book *Running on Empty,* says "blame keeps us victimized." Blaming blocks us from acknowledging the truth about our past while it hinders our current growth.

Learning to accept responsibility for our adult choices, emotions, and behavior is a step toward stopping the destructive results of blaming others. Once we believe that we can change the things about our lives over which we have control, we are on the way to decreasing our anger and helplessness. With God's help we can cease playing this blaming game and begin to live in freedom and acceptance.

Lord, help me face my fears and cease blaming my background for my current circumstances. I trust you to avenge the injustice in my past, to help me deal with my present, and to secure my future.

Read Genesis 3:1–13: "Then the Lord God said, . . . 'What is this you have done?'" (v.13).

"I'm over here, Lord," Adam responded when God called his name. "I was afraid, so I hid."

"What happened?" asked God. "Did you eat from that tree I wanted you to leave alone?"

"Yes, but it was that woman's idea," said Adam.

"It wasn't really my fault," said Eve. "That sneaky serpent tricked me."

Adam blamed Eve. Eve blamed the serpent. It was the first game of pass the buck in human history. Some of us may still be playing this game. We fail to accept responsibility before God for our own feelings, thoughts, and behavior. We say it's our boss's fault that we missed our child's baseball game, when we schedule the appointments. We may blame our spouse for failing to allow us to finish school, when we are the ones who gave up too soon.

Each one of us has a choice. We can choose to accept the things we can't change and learn to act on the things we can change. We gain self-respect when we decide to stop blaming others for our dilemmas and start taking responsibility for our own choices.

Lord, I'm the one responsible for my attitudes and actions. Help me to stop playing the blaming game.

Read John 8:32: "'Then you will know the truth, and the truth will set you free.'"

"Well, at least I'm not a perfectionist," said a harried young man. "Look at my messy workroom. I have unfinished projects scattered all around."

This congenial and talented young man believed he could never do a good enough job, so he continually put things off. Fear of producing a faulty product canceled any pleasure or pride he might have had in his completed project.

Covert perfectionism triggers procrastination. We covert perfectionists may not complete our education, pursue our dream job, or write the book we want to. We may not sing in the choir, buy a house, or risk making new friends, because we are afraid of failure, appearing faulty, being shamed, or making a mistake. Making a decision of any kind paralyzes us and procrastination becomes a way of life. It is painful and depressing.

However, we can learn to believe a truth that can set us free: "I am not perfect, yet Jesus loved and died for me, and I am a valuable person in God's eyes."

Lord, I'm beginning to see how my bondage to shoulds and oughts has perpetuated my procrastination. Teach me your truth and help me learn to accept my human limitations.

Read Luke 19:1–10: "[Jesus] looked up and said to him, 'Zacchaeus, come down. . . .' So he came down at once and welcomed him gladly. All the people saw this and began to mutter" (vv. 5–7).

"When I went to see a counselor to find ways to cope with my chronic medical problems, my family objected," said a friend. "They recite Scripture verses and mutter about 'having faith.' They don't understand. I'm not abandoning God. I just think this is the way he's helping me right now." My friend's family lectured him when his decisions did not measure up to their preconceived "high" standards.

Miriam Elliott and Susan Meltsner, coauthors of *The Perfectionist Predicament,* call people with these behavior traits interpersonal perfectionists. They often demand that others live up to specific ideals at all times, and when they fail to do so, they scold, disapprove, or shame.

Jesus went to the home of a tax collector, and some disapproved, ridiculed, and muttered. Yet Jesus did not allow them to determine how he led his life. He relied on his Father's guidance and continued to stay true to his own values and plans. We who have sometimes wanted others to agree and adhere to our particular ideas and methods can learn to tolerate and appreciate the different way God works in each of our lives.

Lord, help me learn to live and let live.

Read 1 Corinthians 13:7: "[Love] believes all things"
(NASB).

My friend Ann gathered the courage to confront her
mother with the truth. "Everything I ever did, every
decision I ever made, I had you in mind."

"Are you sure?" Ann's mother asked.

This response sent familiar doubts racing through
Ann's mind. Immediately Ann began to question her
own thoughts and emotions.

Later Ann called me and related the conversation. "I
really wish Mom would accept what I say as my own
ideas," she said. "I know she loves me, but I think she
doubts what I feel or do, because it's not the same as she
experiences."

Others may be hurt when we hint that their ideas,
emotions, or perceptions have little merit or credibility.
How we think and how we act is not necessarily how
everyone should think and behave. When we genuinely
love another person, we believe in him and give credit to
the values and things he holds dear. Freedom flows into
our relationships when we accept the differing ideas and
insights of our loved ones.

*Father, please help me accept others' thoughts and
feelings, even when I don't fully understand.*

Read Song of Solomon 2:7: "Don't excite my feelings of love until I'm ready" (NCV).

Some of us try to control the way our spouse or friends show their love for us. To fulfill our personal dreams, we push our "loving" ideas on them. This type of love is limiting. It inhibits intimacy and contentment. True love resists imposing our perfectionistic concepts of love on one another. Healthy love relationships include these characteristics:

Allowing for individuality. Differing talents or temperaments do not threaten true love. Feelings and thoughts can be expressed without fear.

Not attempting to change the other. We may not like everything about our partner, yet when we consider the total picture, we are able to be more accepting.

Caring with detachment. Healthy love cares, listens, and responds yet does not try to fix or remove the lover's uncomfortable feelings of sadness, disappointment, or anger.

Affirming equality of self and partner. A mature relationship treats the partners as equals. There is no sense of competition or one-upmanship.

When we practice mature love, we accept what the other person is able or willing to give. We allow each other space to grow.

Lord, teach me to love. I don't wish to make inappropriate demands. Thanks for your example.

Read Psalm 68:19: "Praise be to the Lord, to God our Savior, who daily bears our burdens."

Some of us expect our love relationships to be a constant support. Yet just like us, our loved ones have good and bad days. Any of us can become bogged down in a personal muddle that renders us unavailable to the other. These are stressful times, but we need not panic.

We can assure ourselves and others that this is a temporary situation in which we need to step back from helping each other and deal with our individual problems. We do not have to try to control another person's problem to make us feel better about our own situation. We can learn to keep expectations of ourselves, other people, and our relationships healthy and reasonable.

Our daily interactions with loved ones need not be perfect. Every human relationship has ups and downs. We will not always be able to meet each other's needs or desires. Only God can consistently and perfectly help us with our daily burdens. We can learn to lean on him.

Lord, it's a relief to admit we aren't perfect in our relationships. I wish we could offer unconditional support, but it's not possible—or wise. For if each met all of the other's needs and desires, then we might be tempted to leave you out of our lives.

Read Malachi 1:2: "'I have loved you,' says the Lord."

Some of us may be afraid to let love become emotional We have agreed to love objectively. Didn't we say, "I do" or "I will"? Yet we balk at the thought of giving into sentimentality, and we hold at bay our genuine feelings. We love primarily with our heads and not our hearts.

Perhaps we have been conditioned to suppress the demonstrative side of love. Maybe we are afraid that we might look foolish or might express our love imperfectly. Sometimes we perfectionists tie up our emotions into neat little packages. We may try to stuff our true feelings in order to appear more in control, more "right."

God loves us emotionally as well as intellectually. I therefore have permission to reverse my restrictive view of love. I am learning that the necessary elements of love, which include commitment and duty, can live peaceably with love's emotional side. Feeling and verbalizing love is acceptable to God.

Lord, thank you for loving me with everything that you are and not just the duty part. Teach me to recognize and verbalize my feelings. I wish to know the joy as well as the responsibility of loving others.

Read Mark 16:15: "'Go into all the world and preach the good news to all creation.'"

We may communicate to our fellow human beings the truth that God has touched and changed our lives, but it is not our responsibility to make them believe. Occasionally I ask a friend to accompany me to church or Bible study. Several years ago one of my guests looked at her watch at least twenty times during the speaker's talk. "What is she thinking?" I wondered. Because I cannot read minds or hearts, I dared not guess. "That is God's work," I reminded myself.

Months later she called to tell me that she was in the midst of a crisis and felt that perhaps it was time to trust God for what she could no longer handle alone.

It is reassuring to know that I do not have to convince another person to believe in God's Son, Jesus. But it is a great privilege to be myself and share my life and let God do the convincing.

Lord, help me as I talk about what you have done for me. I'll allow you to do your work in others' lives.

Read Mark 14:32–34: "'My soul is overwhelmed with sorrow to the point of death,' [Jesus] said to them" (v. 34).

When as a child I sang a well-known hymn by Philip P. Bliss, I was confused by the first phrase: "'Man of Sorrows,' what a name for the Son of God who came." I did not understand how Jesus could be described as a man of sorrows.

Much later I came to understand the message of the lyrics. Jesus experienced pain and sorrow so we humans can be reunited with God. Only recently, however, did it dawn on me why the words of this song confused me as a child. I thought that displaying sadness and sorrow was a sin, so I could not fathom how God's sinless Son could experience sorrow.

It is not surprising, then, that I grew up believing it was my duty to rescue loved ones from circumstances that might cause them grief. In so doing I would be helping them to refrain from sin.

I no longer believe that experiencing sorrow is sinful. Neither do I think it my responsibility to try to keep another from actual or perceived wrong. This is God's job alone, and I am grateful and relieved to let him complete it.

Father, you are the God of comfort and insight. Your Son experienced much pain. I am comforted that he identifies with my distress.

Read 2 Corinthians 1:3–4: "Praise be to the God . . .
of all comfort, who comforts us in all our troubles."

A middle-aged mother of four said to me, "One day last
week my daughter was sunbathing on the deck, crying
over a recently broken engagement. I wanted to go to her
and take all the hurt away.

Then I realized what I wanted was to steal her sorrow.
It belonged to her, and I had no right to hurry it along or
take it away. I could sit beside her and listen, but I could
not be her Godlike comfort and direction. I had to allow
her to walk through it by herself."

We cannot alter our loved ones' emotions, even
though to try to do so might make us feel better. When
we suggest, "Don't cry now, tomorrow will be better" or
"Cheer up, it's going to be all right" or "It's all for the
best," we negate the reality of another's grief.

However, we can listen (even when the words are
uncomfortable to hear) without censoring or instructing.
We can pray with and for them. We may be God's
instrument, with affirming encouragement, but not the
ultimate source of their comfort. By listening, praying,
and stepping back we allow God room to start the recovery process.

*Lord, your comfort brings lasting inner healing.
Help me to take my hands off and let you work.*

Read Matthew 5:4: "'Blessed are those who mourn, for they will be comforted.'"

My friend's mother died. Soon after, my friend was diagnosed with a similar terminal illness. When I tried to talk with her about the loss of her mother and her own health, she changed the subject. At first I thought she was experiencing the denial phase of the grieving process. But as months turned into years, and her condition worsened, I realized she seemed unable to grieve, either in anger or acceptance.

Did my friend believe God would be disappointed if she acknowledged her grief? Jesus said, "Blessed are those who grieve. They will be comforted."

The word *blessed* means more than happy. It means to be personally satisfied with God so that progressive inner joy comes in spite of circumstances. Yet we will never fully experience God's loving help if we do not admit our need, our disappointment, our loss, our grief.

God does not reject us when we exhibit signs of grief and pain. He invites us to come near him and receive comfort. Since he allows us to mourn, surely we can give ourselves and others permission as well.

Lord, my heart is heavy with my disappointments. I need your comforting arms around me.

Read Psalm 90:10 and 14: "The length of our days is seventy years—or eighty, . . . for they quickly pass. . . . Satisfy us in the morning with your unfailing love, that we may sing for joy and be glad all our days."

Recently I watched a television documentary on the lives of active centenarians. These men and women seemed to live in harmony with time. They accepted life's limitations and adapted to inevitable loss. Statistics indicate that most of us will not live to be one hundred years old. However, we can choose to adopt a balanced and peaceful life-style during the years that we have. Author Ralph Keyes makes the following helpful suggestions:

When rushing, ask yourself: Do I need to hurry? What's the worst thing that could happen if I don't rush around? Is that scenario worse than what my hurrying is costing me?

Don't try to make use of each minute; this only increases anxiety and reduces productivity.

Reduce awareness of time. Make frequent visits to sanctuaries from time: churches, parks, libraries. Pursue clock-free hobbies: gardening, listening to music, baseball, fly-tying, or taking walks.

As God daily assures us of his love, we gain permission and courage to slow down and be glad.

Lord, each morning your love satisfies me, so that I am learning to appreciate and enjoy all my days.

Read 1 Timothy 6:17: "... put their hope in God, who richly provides us with everything for our enjoyment."

Some of us are so intense and serious about doing and making everything right that we fail to enjoy life. We think it is unproductive to have fun—not as important as working, serving, or ministering. Yet playing and enjoying is a worthwhile part of life.

"There was in Jesus a wonderful playfulness and encouragement to enjoy God's creation. He ate, drank, and joined celebrations," writes Gerald G. May, M.D., in his book *Addiction and Grace.* God gave us the capacity to have fun. When we refuse to cultivate this area of our personality, we become one-sided.

Perhaps you need to be encouraged to develop the playful side of life. Sometimes I do. Here are several suggestions: The next time you mark your calendar with a meeting date, schedule in a fun activity, too. In the upcoming month, learn how to play a new game. Share the experience with someone you love. Read a joke book. Laugh aloud. Try to remember what you had fun doing fifteen years ago. Do it again this week.

Lord, help me to become more balanced. Teach me to loosen up and enjoy my God-given life.

Read 2 Corinthians 10:12: "They are only comparing themselves with each other, and measuring themselves against their own little ideas" (TLB).

Some of us play with a determination that defies relaxation. We participate in team sports and become controlled by competition, preoccupied with winning. When we lose, we may silently believe there must be something wrong with us. We try harder. "Playing" becomes a form of overwork. Even our participation in individual sports activities may place excessive emphasis on competition—with ourselves. We must run better than we did yesterday, we should exercise longer, we must reach maximum heart rate even though we're exhausted. We push, not necessarily to be more healthy or relaxed, but to be the best or perfect. We compare ourselves with others and with ourselves.

In our race to compete and win, we sometimes miss the camaraderie of friends, the beauty of nature, the laughter of children, and God's free grace. We find an inner release when we stop the comparison game, realize that our value does not depend on our performance, and learn to enjoy our physical activity.

Lord, help me to play with enthusiasm and joy.

Read Colossians 1:4–5: "We have heard of your faith in Christ Jesus . . . —the faith and love that spring from the hope that is stored up for you in heaven."

Today's successes are pleasurable, they contribute to self-esteem and add meaning to our human existence. But when circumstances beyond our control strip us of accomplishments, material accumulation, and dignity—what then? Can we human beings live without hope for the future? Victor Frankl, a psychiatrist who wrote of his experiences in a Nazi prison camp, said, "The prisoner who lost faith in the future was doomed. . . . Loss of hope and courage can have a deadly effect."

Some of us try desperately to build an earthly utopia for ourselves and our families. But this is not possible. The truth remains that life is often cruel, unfair, and confusing. What can we do? How can we get up and go on?

God's promise of a perfect tomorrow can help restore our will to live today, as well as our ability to forgive the painful yesterdays. Although we cannot see it and we cannot touch it, we can hope. Heaven is ahead.

Lord, my ultimate hope is in you. Knowing I'll live with you someday helps me deal with my disappointment today. In this assurance I can relax and let go.

Read Psalm 18:17–19: "He delighted in me" (v. 19).

"Do you like me, Lord?" I wrote in my journal. "You love me, I know, but do you like me? Show me in your Word where it indicates that you like me."

Early one morning, a year later, I sat down to study at my desk. Something I read caught my eye. "He rescued me, because he delighted in me" (Psalm 18:19).

"That's really nice," I thought. I changed the *he* to *I* and the *me* to *you*. "I rescued you, because I delighted in you." The dictionary defines delight in as "to incline to, to be pleased with, to favor, to like."

I grabbed my journal and wrote these words: "Thank you, God. You answered my prayer, the longing of my heart. Something inside me is opening . . . unclenching . . . flying! When I was a child, someone close to me said he would not love me if I were not in his family. In my childish mind I determined I was loved out of duty, and not because I was worth liking. I must have transferred this belief to you. Now I see that you actually want to like me. Thank you."

God loves me. God loves you. He likes us, too.

Lord, thank you for delighting in me.

Read Matthew 14:25–31: "Immediately Jesus reached out his hand and caught him" (v. 31).

Jesus walked toward the disciples' boat, not on land but on the water. "Lord, if it's really you out there," yelled Peter, "I want to come walk with you on the water."

"Come on, then," replied Jesus.

Peter climbed over the side of the fishing boat, stepped on the waves, and started walking. But when Peter saw the effects of the wind, he panicked and began to sink. Peter was in dire need, and he knew it. "Help me, Lord!" he cried.

Immediately Jesus reached out and caught Peter before he went under.

Some of us have experienced dire emotional, spiritual, or physical need. We begged for help, but those we trusted were unable or unwilling to assist us. Instead they left us to flounder and sink. Consequently it is difficult for us to trust.

But Jesus is not like the unreliable people in our memory. Just as he did for Peter, he will come to our rescue. He reaches out to lift us up.

Lord, thank you for helping me when I need you. You do not hold out on me when I panic, and I appreciate that.

Read Matthew 12:43–45: "'And the final condition of
that man is worse than the first'" (v. 45).

When we stop listening to the obsessive thoughts and
start believing the truth about ourselves, we begin to
have the courage to change our compulsive behavior. But
often we feel uncomfortable and empty within. Everything is so unfamiliar. We may be tempted to retreat into
our old habits. Jesus explained this relapse process. We
decide to turn our backs on the destructive life-style, we
clean up our act. But if we do not fill up the clean, empty
spaces with new, healthy attitudes, beliefs, and actions,
the old patterns rush back in.

It is normal for a familiar fear-producing situation to
trigger former thinking and behavior. Our commitment
to growth and healing, however, helps us stay alert and
continue trusting God even when we experience confusion and emptiness. We may need to repeat our newly
gained truth about God, others, and ourselves for weeks
before we really believe it. The new, freedom-filled person we are becoming is worth the process. God helps us
replace the obsession and pain with joy and gratefulness.

*Lord, some days I'm so empty I feel like the air is
blowing through me. But I'm committed to walking
through this confusion to freedom. Please fill up my
empty spaces with your love and help me to become
the person you made me to be.*

Read Romans 1:15–17: "For I am not ashamed of this Good News about Christ. It is God's powerful method of bringing all who believe it to heaven" (v. 16 TLB).

"Girl Missing, Feared Abducted," "Riots in the Streets of Los Angeles," "Hundreds Die in Explosion." The daily newspapers as well as prime-time television broadcasts include reports on war, famine, floods, kidnappings, abuse, murders, and rapes. We listen and we inevitably ache inside. When all this bad news merges with our personal disappointment, we may become overwhelmed. We may do almost anything to medicate the pain. We work more, do more, exercise more, eat more, or drink more. Yet underneath the obsessive behavior we long for relief, for someone to understand and meet our need.

God is that someone. He cares that we are surrounded by bad news. To show us he is on our side, God paid an extravagant price—his Son. By choosing to accept God's costly gift, we discover future hope and a healthy way to cope now. While waiting for the fulfillment of our hope, God grants us peace and comfort in our daily struggles and powerful support as we serve our fellow human beings.

Lord, thanks for going to such great lengths to show you care. I care, too. Please help me to manifest your love in the midst of the bad news.

Read 2 Corinthians 9:10: "For God . . . will make it grow so that you can give away more and more fruit from your harvest" (TLB).

This afternoon I strolled through a beautiful, lush flower garden. The gardener explained each blossom, seedling, and shrub. There were dainty lilies of the valley, majestic purple iris, sun-splashed petunias, and geraniums the color of red crayons. My childhood favorite, the peony bush, was ready to burst into bloom.

Then the gentle gardener showed me a hosta plant with its crisp green and white leaves. This globular plant presented a classic backdrop for the more brilliantly tinted flowers. "Years ago someone gave me one small hosta plant," the gardener explained. "I put it in the ground right here. That original plant grew and multiplied. And just look what has happened. There are now hostas outlining the entire yard. Every season as each plant grows wider, I break off new shoots and transplant them."

As I walked away I thought, "O Lord, make me like the hosta plant. Its fresh green and white foliage adds character and depth wherever it flourishes. May I be consistent in and out of season. And may I mature and grow a sufficient root system to produce other sturdy, healthy plants."

Growth begets growth, Lord. Please help me to develop and produce with consistency and balance.

Read Psalm 56:3: "What time I am afraid, I will trust in thee" (KJV).

Our tent flap flailed in the wind. Outside the canvas haven, rain came down in torrents. My young cousin and I sat in the corner of the tent hugging each other. We could have retreated to safety in the house since we were in my backyard, but we chose to stay put and brave the storm. After all, we had planned this camping adventure for months.

"You know that verse we learned Sunday at church?" my cousin asked.

"You mean, 'What time I am afraid, I will trust in thee?'" I replied.

"Yeah, that's the one!" she said. We repeated it together until the storm subsided.

Sometimes as adults we feel like life is an out-of-control storm raging around us. We become afraid—of new ventures, of failure, of the unknown, of another person, of ourselves. We can retreat and hide in "safety" or choose to hang in there and face the uncomfortable fear, trusting God for what we need. Passing through frightening and unfamiliar situations on the way to maturity is not always easy. When we are anxious (and we certainly will be at times) we can trust the one who is bigger than the storm.

Lord, I admit I'm sometimes afraid. But when I ask you for help and comfort, I believe you are there.

Read 2 Corinthians 5:1–5: "For while we are in this tent [body], we groan and are burdened, . . . but . . . God . . . has given us the Spirit as a deposit, guaranteeing what is to come" (vv. 4–5).

"I thought if I had enough love, and sincerely followed Christ, I would never let disappointment, pain, or discouragement affect my life or my family's," revealed a friend. "Consequently I felt responsible for making sure we had no problems. Of course this meant I pretended a lot."

Larry Crabb, author of *Inside Out,* suggests, "We learn to pretend that we feel now what we cannot feel until Heaven. . . . There is no escape from an aching soul, only denial of it. The promise of one day being with Jesus in a perfect world is the Christian's only hope for complete relief. Until then we either groan or pretend we don't."

We live in an imperfect world, struggle daily with inadequate physical bodies, insufficient relationships, and incomplete spirituality. In the midst of this troubling situation, we have a perfect God who has given us a comforting and strength-giving helper. This is God's guarantee that one day all the groaning will be over.

Lord, my human limitations bug me. Others' human inadequacies irritate me, too. Trusting in your future plan helps me to deal with the imperfection and to be content while I'm waiting for what is to come.

Read Romans 3:10: "As the Scriptures say: 'There is no one without sin. None!'" (NCV).

"A live body is not one that never gets hurt, but one that can to some extent repair itself. In the same way a Christian is not a man who never goes wrong, but a man who is enabled to . . . pick himself up and begin over again after each stumble," wrote C. S. Lewis in *Mere Christianity.*

Some of us live in fear that someone will discover we are fallible. Perfectionism keeps us from acknowledging our humanness. As we change and grow, however, we can be freed to admit: "If I make a mistake, I make a mistake. It is not the end of the world. If I am wrong about something, I realize it is part of being human. I can meet it head-on, admit it, and rectify it. If I sin, I can confess it to God, seeking forgiveness. If my action or attitude affects another person, I can go to her, ask for forgiveness, and leave the choice to forgive with her."

We are each responsible for our own mistakes, wrong, or sin. No one else is responsible for us. This healthy approach to imperfection builds bridges with ourselves, others, and God.

Lord, I know I'm not perfect. Help me have the courage to rectify my mistakes and to seek forgiveness.

Read Matthew 7:1: "'Do not judge, or you too will be judged.'"

"If Sam really loved God, he would join a Bible study," "Marguerite would lose weight if she really cared," "Sarah's house is a mess; she must really be a loser," "Eric's a jerk. He always disagrees with my ideas," "Janice wears too much makeup for a pastor's wife."

Although we may not say things like this out loud, we sometimes think them. This attitude places us as judge over another's motives, actions, and temperament. Some of us grew up with a condemning authority figure looming over our head. We then were conditioned to be critical. Censorious thoughts are second nature to us. They steal our ability to live in joy and harmony with one another.

When we let go of trying to make everything right, the critical attitude begins to fade. We do not have to be perfect all the time; neither do our loved ones, business associates, children's teachers, or the pastor and his wife. The "judge not" attitude can start deep within us. As we admit the truth about ourselves and cease condemning others for our own inadequacies and imperfections, we are set free to enjoy one another.

Lord, help me stop judging others according to my own biased perceptions. This is new for me. I need your merciful touch.

Read Philippians 4:8: "Whatsoever things are true, . . . honest, . . . just, . . . pure, . . . lovely, . . . of good report, if there be any virtue, and . . . any praise, think on these things" (KJV).

One of the insights that helped me as I was recovering from burnout was the realization that I could admit and tell the truth even though it was unpleasant. I had believed that to please God I needed to pretend I did not mind being taken advantage of or being mistreated. I made it a practice to refrain from thinking about painful things. Because I did not allow myself to think about the uncomfortable truth, I could not acknowledge or admit that change needed to take place.

Paul's words encouraged me first to think about, and then to admit, the truth even when it was unpleasant. Although I was uncomfortable confronting reality, I walked past my fear knowing that there was virtue and value in being honest about my pain and moving on to healing.

I am changing, growing, and experiencing a newfound inner freedom that enables me to think about the true, honest, just, pure, and lovely things God has for me.

Lord, when I attempt to hide reality, I erode the very core of my soul. Please help me have courage to tell the truth about the disagreeableness of life and then to move on to trust you for the good.

Read Genesis 12:1–9: "The Lord had said to Abram, 'Leave your country, your people and your father's household and go to the land I will show you.' . . . So Abram left" (vv. 1, 4).

This unanticipated journey required Abram and his family to leave all that was familiar and comfortable. Although Abram did not know what he would encounter on his trip, he believed God would lead. God asks those of us who try to do and make everything right to leave our self-destructive life-style and head toward balance and freedom. The choice is up to us; we do not have to go.

Embarking on the journey means leaving our familiar attitudes and behaviors of perfectionism, performance/work addiction, and people pleasing. The trip will often be uncomfortable; we may have to leave some of our friends and family behind. God knows the way. He is our guide.

Lord, Abram started over again when he was seventy-five years old. I guess it's never too late to change. Please go with me on this unfamiliar journey.

Read Romans 8:1–2: "There is now no condemnation for those who are in Christ Jesus" (v. 1).

"He's weak. It won't be long now," said the nurse. Maxine tiptoed to his bedside. "Hi, Grandpa," she whispered. "I'll read you the mail."

For years Grandpa taught fifth-grade Sunday school, praying for each student. Many boys began to know God's love from Teacher Parker. His influence rippled over generations. But Grandpa had been troubled lately. He was ashamed of what he called his wild days, including three failed marriages. Now as he neared death, he could not let go. Maxine reached for the greeting cards stacked on the nightstand. She tore the seal on one and read the handwritten message from a former student: "I just want to thank you for teaching me Romans 8:1: 'There is now no condemnation for those who are in Christ.' This means a lot to me. Love, Bob."

A tear trickled down Grandpa's cheek as he closed his eyes and smiled. During the night he died peacefully. There was no condemnatory judgment in God's "welcome home."

Because God forgives us, surely we can forgive ourselves.

Father, because of Jesus you hold nothing against me. Thanks.

Read Matthew 23:37: "'O Jerusalem, Jerusalem, you who kill the prophets . . . , how often I have longed to gather your children together, as a hen gathers her chicks under his wings, but you were not willing.'"

Do you want a glimpse into the heart of the Son of God? Then listen to the words he told the men who scorned and tricked him: "So often I yearned to surround you with my love and protection, like a mother hen shields her chicks from danger under her wings, but you would not let me. Instead you actively opposed me."

These people threw stones at God's attempts to be intimate with them. They closed their ears and hearts to God's invitation of freedom and mercy. Although many of us desire God's help in our lives, we may not be aware of how we hold his love at bay. Hesitant to run under his protective wings, we may be afraid of what might happen if we loosen our grip and become less busy and intense. Perhaps we who feel it is our responsibility to help everyone and everything to be just right are apprehensive about what surrender might mean.

Faith does involve risk. But God longs to free us from our unhealthy attachments and to help us be all we were created to be. We can run to his waiting arms, be safe, and live.

Lord, I am willing, today, to trust you.

Read Romans 8:28: "And we know that in all things God works for the good of those who love him, who have been called according to his purpose."

"It's hard to understand how situations that create fear or discouragement could be as worthwhile as events that produce feelings of peace and delight," said a friend. We agreed there are no simple explanations for life's mixture of good and bad.

For the past fifteen years I've prayed: "God, show me who I am now and who I can become, who you created me to be." In retrospect I see how God has answered this prayer. The painful and confusing times uncovered my need and propelled me to seek relief from self-destructive thoughts and actions. Yet I still find it difficult to comprehend how my poor choices and human weaknesses may trigger positive change. Can both positive and negative situations work for ultimate good?

"All things work together for good to those who love God," wrote Paul. But the Greek word *good* does not mean always pleasant and comfortable. *Good* means beneficial, profitable in the long run, that which contributes to growth. We can move toward acceptance and trust that all things work collectively for our good.

Lord, I wish everything in my life was pleasant, but I don't want my distaste for the uncomfortable to thwart my growth. Please help me.

Read Proverbs 3:5: "Trust in the Lord with all your heart, and lean not on your own understanding."

"How can I make her understand that we can work this out?" the hurting young man asked me. His fiancée had doubts about their upcoming wedding, so she broke the engagement. He was obsessed with lessening his pain, changing her mind, and making the marriage happen.

But can we make someone else behave a certain way? Can we force another to understand or feel what we do? We may try, but we will never be totally successful. To believe we can change another person, even those we love very much, is to experience extreme anxiety. The only truly sensible action we can take is letting go.

Letting go is difficult. Often it is painful. Yet it is personally freeing. When we loosen our controlling grip, we do not send the situation into space to wander aimlessly. When we let go, we surrender to God. We need not worry if everything will be all right. When we let go and hand it to God, we can visualize God taking over.

Opening your heart and mind is like unclenching your fists and releasing that which you hold so tightly. Go ahead. Let go.

Lord, letting go hurts. But I can't hold tight any longer. I'm too tired. I don't have any more answers. I transfer everything to you.

Read Zephaniah 3:17: "'The Lord your God is with you, he is mighty to save. He will take great delight in you, he will quiet you with his love, he will rejoice over you with singing.'"

"All I ever wanted was for my parents, especially my father, to be proud of me," said the business executive. "I never felt I was good enough. When I brought home a B he asked why it wasn't an A. The night I missed a free throw and we lost the basketball championship by one point, he lectured me for three hours. I guess he was disappointed."

Perhaps as a child you wished your father would hold you and sing songs of comfort and love. Maybe you longed for him to take delight in your youthful accomplishments. Maybe you wanted him to go with you when you faced the neighborhood bully. Perhaps you needed him to affirm your love of theater instead of demanding that you play sports. But it did not happen, and you experienced great loss.

The words of Zephaniah are for you. Your heavenly Father is with you. He allows you all the room you need to be just who are, even though you are different from your brother or sister. God is delighted with you. Visualize him rocking you gently, calming your fears, and singing happy songs of love and joy.

I'm loved far more than I thought possible. Thank you, Lord.

Read 1 John 4:18: "There is no fear in love; but perfect love casteth out fear: because fear hath torment" (KJV).

"If I let someone love me, first he'll cut off my hands, then my arms, and finally my heart," my friend said. "I'm afraid." She associated love with pain. Past relationships had stolen her uniqueness, thwarted her personality, and depleted her spirit. My friend camouflaged her deep love-hunger by trying to be perfect. She felt driven to prove herself a worthwhile occupant of God's earth. An everything's-just-fine facade hid a terrified inner child. She was afraid her human inadequacies would cause people to reject and ridicule her. So she hid in fear, and the fear tainted her view of love. John Townsend, author of *Hiding from Love,* says, "We hide from what we need."

One day my friend read, "There is no fear in love, but perfect love casts out fear; because fear has torment." When she learned that the word *perfect* in the passage means full grown, or adult, and not sinless, she renewed her commitment to walk through her conditioned fear responses toward mature love. It is a process, and my friend is still working on it. I respect her for that.

Lord, there's no torment in your love. I realize this mentally, but help me experience it emotionally and spiritually as well.

Read Luke 5:18–20: "Some men were carrying . . . a man who was paralyzed . . . to . . . let him down through the tiles with his stretcher . . . in front of Jesus" (vv. 18–19 NASB).

During my recovery from burnout, I met a friend. God put her in my life to be a "stretcher bearer." When I could not help myself, she was there. I telephoned her when my hands shook and my heart ached. She listened and affirmed my genuine desire to change, to be the person God wanted me to be. When weeks turned into months, months into years, and I still felt nauseated and unable to feel the love of others, she waited patiently for me to get well. She did not offer me quick advice or quote Scripture verses or give reasons for my dilemma. She supported my recovery, even though she never mentioned the word.

At times I think she was confused by my rambling and saddened by my pain, yet I never got the impression she felt responsible for my health. She left the responsibility with me and expected God to work.

Our paths rarely cross now, though we remain friends. She was a part of God's support system when I was most needy. Have there been any stretcher bearers in your life? Whom can you count on now for support and encouragement?

Lord, help me to extend and to accept support.

Read 2 Corinthians 10:15: "We hope that your faith
will grow and that, still within the limits set for us,
our work among you will be greatly enlarged" (TLB).

"I'm tired. Been working nonstop for months. But I'm of
hearty stock, the kind that keeps on going faithfully until
we drop. But no matter. Once we drop, then it's all over
anyway. Right?" said the head chef of a catering company.
Do we need to keep pushing and pushing until we col-
lapse of exhaustion and die? Is that God's plan?

We all get tired in the course of fulfilling our daily
obligations. But some of us completely wear out working
in our service-related businesses, careers, or ministries. It
may be difficult for us to acknowledge our limitations,
step back, rest, and let others take over for a while.

While we are away recharging our worn-out batteries,
the work will go on. It may even grow and prosper.
When we return, we will be better equipped to resume
our day-to-day responsibilities.

*Lord, Paul recognized that he had limits. So do I.
Right now I need to retreat and rest. While I'm
gone, please continue to do your will in my work and
ministry.*

Read Mark 5:24–34: "He said to her, 'Daughter, your faith has healed you. Go in peace and be freed from your suffering'" (v. 34).

For twelve years the ailing woman sought relief from her mounting medical problems. After depleting her money, time, and energy supply, the disturbing symptoms remained. She was tired of it all, and ashamed. One day she touched Jesus' coat and was relieved of her pain.

Like this woman, some of us are tired of trying so hard to get well. Our obsessive thoughts and actions have caused us to become people we do not want to be. As a result we are usually exhausted and often full of shame.

Jesus wants to raise us out of the pit of despair and restore our dignity. We can reach out and touch him. He is there even when we cannot see the evidence of his presence. We can go on in peace knowing that God is in the process of healing us from our inner suffering.

Lord, I need you. Make me whole inside, so I can live in peace.

Read Isaiah 58:6–9: "'The kind of fasting I have chosen [is]: . . . to set the oppressed free and break every yoke. . . . Then your light will break forth like the dawn, and your healing will quickly appear; then your righteousness will go before you, and the glory of the Lord will be your rear guard. Then . . . you will cry for help, and [the Lord] will say: Here am I'" (vv. 6, 8–9).

Perhaps it's not that we want everything done our way. Some of us may rarely make verbal demands, yet we have such an urgent and powerful need for all things to be done right, for everyone to think and act right. This includes ourselves. We want our personal emotions, perceptions, ideas, and behavior to be impeccable. When we fail to succeed in this endeavor, we try harder. Instead of liberating us as we want, this philosophy adds to our oppression and hopelessness.

The truth is, no matter how hard we work, care, love, and serve, life in this imperfect world can never be flawless. When we acknowledge this and genuinely relinquish what is out of our domain to God, we experience less perfectionistic anxiety. We are then free for God to enlighten our mind, heal our wounded personality, cleanse our spirit, and protect us on our ongoing journey.

Lord, I need your help. I want to break the chains of rigidity and live with others in your freedom.

Read Matthew 17:1–5: "'Lord, it is good for us to be here. If you wish I will put up three shelters'" (v. 4).

Jesus invited Peter, James, and John to accompany him on an excursion into the mountains. There Jesus' three friends witnessed a magnificent scene. The face of their leader and confidant, Jesus, shone like the sun, and his clothes turned pure white. Then two Jewish heroes, Elijah and Moses, suddenly appeared in conversation with the glowing Jesus.

"Jesus, this is good!" said Peter. "But if it's all right with you, I have an another idea. Let's put up tent-shelters for the three of you." Appreciating the experience of witnessing Jesus' majestic glory was not enough; Peter wanted to "do" something more. Capable Peter, hoping to perfect the perfect, to hold onto the excitement. Some of us, like Peter, endeavor to add to God's perfect plans. Instead of resting and enjoying his loving presence, we work to impress. We pray harder, study more, and work ourselves into a frenzy saying yes to more serving jobs. But we can stop, admit this tendency, and grow to marvel at the magnificence of his majesty.

Lord Jesus, teach me to relax and enjoy your presence.

Read Psalm 46:10: "'Cease striving and know that I am God'" (NASB).

When we focus on knowing *about* God, we are adding to our to-do list. When we concentrate on knowing and enjoying God, we can begin to relax and appreciate him. Some of us are obsessed with wanting and gaining more. We strive to make certain that we will always have enough.

Enough of what? Everything. Enough knowledge, enough love and acceptance, enough security, significance, goodness, hope, enough of God's love and grace.

When we strive only to know *about* God, we may be in competition to gain more knowledge than others. What we look like and what we say may become more important than God himself. Sometimes our striving means that we keep so busy studying and reading that we neglect the reality of his person. The psalmist wrote a song. Included in the lyrics are the words "Be still and know that I am God." This verse encourages us to quit thrashing inside, to hush, and to relax in who God is.

Lord, sometimes I am in such a race inside that even the thought of slowing down to relax with you is frightening. How can I expect to prove my competence if I cease striving? O God, I need your help.

Read James 5:16: "The effectual fervent prayer of a righteous man availeth much" (KJV).

As a child I memorized this Scripture verse. It quickly became one of my favorite passages, and I determined to become a person whose prayers availed much.

Yet as I grew up, I began to equate the word *fervent* with terms such as *fiery, frenzied,* and *intense.* I thought my prayers might get more results if my heart was tied in a knot. Although not noticeably pushy or boisterous, internally I was driven to prove to God how much I cared. I concluded if I was passionate enough, God would have to act on my behalf.

As I became less obsessed in other areas of my life, a relaxed and trusting attitude spilled over into my prayer life. I discovered it is not my overwrought or inflamed words that move the hand of God. There is a difference between enthusiasm and drivenness. While energy and enthusiasm flow from God, obsession and drivenness do not.

The active, energetic, bold requests to God of a person who has decided to believe Jesus and live within God's boundaries and standards are powerful and effective.

Lord, teach me the difference between fervent and frenzied prayer. I calmly believe you will accomplish what I cannot.

Read Matthew 26:6–13: "While Jesus was in Bethany in the home of a man known as Simon the Leper, a woman came to him with an alabaster jar of very expensive perfume, which she poured on his head as he was reclining at the table. When the disciples saw this, they were indignant. . . . Aware of this, Jesus said, . . . 'Why are you bothering this woman? She has done a beautiful thing to me'" (vv. 6–8, 10).

Mary risked the disapproval of the important men who surrounded Jesus when she worshiped him in her unique way. The men's immediate response was condemning and critical. But Jesus' reaction was freeing, accepting, and encouraging.

Some of us are intent on worshiping or showing our devotion to God in just the right way. However, Jesus' reaction to Mary's act of love encourages us to relax and be ourselves in our relationship with God.

Likewise we can learn to accept our fellow Christians in their genuine expression of heartfelt worship. There are no wasted resources when we worship the compassionate and triune God. God accepts our authentic praise and adoration.

Lord, help me to express my thoughts and praise without embarrassment and to allow others to do the same.

Read Matthew 14:13–23: "Then he gave . . . and [all] were satisfied . . . and . . . twelve basketfuls . . . were left over" (vv. 19–20).

I have a tendency to ration out my giving. Under the outer layers of kindness and caring, I'm afraid that if I give wholeheartedly to others, there won't be enough left for me. Perhaps it's because I've equated giving and sharing with having no limits on what I do for others and never saying no. I believed that to be perfectly loving, I must give up who I am and what God wants me to be. So I abandoned my own ideas, concerns, and even pleasure to prove I was a giving person. Paradoxically this hindered my ability to love others. I eventually realized that I needed to retrieve what was rightfully mine—my perceptions, gifts, and individuality. Then I could risk giving generously out of the abundance of who God created me to be.

When Jesus provided food for over five thousand people, inviting them to eat all they wanted, he still had twelve baskets left over. Jesus was liberal with his love and concern. He did not ration out for fear it would deplete his resources. We can be generous without relinquishing who we are. We can be caring while maintaining our God-given identity.

Lord, I do not wish to be miserly in my dealings with others. Help me to give out of the overflow of who you made me to be.

Read Psalm 97:11: "Joy belongs to those who are honest" (NCV).

Recently my twenty-year-old daughter and I drove to my parents' home in the Midwest. During our visit Dad asked me to look through my things in storage. As I rummaged through the keepsakes, my eyes fell on a small green book. "It couldn't be!" I exclaimed. "My junior high diary!"

Inside the front cover were the words: SECRET! STAY OUT PLEASE! Tiny lettering at the bottom of the page read, "I beg. Ask what it says inside, *maybe* I'll tell you."

While scanning the messy pages, I cringed. "This girl was immature and boy crazy!" I thought. Upon our return home, I invited my daughter to read it. Several hours later a surprised young woman walked into my room. "Thanks a lot, Mom, for letting me read your diary. I've always had the feeling you never went through what I did, like somehow I didn't measure up to what you were in junior high. But you were just like me. Flighty and boy crazy!"

We hugged and laughed. "Actually it's rather embarrassing," I admitted.

"Well, thanks for allowing me to see a glimpse of that part of your life," she said.

Lord, help me be open and honest, even before my family.

Read Ecclesiastes 3:7: ". . . a time to be silent and a time to speak . . . "

I have often felt responsible for the silence in conversations. Though I usually did not fill up the quiet spaces with excessive talk, my stomach churned when the other person did not respond. I believed I must say the right thing at the right time for the right reason. Maybe this is one reason why being with people has often worn me out.

Now I'm learning I am not responsible for both ends of a two-way conversation. Although I endeavor to create an atmosphere conducive to sharing, I am accountable only for my own input. I cannot coerce my partner into communicating.

Silences are becoming more comfortable for me; the anxiety is decreasing. When my fellow conversationalist is subdued, withdrawn, surly, or agitated, it is not my responsibility to talk my way to fixing it. I am learning to let it be!

Lord, please give me wisdom and understanding about the appropriate times to speak or be silent.

Read Deuteronomy 5:8–9: "'You shall not make for yourself an idol in the form of anything. . . . You shall not . . . worship them; for I, the Lord your God, am a jealous God, punishing the children for the sin of the fathers.'"

At first glance the consequences of ignoring this commandment seem extremely harsh. Why should innocent children be penalized for the faulty attitudes and behavior of their parents? Yet history has consistently proved this biblical prediction to be true. Adults tend to repeat the life-styles they learned as children.

We who try to do everything right are probably duplicating the perfectionistic, workaholic, or people-pleasing patterns of our parents. We are in danger of passing on these habits to our children. Is there any hope? Yes, the cycle of overcommitment and workaholism can be broken. The first step is to become aware of the flawed messages we received. Was constant busyness a substitute for emotional involvement? Were accomplishments and accumulation the evidence of a person's value? Was it unspiritual to say no even though schedules were already overloaded? We do not have to repeat these harmful patterns. We can change.

Lord, I don't want doing/working to be my god. Give me courage to start a new generation with balanced life habits.

Read Psalm 145:3 and 147:5: "Great is the Lord and most worthy of praise; his greatness no one can fathom. . . . His understanding has no limit."

"Sue has boundless energy and limitless creativity. I can always count on her to be available when needed. Sue is our company's greatest asset. We couldn't function without her." These comments are high praise coming from an employer. Or are they? Let's take a second look at the descriptives used to commend Sue. Boundless energy, limitless creativity, always available, powerless without her. These phrases describe only one—God.

Although human beings can share in God's energy and creativity, helpfulness and power, we do not possess these qualities in infinite measure. To believe we do is a recipe for physical, mental, and spiritual burnout. We can learn to accept the reality of our humanness, lower our unrealistic expectations, and trust God. When we live within our limits, we encourage healthy growth.

Lord, I often try to keep accomplishing flawlessly—forever. Sometimes I push others beyond their finite limits. Only you are able to create and perform with boundless enthusiasm. Please help me to internalize this truth so that it will change the way I think and act.

Read Genesis 1:1–31: "God saw all that he had made, and it was very good" (v. 31).

"Because God created the Natural—invented it out of His love and artistry—it demands our reverence." These are the words of C. S. Lewis. Some of us seem to question whether the Natural deserves our respect. The natural progression of life, normal limitations of time, our interdependence, the divine idea that humans take care of the balance of creation—these realities get in the way of our goals to do and make everything just right. We're not satisfied with God's given. We want more.

So sometimes we push beyond the natural perimeters of God's creation. We strive to turn the ordinary into the extraordinary, the adequate into the excellent, and the average into the perfect.

But God is content with his "good" creation. We can learn to be at peace with the way God created the world. All that he created, male and female, day and night, simple and complex, deserves our respect and acceptance.

Lord, please help me be content with the "good" and "natural" of your loving creation. In so doing I trust that I'll complement and not detract from your overall plan.

Read Ephesians 4:25: "Stop lying to each other; tell the truth, for we are parts of each other and when we lie to each other we are hurting ourselves" (TLB).

Why did I hide my daily circumstances, as well as my feelings, perceptions, and beliefs? Because I thought it was more loving to keep the peace and to make others feel happy and secure. I worked hard at concealing any unpleasantness in order that everyone would be more comfortable. Although this philosophy seemed to work, it actually robbed us all of the opportunity to experience God's intervention in our problems.

I believed I had to focus on only the pleasant things in life. My thought and behavior pattern was reinforced because others appreciated the fact that I rarely complained or disagreed.

However, I had a false impression about the true meaning of unity and cooperation. God did not want me to conceal the truth when it felt uncomfortable or negative. When I began to honestly admit the uncomfortable part of life, I opened up the door to make room for growth. I experienced a newfound freedom when I realized it is acceptable with God to acknowledge and admit the truth, whether unpleasant or delightful.

Lord, help me have courage to tell the truth about the disagreeable circumstances of life and then move ahead with faith.

Read Proverbs 17:17: "A friend loves at all times."

During the last several years I've renewed a lost friendship. The friendship is with myself. I've learned to listen to myself, to affirm my perceptions and emotions. I smile and even laugh at myself sometimes. I feel less threatened. In the midst of my obsessive, workaholic behavior, I was sad and angry at the person I had become. I treated myself poorly. But now I genuinely want what is best for me. I'm learning to allow myself space to recuperate when I'm tired. When I blow it, I try to forgive myself.

I realize that I'll never be perfect. Instead of depressing me, however, this fact causes me to want to grow. Sometimes in the past I wanted to get away from myself, but I no longer have that desire. I am committed to living the remainder of my days in love and peace with the person inside me. One day recently I wrote in my journal, "Good morning, Joan. Let's be Forever Friends."

Lord, thank you that I no longer live in enmity with myself or you.

Read Proverbs 11:17: "Your own soul is nourished when you are kind; it is destroyed when you are cruel" (TLB).

Recently I read the following words: "It is appropriate for a Christian to burn out, but never [to] rust out." I winced as I read this statement, for it was once my unspoken creed. The fulfillment of this philosophy caused me to become a walking dead person. What good was I to anyone then?

Those of us who try to do everything we can to assist, befriend, encourage, and nurture others often neglect ourselves. We extend kindness to our family, friends, and acquaintances while we ruthlessly drive ourselves to destruction. Why? Do we believe that only other people deserve gentleness and support?

Like our neighbors, we, too, are part of God's creation. Our souls are nourished when we treat ourselves with kindness. Yet there is no doubt that we destroy our very core when we are cruel to ourselves. We will respond to life with less anxiety and increased joy when we are considerate to others and ourselves.

Kind Father, your grace has touched my heart and caused me to breathe again. Help me stop abusing myself and thrive.

Read Psalm 8:5: "You made [man] . . . and crowned him with glory and honor."

Recently I read about a well-known public person who acknowledged that her childhood experiences contributed to an erroneous body image in adult life. She is in the process of reprogramming her mind to accept her human body, integrate the past with reality, and not be ashamed.

According to Genesis 1:27, human beings were created in the image of God. Although this does not refer to the "body" of God (for God is a spirit) it does indicate that God made the human body with sufficient dignity to later house the Son of God, Jesus.

God made and crowned man with "glory and honor." The human body, including its obvious limitations, became a suitable dwelling for the incarnate Jesus. This is both humbling and exalting. Understanding this truth can help us to stop heaping contempt on the parts of ourselves that we do not appreciate. We can learn to embrace gratefully the uniqueness of our body and mind.

Lord, help me to accept the body that houses my God-given personality and spirit, human weaknesses and all.

> *Read 1 Corinthians 6:19–20:* "Do you not know that
> your body is a temple of the Holy Spirit, . . . whom
> you have received from God? Therefore honor God
> with your body."

"I always thought I didn't have time to exercise," said a
friend of mine, a busy professional with a thriving new
business. "Now *because* I exercise, I have more energy
and am more productive."

Many of us insist that our overcrowded agendas do
not allow time for a consistent exercise program. But
Myron Rush, author of the book *Burnout,* writes, "Lack
of consistent exercise is part of the reason for the physical
exhaustion of burnout victims."

Developing a beneficial exercise program does not
necessarily mean training for the next marathon. Decide
what is healthy and reasonable for you. Maybe it means
taking a brisk walk around a nearby lake several times a
week. How about enrolling in an aerobics class, swim-
ming laps at the local pool, jogging with a neighbor, or
reviving that tennis game you enjoyed in college?

You are God's creation, housed in the only body you
will ever have. One way to honor God is by taking care of
the body he has given you.

> *Lord, I need to start a healthy exercise program. My
> calendar is too full now, but help me rearrange my
> priorities.*

Read Colossians 3:17: "Whatever you do, whether in word or deed, do it all in the name of the Lord Jesus, giving thanks to God the Father through him."

Some of us compartmentalize our lives. We divide up emotions, thoughts, actions, and duties and then grade them. "God cares about this item," we say, "but that other is not important to him." Sometimes we feel so split up inside that it becomes difficult to function honestly.

"I want to feel integrated, whole," said a friend of mine. "I'm working at bringing together the different parts of my life. Just recently I've begun to see that God accepts me whether I write bills or tithe; spend time with my children or talk to a salesman; take a nap or give a speech; read my Bible or scan the newspaper; eat alone or attend a business lunch; resolve a conflict or whisper 'I love you'; call a client or pray; go to the doctor or sit and relax. All these things are part of me, and I am God's."

Whether we ask a question, laugh, cry, shout, or whisper, we are never separate from God's protection, acceptance, and grace. Each part of our day, every part of our lives, can be God's part. He is concerned with the whole of our lives.

Lord, help me to really understand that you want to be involved in every part of my life. Nothing is too simple or mundane for you.

Read Acts 7:23–36: "Moses thought that his own people would realize that God was using him to rescue them, but they did not" (v. 25).

Some of us may truly believe that we have been called by God to minister to the needs of others. We wish our loved ones would recognize this calling and support and share our mission. When they don't, the indifference or rejection we feel can leave us hurt and disappointed. We may retreat as Moses did if we think others have misjudged our motives or failed to understand our genuine desires. The resulting isolation we experience is often extremely stressful.

The liberating truth is, others, even those closest to us, have the right not to share our burden for a ministry or cause. The call or passion is ours, not theirs. Our responsibility includes being compassionate, open, and honest with our loved ones, true to the principles or ministry we feel strongly about, and patient with God's overall plan. When we truly believe this, a heavy weight seems to roll off our shoulders, and we are free to accept and love one another.

Lord, I am responsible for my own calling before you. I will not impose that call on anyone else.

Read Psalm 25:8–15: "Who, then, is the man that fears [respects] the Lord? He will instruct him in the way chosen for him" (v. 12).

Recently I purchased a study book with a small desk easel to use when working on the computer. When I got home and glanced at the assembly instructions, I concluded that the manufacturers tried deliberately to make it difficult. "Don't they want me to use their product?" I wondered.

Not willing to take the time necessary for putting it together, I used the book but not the accompanying easel. The unassembled easel sat on my desk for three weeks until one day I decided to pick it up and read the instructions. I followed each step, and to my amazement, it worked. The manufacturers did want me to succeed in using the product. When I followed the sensible directions I benefited. They were not trying to confuse me.

Our Creator is not trying to trick us with baffling directions. We need not hesitate to read his words. The instructions he gives in the Bible are for our benefit. It is exciting to discover that what he says makes sense. God wants us to enjoy this "Life" product.

God, please teach me as I read and study your Word.

Read Psalm 18:18–19: "The Lord was my support. He brought me out into a spacious place."

Marlon sat across the lunch table from me at a writers' conference and confided, "My father would never let me finish a sentence. He kept telling me that I would never make it. I guess I'm still trying to prove that he was wrong." Because Marlon was expected to be the precise image of his father's dream, he was thwarted in his ability to fulfill his own dreams.

Perhaps Marlon's father tried too hard to get his son to become what he himself could never attain. Indeed Marlon tried so hard to please that he developed a lifestyle of excessive doing and overworking. Both of them were confined by the tyranny of rigidity and exacting standards. Some of us may identify with the striving. But we are tired of trying so hard and still falling short. We long for a safe place where we can find relief and support.

God's love offers that safety. His love is wide and unconditional. God leads us out of the prison of unreasonable expectations into a spacious area of acceptance and permission. In this place we gain the dignity and freedom to start again.

Lord, hold my hand as I walk out of confinement.

Read Psalm 108:3–5: "For great is your love, higher than the heavens. . . . Be exalted, O God, above the heavens" (vv. 4–5).

Sometimes it is difficult for us to fathom God. He is too great, too awesome to fully comprehend. Yet he loves us!

Some of us may have grown up thinking God is a surly old man who is angry at us. Yet when we have nowhere else to turn and cry out for help, God is there. He does not mock, ignore, or reject us. As we grow to know and trust God, we find he is bigger than the chaotic world in which we live. He is greater than our disappointments, failures, and human limitations.

From his high vantage point God sees us all—the rich and the poor, the educated and the illiterate, the young and the old, the famous and the unknown. Still he reaches down to touch us with his love and understanding. You and I may respond with the words of a well-loved hymn, "How Great Thou Art."

My God, my Creator, my Friend, I am in awe. How grateful I am for words, even for thoughts; yet they are inadequate. You are high! Be exalted!

Read Genesis 16:1–16: "'You are the God who sees me'" (v. 13).

"Where are you going, Hagar?" asked God's angel.

"I can't take it! The pain's too great. I'm running away," replied the pregnant servant.

"You don't need to hide anymore, Hagar. Go back home," said God through his special spokesman. "I have a plan for you and your unborn child."

After God revealed his plan, Hagar responded, "You are the God who sees me. And now I have seen *you.*"

God saw the wrong that Sarai and Abram committed against Hagar. He noticed Hagar's condescending attitude toward Sarai's pain of infertility. He saw Hagar run away.

God sees all—the good and the flawed. He is able to handle the pressure. When we attempt to see and understand all things, we are overcome by the burden of trying to make it all right. Unlike us, God never gets tired, exhausted, or burned out. His eyes never need to close in rest. He sees all things and all people at all times.

Almighty God, my loved ones are never out of your sight. You know everything that happens to them even when I don't. For this I'm grateful.

Read 1 Peter 1:13: "Keep sober in spirit, fix your hope completely on the grace . . . of Jesus Christ" (NASB).

"What do you think it means to be sober in spirit?" asked our teacher. The question intrigued me, so I looked up the word *sober* in the dictionary. To my amazement, the definition read, "not flurried, not excited, but self-possessed." That sounded like the description of a recovering rushaholic. It reminded me of what I wanted to be—calm, less in a hurry to make things happen, consistent, less driven, and better equipped to accept responsibility for my own choices. "Can I stay sober on a regular basis?" I wondered.

Perhaps the answer to my question is found in daily fixing my hope on God's grace. One day at a time is how the new system becomes a habit. If you and I try to tackle all the days all at once, we become overwhelmed. But by taking one day at a time, we will soon have a lifetime of sober living.

Lord, I only ask that you give me this day my daily bread. Keep me sober just for today. And then tomorrow we'll start all over again.

Read Psalm 90:12: "Teach us to number our days aright, that we may gain a heart of wisdom."

Airplanes, fax machines, microwaves, and computers encourage us to hurry up and accomplish more. How can we find a wise balance in this fast-paced and frantic world?

Ralph Keyes, author of *Timelock: How Life Got So Hectic and What You Can Do About It,* suggests that "we plan life, not time" so our daily lives can become less frenetic. Deciding what we want most from life and weeding out activities that detract from our goals will help us feel more balanced. Our Creator has given each of us one earthly life. He does not push us to fill every moment of this life with planned activity. It is acceptable to God to slow down in order to determine where we want to go, what we want to do, and who we want to be. God encourages us to be discerning and to handle our minutes, hours, and days with wisdom, gratitude, and compassion.

Lord, like the psalmist, I long for a heart of wisdom. I really want to glorify you. Teach me to balance my days wisely as we plan my life together.

Read Psalm 31:14–16: "But I trust in you, O Lord; I say, 'You are my God.' My times are in your hands" (vv. 14–15).

After I had been recovering from burnout for eighteen months, I still felt almost everything (eating, getting out of bed, working, fun, housekeeping, being with other people) was a chore. "Maybe this indicates the extent of my charred mind and soul," I thought. "But I used to enjoy doing almost everything—simultaneously."

One morning at the library I came across this description of type-A behavior. "Never enough time, success-oriented, must do two or more things at once, and tendency to become workaholics," I read. "That's me!" I exclaimed. That self-discovery became an important milestone in my journey toward a less exacting and more balanced life-style. I had tried to live outside the boundaries of time. As I practiced acknowledging the impossibility, I gradually learned to relax and operate contentedly within my human time limitations.

Lord God, my times are in your hands. The thought relaxes me.

Read 1 Timothy 1:16: "I was shown mercy so that in me . . . Jesus might display his unlimited patience as an example."

Those of us who try to do everything right set goals and then do not rest until they are completed. This means that any long-term goal puts us in a perpetual state of anxiety. How can we temper this perfectionistic habit?

David Stoop, author of the book *Living with a Perfectionist,* suggests we set subgoals in our quest to finish the larger objective. I found this an effective exercise.

Several years ago I signed a contract to write 365 stories for a children's devotional book. It was a huge project, but I decided to break it down into minigoals of completing four stories per day. Whenever I started to get overwhelmed with the enormity of the entire project, I reminded myself that since I had finished the daily quota, I could relax. I was then free to enjoy myself and others without preoccupation with unfinished business.

God does not expect us to complete our whole life's to-do list in one week. He is patient with our finite limitations. We, too, can learn to practice patience.

Lord, help me to be satisfied with daily progress.

Read Philippians 4:12: "I have learned the secret of being content in any and every situation, whether well fed or hungry, whether living in plenty or in want."

Sometimes when I'm preparing for a teaching assignment, the right words, activities, and examples refuse to come. I may work all day, even several days, knowing I haven't done my best work. Mediocre "stuff" is all I seem to create. At this time I have a choice. I can become frustrated, quit, and get behind schedule. I can obsess, spending painstaking hours on one point until I go crazy. Or I can choose to keep working whether I think it is excellent or not. The following simple comments from Melody Beattie's book *The Language of Letting Go* have helped me to be more accepting during these frustrating times. "There are days when our best is less than we hoped for. Let those times go too. Start over tomorrow. Work things through, until our best becomes better."

Like Paul, sometimes our best results in poverty, other times in prosperity. Learning to be content with both our best performances and our could-be-better times will lessen our anxiety and help us live more peaceful and accepting lives.

Lord, I can only do my best at any given moment. Help me to be content with my fluctuating "best."

Read Isaiah 12:2: "Surely God is my salvation; I will trust and not be afraid. The Lord . . . is my strength and my song."

Recently my husband and I attended a celebration concert featuring the compositions of Petr Eben of Prague. Many works of this talented composer and musician had never before been performed in the United States due to the restrictions and censorship of the communist government. As a result of his experience, Eben's sacred compositions reflect both the joy and the pain, the peace and the struggle of our human existence.

If we expect that because we work hard enough we will know guaranteed success; and if we suppose that because we give much we will be rich; or if we assume that because we eat healthfully and take care of our bodies, we will never be sick, then we are certainly headed for a disappointing surprise. We live in a world where the future is not always predictable or controllable.

Our carefully calculated plans may not come to fruition as we have hoped. Life is not perfect. Only one thing is sure. God is our salvation, strength, and song in the good and the bad times. He is worthy of our trust.

Lord, you're my hope amid unfulfilled dreams. May I expect great things from you, but not necessarily from life.

Read 2 Corinthians 12:7–10: "But he said to me, 'My grace is sufficient for you, my power is made perfect in weakness.' Therefore I will boast . . . about my weaknesses, so that Christ's power may rest on me. . . . for when I am weak, then I am strong" (vv. 9, 10).

One day as a colleague and I discussed a unique problem she faced with her family, she surprised me by asking, "How come God allows negative situations in my life when I can't do anything about them?" The apostle Paul, too, was plagued by a particularly painful circumstance. He asked God to remove it. God said, "Paul, you don't have to try to work yourself out of this. My no-strings-attached gift of grace is enough. My strength in you is best fulfilled when you realize your need." After talking to God several times about his situation, Paul decided to let go of his striving and accept his human neediness.

Circumstances beyond our control may restrict what we are able to accomplish. We may feel stressed as a result. But when we admit our need, and accept that the limitations and weaknesses are inevitable in this life, then we become strong.

We live in an imperfect world and it deeply affects us all. But God's power offers hope in the midst of the imperfection.

Lord, please manifest your strength in my weakness.

Read Galatians 5:13: "You ... were called to be free.
. . . serve one another in love."

"It doesn't matter what I feel or need," said a distressed
young teacher. "All I care about is the school children
and their uninvolved, overworked parents. I'm willing to
try anything and everything to halt the deterioration of
our families and the educational system."

As a child, this capable young man was neglected by
his workaholic parents. The unresolved anger of his past
propels him relentlessly to help hurting children.

Perhaps some of us, like this teacher, crusade for
worthwhile projects or causes in an attempt to submerge
our own pain. Although we succeed in our effort to avoid
dealing with personal distress, in the process we may
alienate ourselves from the people we want to help.
When our vision becomes an addiction, everyone loses.
In the process we often become exhausted, burned out
and angry. Working for progress and good within our
impoverished world is a genuinely high calling. With
God's help we can minister freely and serve one another
in balanced love.

*Lord, I long to serve you and other people. Please help
me to be balanced and honest in this pursuit.*

Read Luke 23:32–43: "Jesus said, 'Father, forgive them'" (v. 34).

In Ken Gire's book, *Intimate Moments with the Savior,* I read the following words, "Keep me from ever wandering far from the foot of [the] cross. . . . For that is the fountain where love is most pure. . . . That is where love is."

"Is that so, Lord?" I asked. "Is balanced love found at the cross?" That same day I read about the thief who died with Jesus. Not the thief who chose to believe, but the other one—the one who ridiculed and rejected Jesus. He laughed in the face of eternity, yet Jesus loved and died for him. The compassionate invitation to look and believe was open to him as well as to the other dying thief. Jesus' love was pure and true while fair and nonmanipulative.

Jesus could not make the decision for either man. The choice was an individual one. Jesus offered both men his love.

Jesus offers each of us his love as well. His love is equal. Unlike some human love we may have known, we need not perform or do or work to earn it. What a relief to stop the striving and accept God's honest, balanced love! We find it at the foot of the cross.

Lord, thanks for answers to my "What is love?" questions. At the cross I find your pure, fair love.

Read John 7:40–44: "Thus the people were divided because of Jesus. Some wanted to seize him" (vv. 43–44).

Many people loved Jesus, others loathed him. But this did not stop Jesus from fulfilling his purpose in life. He seemed unsurprised by it all. Although he cared about others, their opinions did not alter his plans.

Among the misbeliefs guaranteed to make us miserable is the following: "In order to be happy, I must be loved by everybody." Some of us believe we must work hard and long to make everyone love and appreciate us. Consequently we may give in even though to do so conflicts with our values. Or we may try to control others' reactions to us by saying the appropriate words and doing just the right thing. Sometimes we are amazed that someone else does not react as we do.

Not everyone loved and agreed with Jesus; not all will love and agree with us. This is not surprising news. By fulfilling our God-given purposes in life, we can live satisfying and worthwhile lives, regardless of the reaction of those around us. We do not have to be loved and appreciated by everyone to be happy.

Lord, it's a relief to know that I can be who you made me to be even though others may not agree with me. Please help me to be courageous and consistent.

Read Matthew 19:16–22: "But when the young man heard this statement, he went away grieved" (v. 22 NASB).

As I concluded my presentation and dismissed the audience, a determined young woman approached me. "You're not going to like this, but . . . " She then detailed the reasons she did not like my talk.

My immediate response was, "Yes, but didn't you hear me mention . . . ?" I began to recount the points of my speech. Then I noticed that instead of helping her understand, I was compounding her agitation. Stopping midsentence I said, "Basically you didn't agree with anything I said, did you?"

Her face relaxed as she broke into a large smile. "No, sorry. I didn't," she admitted and walked on.

One of the freedom-producing truths I am learning is that I am not responsible for another person's reactions. I can express my opinions and beliefs, but if someone else does not agree, I need not try to change his mind or manipulate him to agree.

The young man disagreed with Jesus, yet Jesus did not try to force him to change his mind. He honored the man's decision and allowed him to walk away. We do not need to control everyone else's reactions. This liberating truth allows us to pursue our own responses with joy and freedom.

Lord, I release my need to make people comply with me. How relieved I am that I do not have to influence everyone.

Read 1 John 4:14: "The Father has sent his Son to be the Savior of the world."

Some of us hang precariously between two diverse yet interrelated self-concepts. Counselor Pat Springle calls it the Savior/Judas complex. He explains how our self-perceptions change in a split second, depending on whether the person we try to help is pleased or upset with us. When we operate in the savior mode, we see ourselves as indispensable. When our efforts to make everything right falter, we feel like a traitor. Others express displeasure, and we feel unappreciated.

This roller coaster existence is a difficult, painful, and exhausting way to live. When we try to be superhuman and fail (which we are bound to do no matter how talented, intelligent, or spiritual we are), we plunge into despair. The resulting shame we feel numbs us until we try to save someone again. The way to begin changing this yo-yo life-style is to admit our humanness and God's sovereignty. Only Jesus is qualified to be the Savior of our lives, of our families' lives, and of the world.

Lord, I guess I've tried to be indispensable. When things and people don't turn out the way I prayed for, worked for, trusted for, hoped for, I feel like a failure. But I'm tired. I don't want to live this way anymore. Please help me learn the truth about myself, others, and you.

Read Psalm 25:20: "Let me not be ashamed, . . . for my trust and my refuge are in You" (Amplified).

"What a relief!" said Betty. "I no longer have to strive for what will never happen. I now realize I can never be the ideal mother or employee. But my family and boss do not understand it yet."

We people pleasers and perfectionists have taught those around us to play a defective game. Our obsessive doing and performing has made life easier for them yet harder for us. Once we refuse to play this game, others may react negatively. Betty was experiencing this dilemma.

"My son didn't get up when his alarm sounded. I told him I wasn't going to come into his room five times to wake him up. He left late and peeved. Last week when I got the flu and went to bed, my boss complained. I was tempted to get up and go into work. But I stayed put till I was better. My daughter wants help with her 'last-minute' sewing project, but I have scheduled plans, and I'm not changing them. This is difficult for me; I still feel the shame of not 'giving' more. But I'm relieved that the long-kept secret is out. I cannot be everything everybody else wants me to be. In the long run this will be better for us all."

God, it looks impossible now. But I'm trusting you to help us all adjust to a new, healthier system.

Read 1 Corinthians 12:4–7: "There are different kinds of gifts, but the same Spirit" (v. 4).

Recently my husband and I enjoyed hearing the St. Paul Chamber Orchestra. We listened to a piano concerto created long ago by Ludwig van Beethoven. The concert also included music written by Russian composer Alfred Schnittke. There was a striking contrast between the two compositions. Beethoven's concerto blended major and minor tones with magical balance. The Schnittke work introduced unfamiliar sounds and timing. Before the concert, objects were placed on the piano strings to alter the sound. Although the violins echoed similar melodies, they were a fraction of a beat off in timing. The result was somewhat comical. In both compositions each instrument had its part to play. The flute did not imitate the sound of the bassoon. The cello did not mimic the detached notes of the harpsichord. Yet the harmony captivated the audience. It worked brilliantly.

Each of us has God-given gifts, God-planned work to accomplish. We do not need to play exactly the same note in order to make lovely music together. We do not have to think, work, or play the same for the sake of harmony. God is the master composer and conductor. He has a brilliant plan.

Lord, help me to play my part and exercise my gift even when it sounds different from another's.

Read 1 Corinthians 3:1–10: "The Lord has assigned to each his task. I planted the seed, Apollos watered it, but God made it grow. . . . Each will be rewarded according to his own labor" (vv. 5–6, 8).

"I can't do everything!" protested the overworked Vacation Bible School director. She was right. God does not plan for one individual to perform all the tasks.

Some of us believe we should be able to accomplish everything and do it perfectly. We may think that if we just try harder, God will surely grant us the strength to carry on. However, it is not God's intention that we be one-man achievement squads. Each one of us has specific tasks to do that correspond directly with our talents and gifts. We need not do more than is humanly possible. God's design is that we work together to plant and water the *process.* Then he produces the growth. This is God's way to avoid overcommitment, disillusionment, exhaustion, and burnout in the local church or any other human endeavor.

Lord, help me to remember I need only do my part. It's not my responsibility to do it all. Even when others fail to complete their job, I will remain true to your plan and let you work it out. I give the process and the result to you.

Read Mark 12:32–33: "'To love [God] with all your heart, . . . and to love your neighbor as yourself is more important than all burnt offerings and sacrifices'" (v. 33).

Some of us develop elaborate programs to show our concern for others. We plan mission trips, give benefits, form task forces, and initiate new projects.

All these things are essential, because helping others is part of the gospel of Christ. Yet when we attempt to do more than our finite capabilities, time restrictions, and budgets can afford, we may eventually become disillusioned and disappointed. Then we try harder and finally wear out. What did Jesus mean when he said to love our neighbors? Must we accomplish more to prove our concern?

God is pleased with consistent daily expressions of love. We can serve the store clerk, our child's teacher, the phone operator, our mate, the librarian, our child, business partner, or client. We need not shame ourselves into planning additional perfect programs, when a smile, an encouraging word, or the willingness to listen also shows our love. What a relief to know we can fulfill the great commandment without trying to save the whole world.

Lord, help me see the ways I can love my neighbor in the midst of my daily life.

Read 1 Peter 1:22: "Now you have made yourselves pure by obeying the truth. Now you can have true love for your brothers. So love each other deeply with all your heart" (NCV).

As I climbed out of the dark, lonely hole of people pleasing and burnout, I was gradually released to offer genuine concern for my fellow human beings. Now less preoccupied with proving my value by doing and helping, I am usually able to love others with fewer strings attached. Others I've met who have weathered similar changes tend to be less controlling and more willing to listen.

When we take personal responsibility for our own emotional, mental, and spiritual growth by cooperating with God as he shows us the truth about ourselves, we become new and healthy people. We may be concerned that this commitment to personal growth will cause life-long self-preoccupation. But we usually find that the opposite is true. We perform good deeds no longer out of an overwhelming desire to heal ourselves but because of the transforming power of God's love within us. As we mature and develop inner strength and calm, we gain courage to reach out and touch others.

Lord, I realize that I'm not perfect, but I do want to grow. Purify my inner motives, so I can touch others out of the overflow of a changed heart.

Read John 13:34: "A new command I give you: Love one another."

"I've always felt that my family and friends want something from me," admitted a friend. "One demands my time, though I have none to spare, while another takes a large emotional bite out of my heart; another asks spiritual questions I can't answer. It never occurred to me that someone might want to just be with me. Could this be?"

Some of us have a difficult time imagining what it might be like not having to do something. When friends come to visit us, we hurry around making certain everything is just right. We may be preoccupied with saying the right words or leading the conversation to worthwhile topics. We work so hard that sometimes being with other people is exhausting.

Wouldn't it be great simply to sit with our loved ones and enjoy their company without giving advice, stuffing them with food, trying to figure them out, or attempting to make them spiritually fulfilled? What a relief it would be.

Jesus said, "Love one another." Perhaps one way to show our love is simply to take pleasure in one another's company, without any strings attached. It's definitely worth a try.

Lord, please help me to relax and enjoy being with my family and friends.

Read Galatians 5:22: "But the fruit of the Spirit is love, joy, peace, patience, kindness, goodness, faithfulness, gentleness and self-control. Against such things there is no law."

One hot afternoon, while taking my daily walk around the lake, the phrase "against such things there is no law" bounced back and forth in my mind until I whispered the words aloud.

At first I said, "Of course there is no law against love, joy, or peace." Then it dawned on me at a deeper level. I've shamed myself into putting a lid on my expressions of these characteristics. Was it because I believed the good attributes would all go away if I stopped trying so hard, relaxed, and appreciated life? Did I think I was being selfish for enjoying things? Or did I feel I did not deserve them? I'm not certain. Yet on this sweltering day in July, God assured me that there is no shame in experiencing the blessings of love, peace, kindness, gentleness, faithfulness, goodness, and self-control.

Lord, I accept with joy all the positive things you have to offer me. Thank you for the work of your Spirit in my life.

Read John 4:4–30; 39–42: "The woman . . . said . . . ,
'Come, see a man who told me everything I ever did.
Could this be the Christ?'" (vv. 28–29).

The woman's life played like a modern-day soap opera.
She had one of the worst reputations in the area. Married
five times and currently living with another man, she
lived with the stigma of inferiority and brokenness.
These facts did not faze Jesus. He met her, not in a
church, but where she lived. Jesus offered her a gift
unlike those offered by the many men in her past. With
no strings attached, Jesus offered a way to fill up her
heart's insatiable longing for love. Jesus did not point his
finger and say, "I'll pray that you give up your shameful
ways" or "Just follow these rules and everything will be
better." Jesus did not even pressure her with, "You must
decide now; pray this prayer." He showed her who she
was, who he was, offered the gift of eternal life, and left
the response to her.

Jesus treats us as he did the woman at the well; he does
not manipulate our decisions. He offers truth, love, and
room to make our choices.

*Lord, thank you for your patience with my spiritual
process.*

Read Matthew 6:6–13: "'But when you pray, go into your room, close the door and pray to your Father, who is unseen'" (v. 6).

"If we are halfway authentic in our searching, we must take time in silence—in prayer and meditation. . . . Our prayer . . . acknowledges our source of hope, expresses our true desire, unites us with the rest of humanity, and commits our willingness to God." This insight of Gerald May, in his book *Addiction and Grace,* emphasizes the importance of prayer in our process of growing and changing. Jesus' prayer, recorded in Matthew 6:9–13, is a model for our own prayers. Jesus acknowledged the Father's power, admitted humanity's need, and granted permission to make requests of an awesome God.

When we feel the strong pull to go back to our familiar yet destructive habits, we can ask God for strength and courage. When we panic because people and circumstances turn out opposite from the way we'd planned, we can turn to God in faith. Prayer is our connection to the God of the universe and an essential part of our daily journey.

Dear God, I close the door to all that would distract me and come to you in heartfelt prayer.

Read Hebrews 10:19–22: "Since we have confidence to enter the Most Holy Place by the blood of Jesus, . . . let us draw near to God with a sincere heart in full assurance of faith" (vv. 19, 22).

As I learn to be less indispensable, I find my prayer life changing. I've often identified so deeply with others' problems or pain that I have assumed I know what God needs to do to fix it. As I realize that I don't need to have all the answers, I'm less compelled to tell God how to work. In *My Utmost for His Highest,* Oswald Chambers said, "Beware of imagining that intercession means bringing our personal sympathies into the presence of God and demanding that He does what we ask." Requests such as, "Lord, cause John to buy this good book" or "Help my son to pick Oakwood College" or "Take away Sue's hurt and disappointment" may hinder God's plan for them. If we believe that we are responsible for our family's, friends', and associates' well-being and happiness, we may spend our prayer time dictating to God on their behalf.

Only Jesus is Savior and Redeemer. Because of his death and resurrection, we can come before a holy God with total confidence and share our concerns without demanding "just the right" answer. We then have the exciting privilege of watching God work.

Lord, with no strings attached, I ask you to work powerfully in my life and my loved ones' lives.

Read Isaiah 14:24 and 27: "The Lord Almighty has sworn, 'Surely, as I have planned, so it will be.' For the Lord ... has purposed, and who can thwart him?"

God is sovereign. All that God does is right and fair. He will have the final word.

You and I need not hold life (yours, mine, or ours) so tightly, because God carries life and all that is. Although we live in the midst of a chaotic and pressurized world, the Lord Almighty surpasses the chaos and pressure. All time and eternity belong to him. When we attempt to go beyond human limitations and be bigger than big, we play God. Because we are not sovereign, however, it is merely game playing.

God has supreme power, authority, and creativity. Out of his vast resources God lovingly gives us the ability to reason, choose, plan, and implement those plans. In this reality we can relax, trusting him to help us make wise decisions and live balanced lives. What a privilege it is to cooperate with the Indisputable One.

Lord, you created me, I did not create you. You sustain me, I do not sustain my world. How grateful I am to be sharing life with you, now and forever.

Read Matthew 17:17: "Jesus replied, 'How long shall I stay with you? How long shall I put up with you?'"

Some of us may have a difficult time accepting the fact that lasting change is a process. We want instant healing, instant excellence, even instant spiritual maturity. Sometimes avoiding struggle may seem more important than genuine growth. We wish we could wake up in the morning to find it all resolved.

If God had sent his Son to accomplish his redemptive work during a weekend retreat, perhaps Jesus could have escaped much of the discomfort. Instead God chose for Jesus to come as a baby, become a teenager, and confront young adulthood. The faultless Son of God left perfection with his Father to face earth's reality: sickness, death, abuse, and unbelief. His statement "How long?" indicates how agonizing it was for him.

God does not always do things instantaneously. The road to the cross was long and difficult. Our journey to lasting change is often tiresome and hard. The path becomes less stressful when we accept that positive change often takes time in the midst of pain. We can slow down and cooperate with God's timetable. As we gratefully accept each day's new insight, we gain confidence to continue the life-changing process.

Lord, you are not in a hurry. Help me not to be. I will trust you for lasting results in my life.

Read Haggai 2:4: "'Be strong,' . . . declares the Lord, 'and work. For I am with you.'"

This morning when I needed a break from writing, I headed for the park. On a whim (I'm learning to be spontaneous) I decided to swing on the swing set. Pumping my legs took more energy than I thought it would. It was a lot of work to get started, but once I pushed past the difficult stage, I closed my eyes and soared through the air. Eventually I was able to glide for a while without pumping again.

"This is what it was like to initiate change in my life," I thought. It was hard work at first. I pumped and pumped just to get my "swing" activated. Yet once I was moving toward health, the effort was worthwhile. Occasionally I stopped pumping to glide. In order to keep swinging toward change, however, I had to stay committed to the basic work of pumping.

Reprogramming our thoughts and turning new skills into daily habits takes years. Five years into my recovery I still work to maintain balance, yet this healthier life-style is becoming more comfortable; the journey is getting easier.

Lord, I will keep working toward change, because I know you are with me.

Read Ezra 3:3: "Despite their fear of the peoples around them, they built the altar... and sacrificed... to the Lord, both the morning and evening sacrifices."

When the Israelites were released to return to their beloved Jerusalem, they determined to restore the temple to its original God-exalting state. Although they encountered opposition, they remained committed to the temple's restoration. Fear could have hindered them from moving forward into action, but it did not. They continued in spite of what the others said and did.

Some of us have been granted the opportunity to grow and recover from our self-destructive life-style. Our future is uncertain and often terrifying. People may doubt our motives and try to sabotage our efforts to change. Regardless of the thoughts, attitudes, or actions of those around us, we can move on to restoration and healing. God is on our side. When we choose to move toward wholeness and health, God is always available to help us. Just as the Israelites did, we can call upon God's name at any time, morning or evening.

Lord, this life-changing journey scares me. I'm afraid of what others might think or say. I don't want anyone to look down on me. I cringe when I hear their ridicule. But I've come too far to go back now. Help me walk through my fear.

Read Psalm 116:6: "When I was in great need, he saved me."

I was finding it difficult to balance a demanding work schedule with the rest of my busy and changing life. My insides churned, and I tried to fight the confusing emotions. Finally I called a friend who was also trying to change from the making-everything-right life-style. After listening to my rambling, she said, "We try to figure it out, have all the right words and reactions before we share our struggle, even before we give it to the Lord."

Some of us believe we dare not admit to our confusing need until we understand it all. We fight to know what to call it and how to explain it, so people (or God) won't think we're incompetent. We think we must get everything fixed up right before we ask for help.

We have the process backward. God wants to help us now. A hopeful future becomes more than wishful thinking when we accept God's intervention in our lives today. God comforts, supports, cares, loves, and saves us *in* our need. Even before we know what the exact problem is, we can seek God's help. Today.

Lord, I don't know how to explain myself. But I need you. Help me in my confusion.

Read Psalm 27:10: "Though my father and mother forsake me, the Lord will receive me."

Some of us have felt physically and/or emotionally abandoned by those we trusted to take care of us. As youngsters we tried, without success, to gain their love and approval. Maybe we attempted to keep the precarious peace by becoming compliant and doing good deeds. Or perhaps the only way we could gain coveted attention was to strive to overachieve, whatever the cost.

When we were children, we learned to cope with life in the most effective way available to us. As adults these learned skills may manifest themselves by overwork, perfectionism, and people pleasing. The realization that our methods are no longer effective may leave us sad and angry.

However, we do not have to wander through our adult years reliving the disapproval we felt as children. Healing is available. God promises to take us in. We are unconditionally loved and accepted by a heavenly parent. Close your eyes and visualize being hugged and praised by God your Father. He will never leave you.

Thank you, Father. How I've longed for a parent's active emotional involvement in my life. Your love and acceptance is reassuring.

Read Galatians 1:10: "Am I now trying to win the approval of men, or of God? Or am I trying to please men? If I were still trying to please men, I would not be a servant of Christ."

A news reporter asked a chief of staff to the United States president if his job was difficult. "No," replied the chief of staff. "I have only one constituent to please."

"How long will you do this job?" continued the reporter.

"As long as the president wants me," he answered.

Some of us try to please everyone, including mother, father, spouse, child, friend, boss, and pastor. We walk a tightrope attempting to juggle all the desires and demands of everybody around us. Usually we end up pleasing no one, while driving ourselves to overload. This is a self-defeating life-style.

In the end, we who have chosen to follow Christ have only one constituent—God.

Lord God, I am tired of trying to do and be what everyone one else wants. If I keep this up, I'll never become the person you created me to be. I'm going to change my pattern to do what I believe you want for me. Please give me wisdom and courage.

Read Luke 6:20–23: "'Blessed are you who are poor, for yours is the kingdom of God. Blessed are you who hunger now, for you will be satisfied. Blessed are you who weep now, for you will laugh'" (vv. 20–21).

When I decided God wanted me to risk rocking the boat, to change my workaholic behavior, and to tell the truth about my feelings, perceptions, and beliefs, I was scared. To help defuse the fear, I often asked myself, "In this situation, what is the worst thing that could happen to me?"

Some of my answers to this question were: "I could make a mistake. I might not succeed. My husband may get angry. I might not make enough money. Others might disagree and reject me."

Then I'd ask, "Would that be the end of the world?" Eventually my answer became, "I guess not. I know God accepts and loves me, no matter what."

In the midst of need or poverty, pain or rejection, we have the assurance of better things to come. Life is not always fair, sometimes it isn't even fun. Although we cry now, someday we will leap for joy.

Lord, you are my ultimate hope. I look forward to being in heaven with you forever.

Read Romans 6:4: "Just as Christ was raised from the dead through the glory of the Father, we too may live a new life."

Changing our everything-must-be-just-right thinking and work or service addiction is frightening. Even though we want to change, the task often seems overwhelming. We have many questions. "How shall I begin? What do I do next? Can I really change? Will it last?" Consider the following life-changing steps:

   Acknowledge the need. Becoming aware of our need marks the beginning of our journey toward freedom.

   Admit the misconceptions. Believing lies about ourselves, others, life, and God has kept us in bondage to our slavish ways.

   Replace the falsehoods with the truth. Study Jesus' healthy life-style. When we change our thought patterns, new behavior will follow.

   Surrender the entire process to God. Trust that he is able to give new life.

   Remain committed. Walk through the pain that often accompanies the unfamiliar process of change.

God has done the necessary energizing work by his Son's death and resurrection. Now we have the privilege of trusting and cooperating with him for our growth and restoration.

Lord, thank you for the promise of new life. Help me stay committed to this life-changing process.

Read 1 Corinthians 10:12: "If you think you are stand-ing firm, be careful that you don't fall!"

"If I change my workaholic behavior, practice saying no, learn to relax, give up my unrealistic expectations, and stop fixing other people, will I finally be able to forget about this whole thing?" asked a young man in my growth group.

When we are certain we have done everything possi-ble to prevent a return to our former life-style, we may in fact be in danger of a relapse. Regardless of our desire to the contrary, the decision to be less obsessed with doing and making everything right is a day-by-day, lifelong process. Predetermining that "all shall be well with me" from now on leaves room for our perfectionistic behavior to come back and knock on the door.

Trusting God to help us one day at a time makes room for our continued growth. Step-by-step reliance on God is a more effective way to live.

Lord, I know I'll never do this life-style change per-fectly. I will depend on you just for today. Tomorrow I'll trust you all over again.

Read Genesis 5:21–24: "Enoch walked with God 300 years" (v. 22).

Taking a walk with a trusted friend is a pleasurable experience. While on this walk we travel at the same pace, agree on the direction to go, experience the same scenery, and enjoy each other's company. Usually we take a casual stroll, with a beginning and ending point.

Enoch and God took a walk that lasted 300 years. It could not have been a sprint, for a person cannot keep up that high-intensity pace for a sustained period. Enoch and God did not walk together because Enoch had superior abilities, flawless determination, great intelligence, a perfect personality, or a successful business. Instead Enoch trusted his walking companion, and God enjoyed that (Hebrews 11:5).

Like Enoch, we can choose to walk with God, not in a harried I-must-impress-him-with-my-commitment-and-speed attitude. We need only to relax and have confidence in our Partner.

When our walk with God becomes a long-term process, we begin to understand his character, his goals, his ultimate plan for us. Faith enhances our earthly journey and prepares us for the continuation of our walk through eternity.

Lord, I want to walk with you.

Read Luke 22:44–45: "And being in anguish, [Jesus] prayed more earnestly: and his sweat was like drops of blood falling to the ground" (v. 44).

"I wish it were all over," confided a friend. "This is such an agonizing journey." For several years my friend has been confronting the debilitating effects of an unhealthy past and how it has contributed to her workaholic present. The process has produced considerable anguish. Although she is committed to growth, she frequently feels alone.

But she is not alone. Jesus understands. According to Luke, Jesus suffered greatly as he faced the prospect of the cross. It was an agonizing experience, yet his friends left him alone to struggle.

When we experience detours triggered by bad memories and strong self-defeating habits, we may be tempted to abandon the journey. Remembering Jesus' commitment and courage in the midst of pain and anguish helps us to walk through the struggle with him.

Lord, sometimes I'm in such pain that I feel nauseated. But healing is more important to me right now than avoiding my fear. You knew anguish and yet walked courageously through it. Please help me to do the same.

Read Isaiah 38:15–19: "You restored me to health and
let me live. Surely it was for my benefit that I suffered
such anguish. In your love you kept me from ...
destruction. ... The living, the living—they praise
you, as I am doing today."

Work, overwork, obsessive caring, disappointments,
denial, exhaustion, pretending, pain, threatened relationships, physical illness, confusion, isolation, burnout!
Losing career, dreams, personhood, emotions, and normal thinking processes; feeling abandoned by God and
other people. Can I possibly say thank you for this?

Quietly, timidly I'm starting to say, "Yes, Lord, surely
it was for my benefit that I suffered such anguish." The
workaholism, the burnout, the failing business forced me
to admit my need and, regardless of the consequences, to
do something about it. Not with elation or pride do I say
thanks. It was not a pleasant way to learn! Yet God
restored me to health and let me live. And only the living
can praise and thank him.

*Lord, in your love (though I did not feel it) you kept
me from destruction. I am grateful. I have my life
back again. Thank you.*

Read Ezra 3:8–11: "When the builders laid the foundation . . . with thanksgiving they sang to the Lord: '. . . his love . . . endures forever'" (vv. 10–11).

"I wonder if I've done permanent damage to my mind and body," admitted a friend who had just left a destructive career environment. "As I begin this journey out of workaholism and burnout, sometimes I'm hopeful, other times I'm racked with doubt. I guess I'd better wait before I count my blessings."

At one time I, too, was frightened that total restoration was not possible. After all, I had fried my brain and soul.

Perhaps the Israelites experienced similar feelings. They had been freed from the oppressive chains of the Babylonians. Restoring the temple in Jerusalem was their goal, but many obstacles remained. The destruction was massive. Could they ever recover what they once had?

With such a huge task ahead, one might expect the Israelites to hold their praise until the temple reconstruction was completed. Yet as the foundation was being laid, they shouted, "God is good!"

Learning new ways to live is risky. There is much work to be done and many obstacles to overcome. Even in our confusion and doubt, however, we can be grateful for evidence of growth and praise God.

Lord, your love endures forever—before, during, and after the restorative process.

Read Romans 14:12: "So then, each of us will give an account of himself to God."

When we who try to do and make everything right decide to cease being responsible for everyone and everything, many questions may flood our mind and heart. "How shall I pray now? If I don't tell God what to do in my friend's life, will God still work specifically? Will growth or change ever take place if I don't get involved? Isn't it my responsibility to do all the good I can? Is this new life-style selfish? How can I show others and God that I am concerned? What shall I do with my questions? Dare I surrender it all to God?"

These are normal inquiries when we change from our caretaking, rescuing, fixing, and people-pleasing life-style. We are responsible to the other people in our lives, but we are not accountable for them. Just as others must make their own choices before God, so must we.

Lord, I feel so empty now. I still want to help others, but because my attempts are not working, I hand it all to you. Even though it feels uncomfortable, I will step back and let you do your job.

Read Psalm 145:8: "The Lord is gracious and compassionate, slow to anger and rich in love."

"How do I know God isn't mad at me?" I still ask myself this question occasionally, even though I'm less obsessed with performance, people pleasing, and "good deeds." Sometimes I worry that my human imperfections and inadequacies displease God, and my restlessness threatens to rob my peace. This morning, however, I received the following reassuring answer to my question.

I know God isn't mad at me because he didn't forsake me when I was deep in the throes of work addiction and perfectionism. God wanted me to be healthy. He waited patiently for me to decide to reverse my direction. Since he stood beside me in those ugly times, then surely he is with me now as I continue to pursue balance and health. He isn't angry with me for failing to achieve flawless thoughts, feelings, attitudes, or actions. I can never attain spiritual perfection in this life.

"You know that about me, don't you, Lord?" I responded. "And you still love me. Help me as I cease striving to make it all right. You are the unerring one. I know I'm righteous in your eyes because of what Jesus did on my behalf. My heart is grateful."

Lord, you are gracious, kind, compassionate, slow to anger, and rich in love. In this reality I rest.

Read Galatians 4:9: "But now that you know God
. . . how is it that you are turning back to those . . .
miserable principles? Do you wish to be enslaved by
them all over again?"

"Our speaker isn't here yet," I whispered to a colleague.
It was 6:55. The meeting started at 7:00. I walked outside
while my partner started the program. I scanned the
parking lot. There was no sign of our speaker. At 7:07 the
speaker rushed toward me in a state of controlled frenzy.
"I need to make copies of my transparencies," he panted.
"Where can I do that?" While he frantically worked to
complete his preparations, I waited at the back of the
auditorium.

Then it dawned on me. "Joan, this is how you once
lived. From one rush to another; one crisis to another.
Jumping from fire to fire as you doused each one just in
time to avoid burning your feet. You do not want to live
like that again!"

At times we may be tempted to return to our old patterns. Then something happens to remind us that those
were wretched days. We are not less spiritual because we
cease rushing and doing and fixing and worrying and
working. This crazy life-style proves nothing. We know
God, and we do not have to live like this.

*Lord, I've tasted freedom. Never do I want to go back
to the bondage of those miserable ways again.*

Read Lamentations 3:19–22: "I remember my affliction and my wandering, the bitterness and the
gall. . . . Yet this I call to mind and therefore I have
hope: Because of the Lord's great love we are not consumed, for his compassions never fail. They are new
every morning; great is your faithfulness."

Several years ago I scrawled these words on a piece of
scrap paper: "I am an open, bleeding wound that is not
allowed to heal. I feel as though I have a broken leg, but I
just keep walking on it. (The difference is that my mind
and soul are what is broken.) I'm standing on the outside
of life watching myself go through the motions, but I
want to participate again. I want to feel like a person, to
be whole once more. God, I want to know and feel your
love. I long for my performing and doing to become one
with who I am. I know that it can be."

That last sentence amazes me. It indicates that I had
not completely lost hope, even though I was sad, disappointed, and bitter. One day at a time God's love
reached out to me. He bandaged my wounds and set my
broken heart. It took time, but I am participating in life
again. Every morning, whether it is sunny or cloudy,
God renews and helps me. He wants to do the same for
you. He is faithful. Let God's love renew you.

*Lord, I don't know just how you will do it, but I am
hopeful. Continue to restore me. I want to live.*